Robert Sachs has studied oriental disciplines for over twenty-five years. He is a trained counsellor, holding a Master's degree in Social Work (MSW) and he works in both Europe and the United States as a stress management consultant and educator in preventative health care. He uses Nine Star Ki successfully for diagnosis and recommendations for individuals, groups and organizations. He is a featured host and guest on talk radio shows in the United States and abroad, providing Nine Star Ki insights to listening audiences.

Robert is also the author of *Health for Life: Secrets of Tibetan Ayurveda*, *Rebirth Into Pure Land*, and *Perfect Endings: A Conscious Approach to Dying and Death*. He and his wife, Melanie, run Diamond Way Ayurveda. They live with their three children in California.

By the same author

*Health for Life: Secrets of Tibetan Ayurveda*
*Rebirth Into Pure Land*
*Perfect Endings: A Conscious Approach to Dying and Death*

# NINE STAR KI

## YOUR ASTROLOGICAL COMPANION
## TO FENG SHUI

Robert Sachs

A catalogue record for this book is
available from the British Library.

ISBN 1-84333-019-9
Printed in China

© Vega 2001

A member of the Chrysalis Group plc

First published in 2001 by
Vega
64 Brewery Road
London N7 9NT

Visit our website at www.chrysalisbooks.co.uk

# Preface

Heather is an English school student. She is concerned about her final exams and where she should look for an adult career. Her family has expectations and plans regarding her future, but she feels drawn towards certain choices that are not in step with these expectations.

John is a university professor on sabbatical. He has decided to make some career changes, precipitated by an old interest and a desire to write. To initiate this transition he plans to travel. Yet, he is uncertain of what to do first and the right timing for the changes.

Mike and Sandra's marriage has been going sour for the last few years. Each feels pressured by the other and they feel as though they are on a merry-go-round of predictable situations and reactions. They do want to make things work, but Mike can't pull himself away from the feelings of an earlier divorce and custody battle. Sandra is torn between needing Mike for emotional support and wanting to establish a niche for herself through her work.

Denise is a supervisor in a hospital laboratory. She does not understand or get on with a number of her employees. She sees that changes need to be made, but feels confused about what steps she should take to create a more cohesive and productive staff team.

In all of these situations, Nine Star Ki offers clear guidance. There are, of course, many types of therapies and work strategies that can facilitate growth and change in the scenarios presented. However, few have a world view that is as embracing, dynamic and adaptable as Nine Star Ki (pronounced 'key').

That is my experience. As a social worker and a therapist I have examined numerous psychotherapeutic and management models. Each has offered me useful ideas and ways of handling the diversity of clients that I encounter. The Law of Five Transformations, the underpinning of oriental philosophy and healing, and Nine Star Ki in particular, however, give my practice a stronger organic base – something I can work out of that feels grounded, more balanced. My confidence in this model, in turn, is reflected in my clients, who feel this confidence and become inspired to tap into their own inherent abilities to learn for themselves from this model.

Individuals wanting to develop and grow, both in themselves and with others, therapists wanting to be more effective as agents of change, business-minded people wanting to make appropriate and timely business decisions – all will benefit from this book. Not acting from projection or cultural/habitual patterning, but from a living, vibrant truth of a basic kind, one's decisions and actions in the world become more efficient, productive, and self- empowering.

# PREFACE

This is what this book offers.

There are many people that have helped in the production of this book. To all the ancient and modern sages adept in Nine Star Ki I am indebted. To teachers Michio Kushi and Rex Lassalle, many thanks. Much gratitude goes out to Colleen Reed, Wendy Buckles, Susan Biggs, artist Morag Charlton, Rebecca Wood and Judy Lawrence for technical assistance and advice. Many thanks to many others not named who showed confidence in and support for this project.

And an especial thank you to all who read this volume and find it useful in their lives.

Robert Sachs

# Foreword

Nine Star Ki, or as it is known in Japan, *Kyu Sei Ki Gaku,* is a part of an ancient cosmology that was common to people throughout the world. It is based on understanding the way that yin and yang, or the two most basic forces in nature, interact to produce all changes in the universe. This universal cosmology, together with applications such as Nine Star Ki, developed at a time when people were living closer to the rhythms of nature and observing the Tao, or order of change, in their daily lives, including their way of eating. Their traditional diet of non-chemicalized whole grains, vegetables, beans and other natural foods enabled them to develop insight into the movement of life energy, or ki, in the planetary environment and in human affairs.

The ancient sages understood that despite what seems to be endless diversity, all things on earth and in heaven move and change in accordance with a simple order. Once this order is understood and confirmed in daily life, it becomes possible to know how future events are likely to unfold. It was through intuitive awareness of the law of change that the study of destiny – which represents the pinnacle of Oriental thinking and philosophy – was born.

Nine Star Ki, and Oriental Astrology in general, continues to be one of the most popular subjects presented in our macrobiotic seminars around the world. Thousands of people have studied Oriental Astrology and have found it to be a useful and practical guide to understanding human relationships, personal health, current events, and human destiny in general. It offers everyone a compass for navigating the troubled waters of modern times.

*Nine Star Ki* is a most welcome and useful Nine Star Ki sourcebook, shedding further light on the personality types of the Nine Ki characters as well as being excellent in its analysis of the interactions between the numbers that make up human personalities. This book and our own on the subject of Nine Star Ki provide readers with the opportunity to discover how the principles of Oriental Astrology apply to their daily lives.

In closing, we would like to thank Bob Sachs for his effort in compiling this book and for making this practical and useful knowledge available to people in the modern world.

MICHIO KUSHI
East West Foundation, founder

EDWARD ESKO
Kushi Institute, Counsellor

To Michio Kushi,
who opened my eyes to the depth, beauty and power
of worlds seen and unseen through his knowledge,
patience and kindness.

To friend Rex Lassalle,
who prodded me on in the study of Nine Star Ki
and the empowerment of myself.

To my beloved life companion, Melanie,
who has always been there to support me
in our us-ness.

To my children, Kai, Tina and Jabeth,
who cheered when the book was finished.

May all beings who are touched by this book
find it beneficial.

# Contents

NINE STAR KI

## APPENDICES

# List of Figures

# How to Use This Book

This section is provided for your convenience. Although it will take you a short time to learn how to make Nine Star Ki calculations, the following steps will help you to use the book immediately. They can also serve as a reminder while you perfect your calculation skills.

1. Establish the month, day and year of birth of the person on whom you would like to do a Nine Star Ki evaluation. You do *not* need the exact time or location of birth.

2. The years and months of the Nine Star Ki system are in accordance with the Chinese calendar. Thus the beginning of the year is in early February. Looking at the year chart (Figure 5) on page 27, find the Nine Star Ki number associated with the year of birth. Anyone born between 1 January and 4 February should take the number from the previous year (for example, a person born on 6 January 1947 should consider their year to be 1946 and therefore look at the Nine Star Ki number associated with 1946). The year number is referred to in the text as the adult natal or adult natal year number. This number is associated with your greatest potential for growth and

development. Read the description of this number in Part 2 of the book.

3. Look for the number associated with the month and day of birth in Figure 6 on page 33. This is called the child natal or child natal month number. This number is associated with your upbringing and your reactions to outside influences during earlier years, hence your conditioning, socially, physically and emotionally. Apart from its influence on the first eighteen years of life, this number's traits become active in later years when under stress. Traits of the month can be more easily taxed if they are over-emphasized. Read the description of this number in Part 2 of the book.

4. The adult and child natal numbers together are the most significant part of the Nine Star Ki chart. There are relationships between these numbers that influence your behaviour, health and relationships. Figure 12 on pages 54–8 will help you to find important passages in the text which are relevant to the adult-child number configuration you are examining. Read these passages.

5. Take time to reflect on the material. How much do you respond from your adult natal or child natal number? In what circumstances? Be open. Be accepting.

# PART 1

# Introduction

# Humankind In Time and Space

INTERESTING TIMES

There is an old Chinese saying that goes 'May you live in interesting times'. If someone were to say this to us, many of us might think of adventure and unknown opportunity. However, the Chinese meant it almost as a curse. 'Interesting times' refers to times of transition in which the stability and harmony of daily life are disrupted and, along with these, the biological, psychological and spiritual constants within culture that normally help us to feel stable and harmonious within our greater environment.

As we move into the twenty-first century, global transitions proclaim that we do – in truth – live in 'interesting times'. Significant changes in the earth's environment, either occurring naturally or induced by our continued meddling with the world's ecology, set the backdrop for vast changes in human life as we have previously experienced it. We are witness to the dissolution of nation-states and the emergence of what some call the 'global village'. The boundaries between cultures are becoming increasingly blurred and reformed, resulting in hybrids that are more global in nature and which some venture to call the 'new world order'. More and more of us no longer live and die in the village, town or city of our birth. Our increased mobility opens us up to endless choices about where to live, who to relate to, what to do with our lives and how to spend our days.

This sense of 'opportunity' can be both exciting and quite frightening. On one level, we have, individually and collectively, the chance to create ourselves and society anew; to recommit ourselves to breaking the old personal and societal historical patterns that have devastated many of this earth's natural resources and left millions dead from unbridled greed or hatred. At the same time, with so much change happening in almost every facet of life and in almost every corner of the world, it is worth raising the question as to whether our bodies and minds have the fortitude to endure, transform and prevail in a new vision – a 'New Age'.

There can be tyranny in unprecedented freedom; with so many options, we may not always know what to do or how to prioritize what is important in life. In the late 1970s, a Tibetan Buddhist teacher, Namgyal Rinpoche, spoke to a small group in London about what we might expect from the Aquarian Age. Many of us in the audience who had been cradled in the flower-power vision of the sixties wanted to see the heralding of an enlightened society. Namgyal

Rinpoche agreed that this was one possibility. However, he suggested that the more likely outcome would be the creation of massive institutionalization in which diversity would be valued less than homogenization, as has been envisaged in the works of George Orwell and in films such as *Brazil* and *Gattaca*. This state would not necessarily come about as a result of wanting to create oppression, but as a response to a collective wish for stability.

Similarly, we might view the emergence of Eastern and Western forms of religious fundamentalism in more recent times as an attempt to create a simple, secure framework in which to contain the collective angst of what seems to be a species out of control. When the institutions within society are in harmony with the universal principles, as revealed and elucidated in the world's wisdom traditions, the nobler qualities of people are able to emerge while society acts as a sort of safety net and a source of protection. When institutions fail to change or adapt with the times, and when they are focused on the containment of seeming chaos, people will experience oppression and respond with attitudes and behaviours often defined as anti-social. When religions rigidly define morality – what our relationship to the Divine should be – but are unwilling to address the ambiguity in everyday life with other than simplistic, patronizing answers, there results a shrinking pool of acceptable behavioural archetypes from which people can choose in order to self-actualize themselves. The consequence is more and more marginalized people in need of therapy, medication and emergency care and attention.

In the West, such 'interesting times' are often associated with the 'end of time', the Apocalypse or Armageddon. In the East, such a period is just considered a 'Dark Age' – not unlike the Dark Ages of times past in which planetary movements and increased levels of awareness have demanded changes of paradigms and behaviours, giving rise to 'new' world orders. In other words, as we enter the twenty-first century we are going through a 'growth spurt' of sorts. We are being asked to re-envisage ourselves and our world. And, to sweeten the pot, just to ensure that we take this mission seriously, we have added to the dynamics of these turbulent times the very real possibility of total global annihilation through self-inflicted nuclear or viral madness.

In such an atmosphere in which conditioned, contemporary wisdom often seems lacking, it is only logical and natural for people to seek out wisdom which transcends the times and cultures we are all emerging from. Fortunately for us, many ancient traditions contain wisdom and practices that we can call upon in order to address our present individual and collective predicament. Out of the Orient, three systems of knowledge, all linked by a common root, have made their way into contemporary awareness: the divination system of the I Ching, Feng Shui (the geomantic tradition of the East) and Nine Star Ki astrology.

# FROM TORTOISE SHELL TO LAMAISTIC CALENDARS

According to one tradition, two thousand years before the Common Era, a series of floods threatened civilization along the Yellow River in China. Fu Hsi, a man of extraordinary talents, appeared at this time and through his knowledge of rivers and engineering, improved the movement of the river, thus re-establishing order in the region. For this he was made Emperor, and prosperity increased for all.

While making his river improvements, Fu came across a tortoise, a symbol of long life and happiness. He was overjoyed to have discovered it, especially as tortoises were believed to carry the force of and to be messengers of the Divine.

Upon closer inspection of his tortoise, Fu Hsi noticed unusual white and black markings on its shell. These markings varied in their position and number, filling the box-like configurations or 'chambers' common to tortoise shells. Each of nine chambers that bore these markings had a certain number of black and white linear marks, creating an interesting mathematical puzzle. Seeing this as a divine sign, Fu decided that a theory should be developed around this nine-chambered configuration; a theory that could be applied to understand nature and human actions. After he consulted with sages, the result was a theory that embraced and organized all systems of knowledge.[1] This theory lies at the root of the I Ching, Feng Shui and Nine Star Ki.

Beyond this legendary origin,

experts cannot agree on any set chronology for the systems of wisdom that emerged from the initial divine intervention. In their *Anthology of I Ching*, W. K. Chu and W. A. Sherrill contend that the nine chambers on the tortoise shell were the basis for the Later Heaven Sequence or Lo Map, a map symbolically representing the interaction between the trinity of celestial influences, earthly environment and humankind. The Lo Map is the basis of the Chinese art of placement, the geomantic tradition of Feng Shui, and directionology or considerations for movement and travel. The Lo Map is also considered to be the basis of the *Lo Shu* or 'Magic Square' whose symbology has been given different names in different cultures: the Nine House astrology of China, Nine Star Ki of Japan, and the system of *Mewas* or 'birthmarks' in Tibetan astrology.[2]

The exact – or even approximate – dates of the initial utilization of the *Lo Map* and *Lo Shu* for geomancy, directionology and prediction remain obscure. However, it is known that the Sun Almanacs, dated to the tenth century CE, contain fragments of Magic Squares and have been deciphered to reveal an elaborate system of numerology practised at that time. These almanacs were found in the ruins of lamaistic monasteries in the Tun Huang region of China, thus revealing the links between Tibetan and Chinese utilization of this system.[3] The proliferation of these practices, including Nine Star Ki, to Japan and other regions of the Far East remains a mystery. More than likely, with ordinary commerce and trade, travellers shared their knowledge and beliefs. Such sharing, combined with our human curiosity, has undoubtedly contributed to a richer body of knowledge of life that cannot be credited to any one culture.

Feng Shui, as it has been thus far defined in history, is generally associated with the influences of earth or nature on humanity as regards place. However, the celestial influences also reflected in the Magic Square and the laws that govern its symbols and movements over time are the domain of what we shall call Nine Star Ki – its most commonly recognized name in the West. Whereas traditional Feng Shui sets the stage and advises us on how to make the most of the world we find ourselves in, Nine Star Ki refines this knowledge through its understanding of time and the impact of celestial forces on the raw material

of nature and all manifest forms. Nine Star Ki allows us to recognize the specific, core strengths and challenges which lead us to think, act and respond the way we do. With such increased self-knowledge, the recommendations and cures offered by Feng Shui become even more personal, dynamic and effective.

Tibetan tradition views Feng Shui or Sa-Che (its Tibetan equivalent) and all systems of astrology, including Nine Star Ki, as a worldly dharma or truth. Worldly truths or dharmas are intended to be an aid on the path to spiritual unfolding, the domain of the higher dharmas. To put it another way, we need to create an ideal physical environment and utilize our human resources and resourcefulness as best we can in order to accomplish the universal mission of true spiritual pursuit, achieved by mending the illusion of separation from the Divine. The value of Nine Star Ki in this mission is best illustrated by where Tibetans place the *Mewas* (the Tibetan name for the Nine Star Ki archetypes) in their elaborate astrological system.

Honouring the system's origins, Tibetans create yearly astrological calendars on the drawn image of the underside of a tortoise's shell. According to some Tibetan historical records, Fu Hsi was indeed a very special person and the tortoise he found was no less than an emanation of the Bodhisattva Manjusri. Tibetan tradition reveres Manjusri as being the source of all knowledge, including astrology, and the Bodhisattva or saint prayed to for guidance in learning anything that benefits sentient beings.

A Tibetan astrological calendar is formed in concentric circles according to one of the more standard presentations (see Figure 1 for an example). Going from the outside in, its rings contain the symbols of the twelve astrological animal signs, the symbols of the elements influencing the characteristics of the archetypal animal of the year, the Par-kha (called *Pa Qua* in Chinese or *Bagua* in the Japanese) or basic trigrams known in the I Ching and, finally, in the centre the Magic Square, arranged with numbers that are ascribed to the elements or transformations (which will be discussed in the following chapters), set in houses based on the particular year. Each animal sign reveals general characteristics which influence the personality of those born under it. However, the element associated with the particular year governed by the sign

*Figure 1. Tibetan astrological calendar*

reveals certain, specific modifications to those characteristics. In some respects they can best be described as inclinations which set the mood of the animal governing the year. The combination of animal with element is also important when assessing compatibility with others.

The Bagua (Par-kha) are the eight trigrams that symbolically represent the most essential energetic interactions in the irreducible and ever-interacting cosmic forces of yin and yang (see below). The characteristics attributed to these series of trigrams configures as a series of broken (yin) and solid (yang) lines, ranging from the most subtle to the most dense or material. They are the encoded representations of universal knowledge and order, and are thus symbols for all the phenomena we experience, including ourselves as experiencers. Feng Shui and the astrological traditions of Tibet, China and Japan identify with each of these trigrams resources that every one of us needs to access and work with effectively if we are to transform our mundane lives and realize our full potential as spiritual beings incarnate. In the East, accessing these resources means success on all levels: to feel inspired, to be aware of our true potential, to have convictions and to be aligned with and focused on our life's true purpose. It means being able to identify and access support for our efforts, to experience unconditional love and friendship and to be able to reciprocate in kind; it entails mastering all the fame, success and riches we encounter to benefit others most effectively whilst continually nurturing who we are so that we, in turn, become a wellspring – an inspiration to others. In so doing, we will fulfil what can be each of our destinies. Destiny here does not imply pre-determination, but rather a recognition of our inherent capabilities to become enlightened or self-actualized.

In the centre of the Par-khas stands the Magic Square, the chambers or houses of which also have their corresponding trigram. Similar in nature to the Par-khas surrounding them, they are more specifically aligned to a facet of our destiny rooted in time. In each chamber, one of the nine numbers also has an assigned trigram. Unlike the Par-khas around the Magic Square, which remain stationary, and the trigrams associated with a given chamber or house, the trigram of a given number moves through the various houses of the Magic Square over the course of the years. The configuration in a yearly chart thus reveals the dominant energy for that particular year. The configuration of the numbers, with their traits and their qualities as revealed in the Magic Square, modifies how we should approach and work with the various different aspects of our destiny, and how we process information, interact and communicate through the animal personality that we are. A modern analogy is that the animals, the elements and Par-khas are like software programmes that are installed into a computer. All of them are loaded and function in accordance with what the mainframe or hard drive of the computer permits. The Tibetan term *Mewa* or 'birth mark' is quite an appropriate name for this data. Birth marks are what you are born with. They do not go away. Similarly, the *Mewas* or the Nine Star Ki data for a person are *immutable*. They do not change. It will be the matrix through which all of life's experiences will have to pass in order to be processed and acted upon. If you learn how to understand, accept and work with the strengths and weakness of the matrix that is you, you can become master of the most difficult of matrices. It will allow you to utilize more effectively whatever knowledge or experience you encounter at any level, from the most mundane to the most exalted and spiritual.

## AN ANCIENT SYSTEM OF ASTROLOGY FOR MODERN TIMES

At a time when humankind was more keenly aware of its intimate relationship with nature than it is today, astrology was a part of life. Life situations, crises and opportunities for material and spiritual growth could be perceived and acted upon more clearly as the interaction between microcosm (humankind) and macrocosm (heaven and earth) was revealed by those adept in this ancient science.

If such information was useful to societies that lived closer to nature, it is even more vital today when the pace and stimulation of modern living makes us lose touch with what truly keeps us alive and gives life meaning. And while every system of astrology has something to offer us,

the calculations and information available in Nine Star Ki Astrology are relatively easy to learn, thus making it a system suited to modern times and our way of life.

The same applies to the theory supporting Nine Star Ki. Some may want a scholarly approach to this theory, in which case Appendix 2 will be interesting and informative. For those of you wanting key concepts so that you can just get on and work with the Ki, the following definitions will suffice for interpreting the basic data of the Nine Star Ki archetypes.

### Yin, Yang and Ki

*Yin* and *yang* are the names given to polar opposite forces in nature.

Considered to be *the* primal forces from which everything is created and dissolved or destroyed, each is ascribed certain properties, properties that remain constant even though different Oriental traditions will use the terms yin and yang in seemingly contradictory ways. The properties associated with these two terms in this volume are in keeping with those of Oriental philosopher George Ohsawa and the Macrobiotic tradition.

The distinctions drawn between yin and yang can be seen in Ohsawa's classification of their traits and tendencies.[4]

On a more psycho-spiritual level, yin is classified as intuitive awareness and compassion. The Chinese deity Kuan Yin best exemplifies this. Yang is classified as intellect with the will towards action. Even though such distinctions are drawn, it must be understood that yin does not exist without yang or vice versa. Both are present and needed in varying degrees for all things in nature – whether they be rocks or thought forms – to exist.

*Ki* refers to life force. This life force is present in the interaction between yin and yang. It is only detected by its presence in this interaction and bears a particular signature based on the specific balance of yin and yang in this interaction. Yet to say that it is the same as yin and yang would not be correct. The cultivation and direction of ki or life force is the primary purpose of the meditative, healing and martial arts traditions of the Orient. Still, like life itself, it escapes the scrutiny of the question, 'Why?' However, the question, 'How?' is permissible and thus creates opportunities for study and mastery.

|  | **Yin** | **Yang** |
|---|---|---|
| tendency | expansion | contraction |
| position | outward | inward |
| structure | space | time |
| direction | ascent | descent |
| colour | purple | red |
| temperature | cold | hot |
| weight | light | heavy |
| catalyst | water | fire |
| atomic particle | electron | proton |
| light | dark | bright |
| vibration | short wave | long wave |
| work | psychological | physical |
| attitude | gentle, negative | active, positive |
| biological | vegetable | animal |
| sex | female | male |
| nerves | orthosympathetic | parasympathetic |
| elements | K, O, P, Ca, N | H, As, Cl, Na, C |

*Figure 2. Yin and yang traits and tendencies*

## The Five Transformations

As the forces of yin, yang and ki interact in varying degrees and proportions, specific phases are created through which all things must pass. Sages observed five distinct phases in the cycle from birth to death. These are:

1. creation
2. gestation (or vibrancy)
3. consolidation
4. maturation
5. dissolution and dormancy.

An example of this is a seed which sprouts, grows, forms into fruit, reaches full ripening and then falls to the ground, from whence the cycle is repeated. All things in nature, from the most inert (minerals) to the most subtle (thought vibration) go through all five phases. Not only that, sages could see sub-cycles in each phase. So for example in the case of a piece of fruit, the seed has to mature and decay before the sprout can emerge, and so on.

The ancients observed that in each phase, regardless of whether it is a part of a long or a brief cycle, there are distinct properties inherent in it. Over time, the aggregates of a certain phase were given names that metaphorically symbolize the dynamics of that phase.

1. The energetics and properties present in birth, creation, or first impulse are known as *tree* or *space*. Tree implies something breaking through the ground for the first time, arising from dormancy. Space implies the invisible potential from which all things are born. In some literature you will find this phase referred to as 'wood' or 'ether'.

2. The energetics and properties present in gestation are known as fire. Fire implies the vibrancy of life – glowing with potential. It is seen in the bud of a flower that is ready to burst into bloom. This is the phase that is outwardly most active – as if everything is being worked on all at once. Fire is very consuming and noticeable from afar.

3. The energetics and properties present in consolidation are known as *earth*, where things are settling down from fire. Things are at their densest and fully present in the form in which they will eventually mature; the first glimpses of a finished product. Earth bears the quality of accomplishment through effort.

4. The energetics and properties in completion or maturation are known as *air* or *metal*. When something has reached its ripest, it has reached its capacity. In a living organism, this means that the level of oxygen it can hold has reached its fullest capacity. Beyond this point it will begin to lose this capacity and its use of air will likewise diminish. Metal implies something that stands on its own. There is a quality here of certainty; almost a relaxed boldness.

5. The energetics and properties in dissolution and dormancy are referred to as *water*. The signposts of water are in the dissolution of what was fully grown, its death and the storing in dormancy of the potential for what will come next. This dormant potential portends the future. Thus the death of any one thing always carries with it the signature of a birth-to-be.

The chart below summarizes these phases.

Earlier translations of Chinese literature have called these the *elements* of life. However, because elements to us implies irreducible building blocks like in our atomic chart, modern theorists of Oriental knowledge have elected to use the word *transformation* to convey the irreducible yet *dynamic* nature of each phase and its characteristics.

Thus all things in nature possess the Five Transformations. Different species are dominated by different transformations and even within one species, the blending of transformations varies with time and circumstances. Relating this to human life, we are born and eventually die, in which case all transformations show themselves in the grand life cycle. But even daily, cells in different organs and tissues are born and die.

| Phases in the Birth to Death Cycle | The Elements |
|---|---|
| Creation | Tree/Space |
| Gestation | Fire |
| Consolidation | Earth |
| Maturation | Air/Metal |
| Dissolution | Water |

*Figure 3. Elements associated with phases in the birth to death cycle*

Some of these changes are by genetic design; some are dramatically influenced by how we live. And sages could see the Five Transformations at work on the physiological, psychological and spiritual dimensions of our being. Some of their findings and classifications are found in the chart in Appendix 1. For further information on this subject, see Appendix 2.

## NINE STAR KI ASTROLOGY: LEARNING FROM CYCLES IN NATURE

Wise people of the past who fully comprehended the relationship between heaven, earth and mankind observed that every nine years there is a predictable cycle in which each transformation becomes dominant for a given period of time. The chart in Figure 4 shows the relationship between the number of the year in the nine-year cycle and the transformation most dominant at that time. (The chart also shows whether a year and its associated transformation are considered more yin or yang at that time, and the trigrams that came from the encoding first found on Fu Hsi's tortoise.) The significance of these trigrams in Feng Shui and Nine Star Ki will be discussed in the following chapter.

These people also observed monthly, daily and hourly cycles. Thus the nine-year relationship to the transformations was similarly reflected in smaller increments of time.

| Transformation Phase (Element) | Yin/Yang | Number | Trigram | |
|---|---|---|---|---|
| Fire | Yin | 9 | ☲ | (Li) |
| Earth | Yang | 8 | ☶ | (Ken) |
| Air/Metal | Yin | 7 | ☱ | (Tui) |
| Air/Metal | Yang | 6 | ☰ | (Ch'ien) |
| Earth | Yin/Yang | 5 | O | none |
| Tree/Space | Yin | 4 | ☴ | (Sun) |
| Tree/Space | Yang | 3 | ☳ | (Chen) |
| Earth | Yin | 2 | ☷ | (Kun) |
| Water | Yang | 1 | ☵ | (Kan) |

*Figure 4. The relationship between year number and transformation phase*

By virtue of the time that we are born, certain transformations are more dominant in our nature than others. All the descriptions of the numbers and the transformations they represent that follow in these pages are based on centuries of observing human life and behaviour.

And as will be seen, the sages were able to look into the deepest aspects of our being and see the subtle influences of the Five Transformations in our likes, dislikes, personality quirks, interactive skills and aspirations. Further information on this subject is provided in Appendix 2.

## Of What Use is Nine Star Ki in my Life?

Nine Star Ki is a very versatile and accessible astrological system. And what makes this book a unique volume on this system is that along with useful personal information for understanding ourselves and others, equal attention is given to understanding the processes of interaction, the dynamics between people.

People can approach it from a variety of levels, from personal to professional.

1. *For those with a personal interest*, there are four basic relationships addressed. First and foremost is one's relationship to oneself. For self-growth and development, Nine Star Ki will reveal to you your *core* or primary strengths and weaknesses on physical, psychological and spiritual levels. Knowing what your primary strengths are, you can tap into them to develop deeper intimacy with others, to become more effective in work or business, and to know how to best access your resources of spiritual development for greater fulfilment. Knowing your weaknesses, rather than berating yourself for character defects, you will understand – on an energetic level – what you need to cultivate in your character and being. As regards prediction, you will – with practice – understand why certain years and months affect you the way they do, thus enabling you to plan careers, holidays, or any other form of life change, with a greater sense of focus and purpose. And your ability to understand and communicate effectively with others will be greatly

enhanced as your perception becomes more aligned with how things really are for you rather than how you have been conditioned to see yourself and others.

2. *If you are a therapist or agent of change for others* (including doctors, lawyers, etc), you will find in Nine Star Ki an excellent short cut to understanding the people you counsel. Knowing a person's Ki characteristics and addressing them accordingly will create a stronger bond and enhance communication and transformative processes and techniques on all levels. An entire section of this book is devoted to the application of Nine Star Ki to group dynamics. Thus working with family systems and structured groups in any context will be more realistic and accurate. You will be more effective in facilitating change and growth on personal and interpersonal levels. Consequently you will save time and find your work less stressful and more rewarding.

3. *Businesses and business-minded people* will learn how to bring out the best in themselves and others, such as employees. You will understand what makes any kind of team or organization function the way it does. You will be able to select the right person for the right job, delegate more effectively, and determine what traits in an organization need to be cultivated for greater effectiveness, productivity and growth.

4. For those of you who use Feng Shui personally or professionally, Nine Star Ki will allow you to address significant areas in your life that will

further your overall success and create environments and spaces which enhance personal effectiveness at all levels. A unique feature of this second edition is the inclusion of information about the Bagua or Parkha, what it highlights about our destiny and how each of the Nine Star Ki archetypes interacts with and will most auspiciously be transformed in relation to the Bagua using the alchemy of the Five Transformations.

The next chapter is a description of how to calculate the year and month Nine Star Ki numbers that are relevant to you, what can be learned from understanding the transformation phases that are associated with them, and how to interpret the various combinations of year and month Nine Star Ki numbers that are created at the time of birth and over the passage of time. This knowledge can then be applied to yourself for your own growth and development, for understanding and nurturing others, and for working more effectively in any group situation.

Ki as used in this book refers to energy – life energy. As it is pronounced 'key', there is an obvious, even deeper meaning to the title. *Life is energy in transformation.* If one can learn the mechanisms underlying this transformational process, one indeed has the 'key' to a deeper, fuller, richer life.

# How to Calculate Your Nine Star Ki Numbers

Although there are both hourly and daily times in which one of the five transformations is dominant, in order to focus on more basic constitutional or long-lasting traits and conditional or circumstantial tendencies we shall focus only on the Nine Star Ki numbers and associated transformations connected with a person's birth year and month. The descriptions of the Nine Numbers in Part II are used for understanding both natal year and natal month tendencies. However, there is a significant difference in how the year and month numbers impact our lives. This follows in the description of how to calculate both of these numbers.

## CALCULATING YOUR ADULT NATAL YEAR NUMBER

The number and transformation phase ascribed to a person's year of birth has to do with their optimal potential. As a person becomes an individual in their own right, the qualities of the natal year become more and more apparent in their physical expression, attitudes and actions. The emphasis here is on strengths. This does not mean that there are no challenges in the person's life, paradoxes in the personality, conflicts, and such like. Rather, when a person begins to actualize their natal year potential fully the seeming quirks characteristic of that year and resulting interactions with life's events become the texture that makes their life interesting and fruitful. To distinguish these year traits from month traits, they are classified as 'adult' traits or potentials as opposed to the month influences which are classified as 'child' traits or potentials. (You should get used to seeing year traits described as 'adult

natal year' traits and month traits as 'child natal month' traits.)

The natal year is about self-actualization. Therefore it is not something one just falls into easily. Indeed conditional patterns from childhood and circumstances may prevail and the adult natal year potential remain dormant. To overcome these limitations on one's potential requires personal commitment to openness and growth. As this volume focuses on how the Par-kha or Bagua influences our potentials for self-actualization, the most important Nine Star Ki number in this particular application is the year number. This will be elaborated on further in this chapter.

A list of the numbers associated with particular years is given in Figure 5. Please bear in mind that the year is

*Figure 5. (Opposite) Year and the yang, or descending, natal year numbers*

## HOW TO CALCULATE YOUR NINE STAR KI NUMBERS

| Year | Number | Year | Number | Year | Number | Year | Number |
|------|--------|------|--------|------|--------|------|--------|
| 1896 | 5 | 1925 | 3 | 1954 | 1 | 1983 | 8 |
| 1897 | 4 | 1926 | 2 | 1955 | 9 | 1984 | 7 |
| 1898 | 3 | 1927 | 1 | 1956 | 8 | 1985 | 6 |
| 1899 | 2 | 1928 | 9 | 1957 | 7 | 1986 | 5 |
| 1900 | 1 | 1929 | 8 | 1958 | 6 | 1987 | 4 |
| 1901 | 9 | 1930 | 7 | 1959 | 5 | 1988 | 3 |
| 1902 | 8 | 1931 | 6 | 1960 | 4 | 1989 | 2 |
| 1903 | 7 | 1932 | 5 | 1961 | 3 | 1990 | 1 |
| 1904 | 6 | 1933 | 4 | 1962 | 2 | 1991 | 9 |
| 1905 | 5 | 1934 | 3 | 1963 | 1 | 1992 | 8 |
| 1906 | 4 | 1935 | 2 | 1964 | 9 | 1993 | 7 |
| 1907 | 3 | 1936 | 1 | 1965 | 8 | 1994 | 6 |
| 1908 | 2 | 1937 | 9 | 1966 | 7 | 1995 | 5 |
| 1909 | 1 | 1938 | 8 | 1967 | 6 | 1996 | 4 |
| 1910 | 9 | 1939 | 7 | 1968 | 5 | 1997 | 3 |
| 1911 | 8 | 1940 | 6 | 1969 | 4 | 1998 | 2 |
| 1912 | 7 | 1941 | 5 | 1970 | 3 | 1999 | 1 |
| 1913 | 6 | 1942 | 4 | 1971 | 2 | 2000 | 9 |
| 1914 | 5 | 1943 | 3 | 1972 | 1 | 2001 | 8 |
| 1915 | 4 | 1944 | 2 | 1973 | 9 | 2002 | 7 |
| 1916 | 3 | 1945 | 1 | 1974 | 8 | 2003 | 6 |
| 1917 | 2 | 1946 | 9 | 1975 | 7 | 2004 | 5 |
| 1918 | 1 | 1947 | 8 | 1976 | 6 | 2005 | 4 |
| 1919 | 9 | 1948 | 7 | 1977 | 5 | 2006 | 3 |
| 1920 | 8 | 1949 | 6 | 1978 | 4 | 2007 | 2 |
| 1921 | 7 | 1950 | 5 | 1979 | 3 | 2008 | 1 |
| 1922 | 6 | 1951 | 4 | 1980 | 2 | 2009 | 9 |
| 1923 | 5 | 1952 | 3 | 1981 | 1 | 2010 | 8 |
| 1924 | 4 | 1953 | 2 | 1982 | 9 | 2011 | 7 |

based on the Chinese lunar calendar and the start of the year is based on the mid-point between the winter solstice and the vernal equinox (first day of winter and first day of spring respectively). This means that the year begins roughly on 4 February. Thus if you were born between 1 January and 3 February, use the preceding year as the way to find your associated adult natal year. At the same time, if your birthdate is close to 4 February, say between the 1 and 6 February, I suggest you look at the characteristics for the two natal year numbers that meet at that point in time and assess for yourself which of the two archetypes you identify with the most.

Of course, once you become proficient in knowing the traits of the transformations, you may want to calculate the numbers without the use of the chart. To do so, there is a formula to work to. This formula will work for all years from 0 to 3000 C.E. (Credit is due to Robert Metz from San Luis Obispo, California for contributing his computer and mathematical skills to work on this formula.)

Let's take an example: 1947. To get the Nine Star Ki number for the year 1947, take all four digits (1, 9, 4, 7) and add them together:

$1 + 9 + 4 + 7 = 21.$

Now take the number 21 and add its two digits together in order to reduce it to a single digit:

$2 + 1 = 3.$

This 3 is then subtracted from the number 11:

$11 - 3 = 8.$

This 8 is the Nine Star Ki number for the year 1947.

Another example could be 1960:

1 + 9 + 6 + 0 = 16,

1 + 6 = 7, 11 − 7 = 4.

Thus 4 is the Nine Star Ki number for 1960.

To summarize the points in this formula:

1. Add all the digits of the year to get a single number.

2. If the number derived has one digit, leave it as it is. If it has two digits, add these two digits together to reduce the digits to a single digit number.

3. Subtract the number derived from 11.

4. The number derived at this point is your Nine Star Ki year or *adult* natal number.

There are instances when the number calculated from adding all 4 numbers is 10. For example the year 1900: 1 + 9 = 10. When reduced to one digit, we are left with a 1, which when subtracted from 11 equals 10. The solution here is to reduce this number to a single digit: 11 − 1 = 10, 1 + 0 = 1. Thus, the year number for 1900 is 1.

With this formula, you can go back in history and look at historical figures, perhaps even your own ancestors. And if this book is picked up by someone in the year 2786, it will still work!

But, as mentioned earlier, remember that if you are looking for the year number for someone born between 1 January and 3 February, the Nine Star Ki year is calculated based on the previous calendar year. For example, if the date of birth is 15 January 1971, you would not use 1971 for your calculation, but rather 1970: 1 + 9 + 7 + 0 = 17,

1 + 7 = 8, 11 − 8 = 3.

Oriental masters observed that there are both descending and ascending numbers through time. The descending or yang order shown here is the one most commonly used. Appendix 4 explains the significance of the ascending order and supplies useful charts for years and months. In these changing times, I advise all those who are serious about using Nine Star Ki to familiarize themselves with both orders.

## CALCULATING YOUR CHILD NATAL MONTH NUMBER

The number and transformation phase ascribed to a person's month of birth has similar potential to the natal year, but is more bound by time and conditioned by events. It is in the first two cycles of nine – up to the age of eighteen years – that the natal month's transformation phase is most noticeably dominant, that is when a person is more dependent upon others and has less obvious control over their circumstances. Thus reactions and responses to others and to events are determined by the qualities and characteristics of the natal month's transformation phase.

It is also the foundation from which the potentials of a person's natal year will emerge. Consequently the transition from natal month to natal year aspects can vary considerably – smooth, rocky, chaotic, etc. This is not only because of the reactions and responses a person has gone through in dealing with others and with circumstances. There are also definite ways in which two transformation phases interact with each other, in which case what the person experiences in going from a more dependent to independent way of life and being may be strictly an internal (psychological) process.

In times of stress in adult years, responses and reactions of the natal month will re-emerge. This can also happen if, in early years, because of particular circumstances, usually crises and traumatic events, a person was thrust into a more independent, hence a more adult, mode. In such a case the adult year characteristics may dominate the child month characteristics in an unhealthy way, and it is only logical that they should re-emerge when there is no crisis. This may, in fact, be the origin of the adult-child response, and what is actually referred to as the 'child within' in literature on co-dependency and dysfunctional families. Another circumstance in which the natal month qualities may re-emerge in later years is when a person is in a position where they may again become dependent upon others.

When the natal month's transformation phase and its associated organs, systems, etc. are reactivated in this manner, it usually becomes the ground for physiological and psychological stress and disease. Rarely do the bodily systems, organs or psychological functions associated with the natal year become over-stressed or diseased, unless there are external pressures or life-threatening situations arising from outside causes. In general, and more often than not, when a person finds that their natal month transformation is being reactivated, along with it come unresolved childhood patterns and reactions. Once again perceiving ourselves to be victims of circumstances, we lose our ability to express ourselves and open the door to any number of problems in the many aspects of our lives.

The remedy for such a turn of events is to acknowledge the situation, that we are in our natal month expression, look for ways that would help us to develop or bring such a phase to a positive resolution, and move on. The strategies to make a transition from natal month (child) to natal year (adult) expression are numerous. The key ingredients for a successful blend, where both child and adult aspects are being nurtured in a balanced fashion, are kindness to oneself and humour.

There is no simple formula for calculating the natal month number, so a chart is provided opposite. It should be noted that there is some variation in the monthly charts between the Chinese and Japanese systems of Nine Star Ki. Again, this is because of the variance in the start of the year according to these traditions. If we were to add to this the variance from the Tibetan methods of calculation, we would possibly spawn an interesting cosmological and philosophical discussion but paralyze ourselves into inaction because of confusion. Therefore, I have chosen the year and month charts most commonly used and accepted. Like the year number, if you find that your day of birth in the month comes one or two days either side of the ending and beginning points for the months as indicated in Figure 6, look at the two adjacent month numbers and assess for yourself which one you identify with the most. For example, if a person is born on 7 August in a 1 year, they should look a the characteristics ascribed to both 3 and 2 natal numbers.

| When your Nine Star Ki Birth Year Number is... | 1, 4 or 7 | 2, 5 or 8 | 3, 6 or 9 | For birthdays between |
|---|---|---|---|---|
| **Your Nine Star Ki Birth Month Number is** | 8 | 2 | 5 | 4 Feb 5—5 Mar |
| | 7 | 1 | 4 | 6 Mar—4 Apr |
| | 6 | 9 | 3 | 5 Apr—5 May |
| | 5 | 8 | 2 | 6 May—5 Jun |
| | 4 | 7 | 1 | 6 Jun—7 Jul |
| | 3 | 6 | 9 | 8 Jul—7 Aug |
| | 2 | 5 | 8 | 8 Aug—7 Sep |
| | 1 | 4 | 7 | 8 Sep—8 Oct |
| | 9 | 3 | 6 | 9 Oct—7 Nov |
| | 8 | 2 | 5 | 8 Nov—7 Dec |
| | 7 | 1 | 4 | 8 Dec—5 Jan |
| | 6 | 9 | 3 | 6 Jan—3 Feb |

*Figure 6. Months and the yang, or descending, natal year numbers*

Although this is the chart we refer to generally, as it divides the year into twelve equal portions and ascribes numbers accordingly, Sherrill and Chu's monthly chart in *An Anthology of I Ching* is based on the Chinese system of twenty-four seasons. An explanation for this variation and the chart itself can be found in Appendix 3.

## THE GENDER OF THE NUMBER

We saw previously that each number has associated with it a transformation and that each transformation is proportionately more yin or yang in its properties, relatively speaking. Some transformations are more dominantly yin or yang, and others have combinations of yin and yang that vary in accordance with time – again, relatively speaking. Thus, for example, whereas fire is associated with yin and water with yang, earth, tree/space and metal/air have both more overtly yin and yang aspects. Thus one finds that in the passage of time, numbers associated with one element (such as tree/space) will have a yang (3) and yin (4) period of time.

The yin and yang nature of each of the numbers is significant for personality characteristics and physiological/psychological tendencies. Thus, using the concept of female (f) as representing yin and male (m) as representing yang, each number when calculated is listed with its yin or yang aspect by putting an 'f' or 'm' beside it. Thus a person born in a 1 Water year will see it represented as *1(m)*, the 'm' representing male or yang, whereas in *7(f)*, the 'f' would signify female or yin.

These gender aspects to the numbers *do not vary* according whether the person is male or female. They remain constant and there is some significance in there being a dominant male or female energetic in the numbers for a man or a woman.

Classical acupuncture theory classifies yin and yang as having certain archetypal characteristics. The polarity of these two is often described in terms of gender. Such categorization is not accidental or arbitrary. The deeper significance of this gender distinction is discussed at length in Part III.

## THE HOUSE OF THE CHILD NATAL MONTH NUMBER

Similar to occidental and other oriental astrologies, the Nine Star Ki system includes the notion of 'houses'. These houses are from the concepts inherent in what is called the Magic Square. Simply stated, the Magic Square represents the qualities, order and movement of all phenomena here on Earth as expressed in the Law of Five Transformations.

| SE | S | SW |
|---|---|---|
| 4 | 9 | 2 |
| 3 | 5 | 7 |
| 8 | 1 | 6 |

(E on the left, W on the right; NE bottom-left, N bottom-centre, NW bottom-right)

*Figure 7. The Magic Square (Lo Shu)*

Figure 7 is the classic Magic Square as traditionally depicted. What makes the square 'magic' is that with 5 in the middle, if you take any three numbers in a row in any direction within the square, they will add up to 15. The numbers as they are represented in this square with 5 in the middle is the standard representation. Thus not only are the numbers in their traditional positions, the number in each one of the square's positions is the house number of that position. (Figure 8.)

| SE | S | SW |
|---|---|---|
| House of 4 TREE | House of 9 FIRE | House of 2 EARTH |
| House of 3 TREE | House of 5 EARTH | House of 7 METAL |
| House of 8 EARTH | House of 1 WATER | House of 6 METAL |

E (left of middle row) · W (right of middle row)

NE · N · NW

*Figure 8. The Magic Square showing the houses and their transformation phases*

The Magic Square or *Lo Shu* was also given an octagonal or eight-sided appearance, known in Yoshikawa's *The Ki* as the Universal Chart. Because both representations are useful, I will use both, as they are both easy to comprehend and work with, and it will accustom you to using both.

Each year and month, the number in the centre of the Magic Square changes to the natal number of the year or month. Thus in a 9 year, 9 is in the centre; in an 8 year, 8 is in the centre, and so on. When this happens, all the other numbers migrate or change position in the Magic Square. Figure 9, showing the octagonal versions of the Magic Square, indicates what numbers are where when the number in the centre changes.

Although the numbers change

*Figure 9. Universal Charts*

their positions over time, the houses remain the same. Thus as each number and its associated transformation phase enter a particular house, there is an interaction that takes place between the basic qualities of the number entering that house and the house itself. Please bear in mind that the term 'house' as used in Nine Star Ki should not be equated in any way with the 'ninth house' or 'tenth house' etc. as referred to in Western astrology. The only similarity is in the term.

Every person's birth (natal) year is located in the 'house of 5' at the time of their birth and every nine years after that. To determine the house of the natal month, one needs to find where the natal month number is situated when the person's natal year is in the middle of the Magic Square.

Here is an example. A man is born on 1 March 1957. The natal year number for 1957 is 7 and the natal month number is 8. If you refer to Figure 9, you will see that when 7 is in the centre (where 5 was originally), 8 is in the position where 6 was. So 7 is said to be in the house of 5, and 8 in the house of 6.

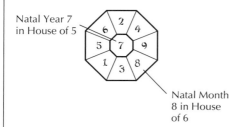

Natal Year 7 in House of 5

Natal Month 8 in House of 6

*Figure 10. Chart for someone born on 1 March1957*

The significance of the direction ascribed to the various houses is discussed in the chapter on 'The Houses'.

## WRITING DOWN YOUR COMPLETE BIRTH-DATE IN NINE STAR KI CONFIGURATION

If we were to take our previous example of a man born on 1 March 1957 and write out the Nine Star Ki numbers, it would appear as follows:

| Year | Month | House |
|------|-------|-------|
| 7f | (8m) | sixm |

Because the yin or yang nature of each of the numbers is significant for personality characteristics and physiological/psychological tendencies, using the concept of female (f) as representing yin and male (m) as representing yang, the birth-date can be written in the following manner:

7f (8m) sixm

Figure 4 on page 21 will help you

become familiar with which numbers are female (yin) and male (yang).

Familiarize yourself with writing out Nine Star Ki birth numbers in the manner shown. In this way, you can create constant birth-date charts that are immediately understood by those studying and using the Nine Star Ki system.

When the numbers are written in this manner, the following questions can be considered regarding the person being analyzed. Using our example of 7f (8m)sixm:

1. What are the characteristics of the natal year, 7?

2. What are the characteristics of the natal month, 8?

3. What is the relationship between the transformation phases of the natal year, 7, and the natal month, 8?

4. What dynamic is in operation with the natal month, 8, being in the house of 6 at the time of birth?

5. What influence do the gender f or m for the natal year, 7f and natal month 8m have on the man's character and his interactions?

To make such an investigation easier, there is an Easy Reference Table at the end of this chapter to enable you to find the pages in the text which will help you answer these questions. These are the basic questions for which the profiles, narratives and descriptions of numbers, house and gender dynamics in Part II have been designed. With greater proficiency in this system and deeper understanding of the Law of Five Transformations, you will be able to understand your changes and experiences, and those of other people, as the numbers migrate into the various houses during the months and years. Consequently, knowledge gleaned of yourself, of others and of relationships is not static but dynamic. Nature, in accordance with the Law of Five Transformations, provides us with a rich and varied assortment of elemental and energetic experiences from which we can learn of the mystery of life.

## A Point of Distinction Regarding the Third Number

My emphasis is on personal transformation as the most important *raison d'être* for Nine Star Ki, but readers of other Nine Star Ki books may have noted that many use the Yoshikawa tradition in determining the 'third'

number in a Nine Star Ki chart. Rather than finding what house the child or month number resides in in the *Lo Shu* associated with a person's Nine Star Ki year, Yoshikawa takes as his third number the house in which the person's year number resides in in the person's month chart. Thus, using my example from Figure 10, Yoshikawa would not use the Universal Chart for '7' (the year), but the chart for '8' (the month) to identify a third number. His third number would therefore be a '4'.

Please note that this is not a contradiction. The third number indicated in my calculations emphasizes a different aspect than that indicated in the Yoshikawa method. Yoshikawa calls his third number a 'tendency' number. In his *Feng Shui Astrology*, author Jon Sandifer states that this tendency number has more to do with the traits or qualities that another person might observe in us on first impression. He calls it an 'energetic' number.[5] In my own studies, I have seen this to be more evident when the child or month number is more to the forefront in a person's interactions. Thus, as a person self-actualizes, the presence of this aspect becomes less obvious and significant.

## THE BAGUA, THE NINE YEAR NUMBERS AND FENG SHUI

In the first edition of this book, the focus was on personal and interpersonal transformation. To accomplish this transformation, the emphasis was on our own inherent potentials and how to work with them through diet, exercise and psychological and spiritual attunement. The brief mention of directionology with respect to personal movement and travel was as close as that text came to discussing the spatial dimension of the Bagua that is addressed in Feng Shui. However, the growing concern for the environment and for the appropriate use of space in all spheres of activity – be it personal, professional, spiritual or political – means that applying how the Nine Star Ki archetypes interact with the spatial dimension of the Bagua is essential for the successful application of both Nine Star Ki and Feng Shui.

As mentioned earlier, both Feng Shui and Nine Star Ki have as their essential foundation the Lo Map. The basic configuration of this map, with its nine chambers, is by no means random. The knowledge gleaned from the symbols of each chamber, including the trigrams which make up the Bagua, its nine numbers and associated characteristics, is far reaching. Whilst the number and trigram of the yin or yang aspect of each transformation represented in each of the chambers remains constant, Nine Star Ki and Feng Shui focus on a particular aspect of how these function in time and space respectively.

Out of the vastness of the encoded material contained in the Lo Map, Feng Shui accesses data that provides a basic grid of what resources we can encounter if we envision whatever space we find ourselves in as the *Lo Shu* itself. Feng Shui focuses on the stationary dimension of this configuration and the *Lo Shu* as identified by the Bagua. There seem to be a variety of ways in which this is done. As each of the chambers of the *Lo Shu* are ascribed a particular compass direction, some Feng Shui prac-

titioners rely on true ordinal and cardinal directions when making recommendations. Others orient the Bagua in accordance with the main entrance to a space, house, building, etc. In either case, the purpose is to address how to maximize the potentials inherent in each direction for the fulfilment of a particular dimension of our life's destiny. This is accomplished by accentuating, embellishing or altering the space of a given direction.

To clarify further: every chamber of the *Lo Shu* has a trigram and an essential, unchanging number. The number associated with a given chamber acts like a 'house' in Western astrology – as explained earlier and will be elaborated on further in the chapter on 'The Houses'. The configuration of the *Lo Shu* with the Bagua and nine stationary numbers is as follows:

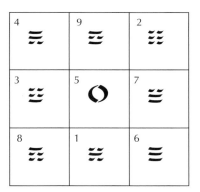

*Figure 11. Configuration of the* Lo Shu *with the Bagua and nine stationary numbers*

With respect to the resources we need to access and develop in order to realize our potential fully, each of the nine chambers offers the aspects listed below. Please bear in mind, that concerning the energetics of direction, this information can be taken both literally and metaphori-

cally. A Feng Shui master or consultant may derive from this information data to enhance a particular room in a house or office. A Nine Star Ki master or consultant can take from these qualities and attributes material that represents the transformations a person needs to work with in order to manifest a more rounded sense of success and self-actualization.

## ☵ Kan (The Abysmal), the North, House of One

The transformation of water here has to do with where the flow of our life is leading us. It is the direction and energetic that beckons us to look back and clearly assess what our potentials are to date, to ponder how best they can be used, and get a deep sense as to where they can lead us from this time forth. At the most superficial level this has been called

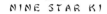

the chamber of the Bagua associated with career. More than career, however, the implications of this house are to remind us of our spiritual being and summon us to use our life's potential as a calling.

## ☷ Kun (The Receptive), the Southwest, House of Two

The transformation of earth in its most yin aspect has to do with our stepping out to embrace the world. Thus, this direction and its space are associated with relationships. True, Kun has to do with such relationships as marriage and partnerships, but its deeper meaning is about the unconditional aspect of relating. Thus, there is a sense of connectedness and cooperation that moves beyond barriers to a greater intimacy with all things. Being the most yin trigram and symbol of the primal mother, however, it implies

that in this situation we are not seeking mutuality, but rather a deep sense of connection and intimacy as nourishment for furthering our purpose in the world.

## ☳ Chen (Thunder or The Arousing), the East, House of Three

The yang aspect of the transformation of tree has been interpreted as meaning ancestors, including parents and teachers. The deeper meaning behind ancestry is that they are *sources of inspiration.* From their past efforts the seeds of possibility arise and become ours. What is needed on our part for these seeds to grow is for us to cherish what we have been offered and to have a sense of vision. The trigram Chen means thunder or the arousing. Tapping into the resources of ancestry, we access the best and most vital aspects of what has gone before, and are given the opportunity to mould it into new ways as yet uncharted. Ultimately, the ancestral source of all things manifest is the unmanifest – the 'uncarved block' of the Tao Te Ching or the Tibetan's mother of all existence, Vajrayogini. Vajrayogini expresses an emptiness that is pregnant with possibility. And the mark of Vajrayogini is the emptiness that is not separate from form. Realization of this truth puts us in touch with the source from which the alchemy of the Five Transformations unfolds.

## ☴ Sun (the Wind), the Southeast, House of Four

This is the tree transformation in its yin aspect. It has been called the trigram of prosperity or luck. What we should understand by these attributes is that they do not imply that this region of

the Bagua is about acquisition or riches that can be used or plundered. The trigram of the Wind tells of a force arising. Here we become aware of what resources are available to us and the possible riches they can bring. We need to acknowledge them and plan how we are going to use them in a creative and mindful way. We need to pay attention and be patient. If we are not, then it is like having a vegetable garden and pulling up the plants periodically to see how well they are growing.

## ◐ No trigram, (the Centre), House of Five

There is no trigram associated with this particular aspect of the earth. As kun or 2 is the yin aspect of earth and Ken or 8 is the yang aspect of earth, the trigram-less 5 stands between, almost as an androgine, but more appropriately as a dynamic balance between the forces of yin and yang inherent in all the other trigrams. This central position has been postulated thus far as meaning 'directionless'. I would like to contend, however, that we look at this central point more from a three-dimensional perspective. Thus the centre is where the axis of Zenith and Nadir, the positive and negative, the 'great' north and south poles reside. This central axial position thereby becomes the energetic resource for all transformations, their directions and their health. But health here does not imply mere physical or psychological wellbeing. In truth, health here has more to do with balance and integration of all aspects our being in a healthy, beneficial way. And so, whatever is at hand, we know how to use it most effectively.

Feng Shui experts encourage people to keep the centre of a room or the centre room of a house (if the Bagua is superimposed over the entire house) free of clutter, both below and above (including such 'clutter' as dingy marks, cracks in the plaster, or a bad paint job on the ceiling). Like the palm of our hand, we keep it open so that it can give, receive or protect and preserve. Avoiding extremes and learning in life to extend ourselves into the world and, at the same time, taking care of ourselves are aspects of the balance that is sought from the resource of the centre.

## ☰ Ch'ien (The Creative), the Northwest, House of Six

This is the yang aspect of the transformation of metal. The resources available from this direction are outside help and support. Though the trigram means the creative and is considered the force of heaven, it is more akin to our Western notion of a Heavenly Father who busies himself with bringing things into being and with assuring us that the resources needed to sustain these things are available. Thus, unlike Kun or the receptive with its unconditional, nurturing qualities, Ch'ien implies a more conditional sense of nurturing that has as its primary purposes protection, preservation and encouragement. But, as with all things conditional, there is a price. The price in accessing the resources of this energetic rests in the resolve to be likewise a source of protection, preservation and encouragement for others.

## ☱ Tui, (Joyous Lake), the West, House of Seven

This is the yin aspect of the transformation of metal. The resource available from this direction and its associated characteristics is the fruition of our own efforts; what riches we truly possess. What we have done, what we have created up to this point, is what we will find here as children, progeny or the completion of our tasks and projects. As such, from this direction we can cultivate the joy of accomplishment. The trigram of this direction being the Joyous Lake, we can imagine glacial snows melting and rivers feeding into a clear, cool lake. The lake is like the pooling of resources which can be enjoyed as they are, or used for further development.

Feng Shui experts encourage people to activate this house in order to manifest results and whilst there is certainly an aspect of rest and enjoyment that goes with this, it does not imply merely resting on our

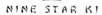

laurels. Rather, we need to be able to balance the enjoyment of fruition with being able to realistically evaluate results; what are they really worth? With such a view, we will escape the tendency towards self-indulgence.

### ☶ Ken (The Mountain), the Northeast, House of Eight

This trigram represents the yang aspect of the earth transformation. Translated as 'The Mountain', Ken represents stillness and contemplation. The purpose of this direction and its associated qualities is to cultivate in us a sense of conviction and the ability to stand firm on our own. To accomplish this, we need stillness and the opportunity to contemplate. This does not imply that we should become hermits or remove ourselves from the world. Certainly we may need solitude in order to reflect or meditate. From such times and opportunities indicated by Ken, we strive to know who we are, where we stand and what we stand for. We can therefore be in the world, being nourished by and providing nourishment to others, without feeling needy or co-dependent. This cultivates in us a quiet depth to our character.

### ☲ Li (The Clinging), the South, House of Nine

The trigram Li or 'The Clinging' represents the transformation of fire, which is yin in nature. Although fire is hot, it cannot exist without the presence of fuel; it must be receptive to fuel in order to burn.

Of all the trigrams, Li most obviously demonstrates the paradoxical nature in the law of complementary antagonisms; briefly stated as 'what has a front has a back; the bigger the front the bigger the back'. Fire is associated with light. Light can be like a spotlight and thus this trigram and its associated direction in the Bagua are associated with fame. However, a spotlight will not only present us to others in the way we may wish; it will also reveal to others aspects of ourselves we may not want revealed or scrutinized. This is the dual nature of fame – which is why I prefer to identify this trigram as meaning exposure. When seeking to be noticed and activating the energy of this direction, are we fully prepared for having each and every aspect of who we are noticed by others?

Another internal dimension of Li lies in how this direction reveals to us more clearly what our guiding light in life is. Such clarity can simplify matters and help us to burn away whatever is unnecessary in our lives.

At the same time, as we do this through the energetics of this direction, our motives and designs become more obvious to those around us. Again, in pursuing Fire, are we prepared for this exposure?

Through placement, spatial recommendations and 'cures', a Feng Shui practitioner attempts to maximize the resources a person needs in order to achieve the success they are looking for in life. At the same time, as we will discover in the chapters following the actual number–archetype descriptions, there are laws in the Five Transformations that concern themselves with how the transformations work together.

In our discussion of Nine Star Ki so far, we have mentioned the importance of the relationship between the transformation of the year and month

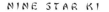

natal numbers, as well as the relationship between the month number transformation and the transformation of the house the natal month number resides in with respect to the natal year chart. We have also intimated and will discuss at length later on in the text how – through the passage of time – both the natal year and month numbers migrate through the various Houses of the *Lo Shu*, creating the weave and hue of our experiences.

As regards our individual process of self-actualization, I have stated that the archetype represented by our natal year number is the most critical. The Bagua of Feng Shui highlights the resources we have available to us for this process. The logical question becomes, if each of the trigrams of the Bagua similarly represents a given transformation, what is the relationship of any given trigram to our Nine Star Ki year number?

To answer this question, each number chapter will introduce basic material that can help individuals best understand and maximize their strengths, and overcome challenges in accessing resources needed for personal success – based on the interaction between their Nine Star Ki natal year number and the Bagua as used in Feng Shui.

When looking at this material please remember that, first and foremost, this is a book about Nine Star Ki. The energetic and basic Feng Shui 'cures' recommended in this volume are intended to satisfy readers who wish to add to the self-knowledge they glean from Nine Star Ki some additional environmental sensitivity, guidance and resources for success. Beyond this, I encourage you to seek out some of the Feng Shui resources listed in the section on Further Reading, as well as competent, professional Feng Shui practitioners. For those of you who are Feng Shui practitioners, the material presented will whet your appetite and provide you with a glimpse into how to make your consultations more personal and effective.

## SYSTEMS OF KNOWLEDGE AND ART

Systems of knowledge, be they analytically based sciences, philosophical theories or spiritual awarenesses derived from various methodologies, become meaningful only in so far as we are able to integrate them into our lives. Meaning is a very private matter and how we derive meaning from our world of experiences is based on factors too numerous or mysterious for any one book to expound fully. In many ways, the inferences and conclusions we draw from our lives – even if those inferences and conclusions seem to be based on 'hard' facts – are woven together like a unique tapestry, a piece of art.

Intuited knowledge and data drawn from an awareness of energetics as is found in the I Ching, Law of Five Transformations and Nine Star Ki may not bear the scrutiny of the scientific methods we currently apply. Indeed the language of such knowledge and data is often a mixture of philosophy, psychology, religion, natural science and metaphor. In fact, it is often the use of metaphor which creates the glue to enable such a variety of concepts to hang together.

Metaphors also create pictures of broader aspects of reality that we may not be able to conceptualize or describe in any other way. We should therefore also not be surprised that in the process of piecing data together contradictions arise within the picture. Unless we are robots, there are bound to be contradictions and inconsistencies in our approaches even to the same situations. This may have more to do with elemental and dynamic processes inherent in our nature than some kind of pathological aberration or sign of being weak-willed. It can be tremendously liberating and empowering to embrace our quirks and contradictory ways.

Thus it is that what is presented as Nine Star Ki data is a blend of knowledge and art, where the colours and textures of data and knowledge gleaned from the I Ching and Law of Five Transformations are pieced together with the glue of metaphor born of intuition and personal experience. In addition to studying the text,

you can deepen your knowledge of the Law of Five Transformations by reading Naboru Muramoto's *Healing Ourselves* and William Tara's *Macrobiotics and Human Behavior.* At the same time you are advised to test what is presented by reflecting upon your own experiences of life. In this way, what is studied becomes more meaningful. It also creates the possibility of new linkages within the body of knowledge and data being discovered, thus benefiting oneself and others.

## A BRIEF WORD OR TWO ABOUT ATTITUDE

To see ourselves truly as we are, we must learn to relax and give up our concern about who we are. We are used to typecasting ourselves or living in the images that others have created for us. Although we think that we are being free in our choices, we are too often bound by the cultural and social concepts of the day. The power of Nine Star Ki is that the traits and characteristics presented come from an ancient tradition based on the deepest contemplations and meditations of the great sages of the past. This makes such a body of knowledge and data more likely to cut through cultural and social nuances and be more precise and time tested. Therefore it speaks to us more directly, in a way that feels more truthful. It may also be an affront to the person we have portrayed ourselves to be.

As mentioned in the previous section, we need to reflect on what the Nine Star Ki presents to us. Reflection does not mean, however, to dissect our experience and the data morbidly. Reflection requires an ability to see things as they are. To do this, we need openness and humour. Reflection without openness and humour would lead us down a path where we become straitjacketed by our limited perceptions, with anything which does not fit within our perceptions being viewed with some level of cynicism. Not to reflect at all and just to accept the Nine Star Ki without personal scrutiny would make us mindless devotees.

The value of Nine Star Ki is its usefulness in helping us to deepen our appreciation of who we are and the transformations we go through in life. It should not be used as a new toy or gimmick to replace truly felt emotion or insight. In that way, Nine Star Ki becomes a facilitating tool rather than an answer to life and living in the world.

| | Adult number page | Child number page | Child number is mother to house it resides in (p.212) | Child number is son to house it resides in (p.212) | Child number is in house that it controls (p.213) | Child number is in house that it is controlled by (p.214) | Child number resides in house of same transformation as itself (p.215) | Adult number supports child number (p.228) | Adult number controls child number (p.228) | Child number supports adult number (p.227) | Child number controls adult number (p.229) | Adult and child number are same (p.214) | Adult and child transformation (not number) are same (p.230) | Males Same/same (p.233) | Males Same/opposite (p.234) | Males Opposite/same (p.235) | Males Opposite/opposite (p.236) | Females Same/same (p.233) | Females Same/opposite (p.234) | Females Opposite/same (p.235) |
|---|---|---|---|---|---|---|---|---|---|---|---|---|---|---|---|---|---|---|---|---|
| 1m (1m) five m/f | 179 | 179 | | | | ● | | | | | | ● | | ● | | | | | | |
| 1m (2f) six m | 179 | 164 | ● | | | | | | | ● | | | | | ● | | | | | ● |
| 1m (3m) seven f | 179 | 149 | | | | ● | | ● | | | | | | ● | | | | | | |
| 1m (4f) eight m | 179 | 133 | | | ● | | | ● | | | | | | | ● | | | | | ● |
| 1m (5m/f) nine f | 179 | 117 | | ● | | | | | | ● | | | | ● | ● | | | | | ● |
| 1m (6m) one m | 179 | 104 | ● | | | | | | ● | | | | | ● | | | | | | |
| 1m (7f) two f | 179 | 90 | | ● | | | | | ● | | | | | | ● | | | | | ● |
| 1m (8m) three m | 179 | 78 | | | | ● | | | | ● | | | | ● | | | | | | |
| 1m (9f) four f | 179 | 67 | | ● | | | | | | | ● | | | | ● | | | | | ● |
| 2f (1m) four f | 164 | 179 | ● | | | | | ● | | | | | | | | ● | | | ● | |
| 2f (2f) five m/f | 164 | 164 | | | | | ● | | | | | ● | | | | | ● | ● | | |
| 2f (3m) six m | 164 | 149 | | | | ● | | | | ● | | | | | | ● | | | ● | |
| 2f (4f) seven f | 164 | 133 | | | | ● | | | | ● | | | | | | | ● | ● | | |
| 2f (5m/f) eight m | 164 | 117 | | | | | ● | | | | | | ● | | | ● | ● | ● | ● | |
| 2f (6m) nine f | 164 | 104 | | | | ● | | ● | | | | | | | | ● | | | ● | |

*Figure 12. Easy-Reference Table. Once you have calculated the Nine Star Ki numbers for a given birth-date, locate that combination in the left-hand column of the table. Reading from left to right on the same line, you will find marks in at least four*

| | Adult number page | Child number page | Child number is mother to house it resides in (p.212) | Child number is son to house it resides in (p.212) | Child number is in house that it controls (p.213) | Child number is in house that it is controlled by (p.214) | Child number resides in house of same transformation as itself (p.215) | Adult number supports child number (p.228) | Adult number controls child number (p.228) | Child number supports adult number (p.227) | Child number controls adult number (p.229) | Adult and child number are same (p.214) | Adult and child transformation (not number) are same (p.230) | Males Same/same (p.233) | Males Same/opposite (p.234) | Males Opposite/same (p.235) | Males Opposite/opposite (p.236) | Females Same/same (p.233) | Females Same/opposite (p.234) | Females Opposite/same (p.235) | Females Opposite/opposite (p.236) |
|---|---|---|---|---|---|---|---|---|---|---|---|---|---|---|---|---|---|---|---|---|---|
| 2f (7f) one m | 164 | 90 | • | | | | • | | | | | | | | | | • | • | | | |
| 2f (8m) two f | 164 | 78 | | | | • | | | | | | | • | | | • | | | • | | |
| 2f (9f) three m | 164 | 67 | | • | | | | | | • | | | | | | | • | • | | | |
| 3m (1m) three m | 149 | 179 | • | | | | | | | • | | | | • | | | | | | | • |
| 3m (2f) four f | 149 | 164 | | | | • | | | • | | | | | | • | | | | | • | |
| 3m (3m) five m/f | 149 | 149 | | | • | | | | | | | • | | • | | | | | | | • |
| 3m (4f) six m | 149 | 133 | | | | • | | | | | | | • | | • | | | | | • | |
| 3m (5m/f) seven f | 149 | 117 | • | | | | | | • | | | | | • | • | | | | | • | • |
| 3m (6m) eight m | 149 | 104 | | • | | | | | | | • | | | • | | | | | | | • |
| 3m (7f) nine f | 149 | 90 | | | | • | | | | | • | | | | • | | | | | • | |
| 3m (8m) one m | 149 | 78 | | | • | | | | • | | | | | • | | | | | | | • |
| 3m (9f) two m | 149 | 67 | • | | | | • | | | | | | | | • | | | | | • | |
| 4f (1m) two m | 133 | 179 | | | | • | | • | | | | | | | | • | | | • | | |
| 4f (2f) three m | 133 | 164 | | | | • | | | • | | | | | | | | • | • | | | |
| 4f (3m)/ four f | 133 | 149 | | | | | • | | | | | | • | | | • | | | • | | |

*columns. Besides the number narratives, these indicate other significant points for the given number combination. Refer to the page number at the top of the column to find the information in the text.*

| | Adult number page | Child number page | Child number is mother to house it resides in (p.212) | Child number is son to house it resides in (p.212) | Child number is in house that it controls (p.213) | Child number is in house that it is controlled by (p.214) | Child number resides in house of same transformation as itself (p.215) | Adult number supports child number (p.228) | Adult number controls child number (p.228) | Child number supports adult number (p.227) | Child number controls adult number (p.229) | Adult and child number are same (p.214) | Adult and child transformation (not number) are same (p.230) | Males Same/same (p.233) | Males Same/opposite (p.234) | Males Opposite/same (p.235) | Males Opposite/opposite (p.236) | Females Same/same (p.233) | Females Same/opposite (p.234) | Females Opposite/same (p.235) |
|---|---|---|---|---|---|---|---|---|---|---|---|---|---|---|---|---|---|---|---|---|
| 4f(4f) five m/f | 133 | 133 | | | • | | | | | | | | • | | | | • | • | | |
| 4f(5m/f) six m | 133 | 117 | • | | | | | | • | | | | | | | • | • | • | • | |
| 4f(6m) seven f | 133 | 104 | | | | | • | | | • | | | | | | • | | | • | |
| 4f(7f) eight m | 133 | 90 | | • | | | | | | • | | | | | | | • | • | | |
| 4f(8m) nine f | 133 | 78 | | • | | | | | • | | | | | | | • | | | • | |
| 4f(9f) one m | 133 | 67 | | | | • | | • | | | | | | | | | • | • | | |
| 5m/f(1m) one m | 117 | 179 | | | | | • | | • | | | | | • | | • | | | • | |
| 5m/f(2f) two f | 117 | 164 | | | | | • | | | | | | • | • | • | | • | • | | • |
| 5m/f(3m) three m | 117 | 149 | | | | | • | | | • | | | | • | | • | | | • | |
| 5m/f(4f) four f | 117 | 133 | | | | | • | | | • | | | | | • | | • | • | | • |
| 5m/f(5m/f) five m/f | 117 | 117 | | | | | • | | | | | | • | • | • | • | • | • | • | • |
| 5m/f(6m) six m | 117 | 104 | | | | | • | • | | | | | | • | | • | | | • | |
| 5m/f(7f) seven f | 117 | 90 | | | | | • | • | | | | | | | • | | • | • | | • |
| 5m/f(8m) eight m | 117 | 78 | | | | | • | | | | | | • | • | | • | | | • | |
| 5m/f(9f)/ nine f | 117 | 67 | | | | | • | | | | • | | | | • | | • | • | | • |
| 6m (1m) nine f | 104 | 179 | | • | | | • | | | | | | • | | | | | | | |
| 6m(2f) one m | 104 | 164 | | • | | | | | | | • | | | | • | | | | | • |
| 6m(3m) two f | 104 | 149 | | • | | | | • | | | | | • | | | | | | | |
| 6m(4f) three m | 104 | 133 | | | | • | | • | | | | | | | • | | | | | • |

| | Adult number page | Child number page | Child number is mother to house it resides in (p.212) | Child number is son to house it resides in (p.212) | Child number is in house that it controls (p.213) | Child number is in house that it is controlled by (p.214) | Child number resides in house of same transformation as itself (p.215) | Adult number supports child number (p.228) | Adult number controls child number (p.228) | Child number supports adult number (p.227) | Child number controls adult number (p.229) | Adult and child number are same (p.214) | Adult and child transformation (not number) are same (p.230) | Males Same/same (p.233) | Males Same/opposite (p.234) | Males Opposite/same (p.235) | Males Opposite/opposite (p.236) | Females Same/same (p.233) | Females Same/opposite (p.234) | Females Opposite/same (p.235) | Females Opposite/opposite (p.236) |
|---|---|---|---|---|---|---|---|---|---|---|---|---|---|---|---|---|---|---|---|---|---|
| 5m(5m/f) four f | 104 | 117 | | | | • | | | | • | | | | • | • | | | | | • | • |
| 5m(6m) five m/f | 104 | 104 | | • | | | | | | | • | | | • | | | | | | | • |
| 5m(7f) six m | 104 | 90 | | | | | • | | | | | | • | | • | | | | | • | |
| 5m(8m) seven f | 104 | 78 | • | | | | | | | • | | | | • | | | | | | | • |
| 5m(9f) eight m | 104 | 67 | • | | | | | | • | | | | | | • | | | | | • | |
| 7f(1m) eight m | 90 | 179 | | | | • | | • | | | | | | | | • | | | • | | |
| 7f(2f) nine f | 90 | 164 | | • | | | | | | • | | | | | | | • | • | | | |
| 7f(3m) one m | 90 | 149 | | • | | | | | • | | | | | | | • | | | • | | |
| 7f(4f) two f | 90 | 133 | | | • | | | | • | | | | | | | | • | • | | | |
| 7f(5m/f) three m | 90 | 117 | | | | • | | | • | | | | | | | • | • | • | • | | |
| 7f(6f) four f | 90 | 104 | | | • | | | | | | | | • | | | • | | | • | | |
| 7f(7m/f) five m/f | 90 | 90 | | • | | | | | | | • | | | | | • | • | • | • | | |
| 7f(8m) six m | 90 | 78 | • | | | | | | • | | | | | | | • | | | • | | |
| 7f(9f) seven f | 90 | 67 | | | • | | | | | • | | | | | | • | • | • | • | | |
| 8m(1m)/ seven f | 78 | 179 | | • | | | | • | | | | | | • | | | | | | | • |
| 8m(2f) eight m | 78 | 164 | | | | | • | | | | • | | | • | | • | | | | • | |
| 8m(3m) nine f | 78 | 149 | • | | | | | | | • | | | | • | | | | | | | • |
| 8m(4f) one m | 78 | 133 | | • | | | | | | • | | | | | • | | | | | • | |
| 8m(5m/f) two f | 78 | 117 | | | | | • | | | | | | • | • | • | | | | | • | • |

57

| | Adult number page | Child number page | p.212 Child number is mother to house it resides in | p.212 Child number is son to house it resides in | p.213 Child number is in house that it controls | p.214 Child number is in house that it is controlled by | p.215 Child number resides in house of same transformation as itself | p.228 Adult number supports child number | p.228 Adult number controls child number | p.227 Child number supports adult number | p.229 Child number controls adult number | p.214 Adult and child number are same | p.230 Adult and child transformation (not number) are same | p.233 Males Same/same | p.234 Males Same/opposite | p.235 Males Opposite/same | p.236 Males Opposite/opposite | p.233 Females Same/same | p.234 Females Same/opposite | p.235 Females Opposite/same |
|---|---|---|---|---|---|---|---|---|---|---|---|---|---|---|---|---|---|---|---|---|
| 8m (6m) three m | 78 | 104 | | • | | | | • | | | | | | • | | | | | | |
| 8m (7f) four f | 78 | 90 | | • | | | | • | | | | | | | • | | | | | • |
| 8m (8m) five m/f | 78 | 78 | | | • | | | | | | | • | | • | | | | | | • |
| 8m (9f) six m | 78 | 67 | | • | | | | | | • | | | | | • | | | | | • |
| 9f (1m) six f | 67 | 179 | • | | | | | | | | • | | | | | • | | | • | |
| 9f (2f) seven f | 67 | 164 | • | | | | | • | | | | | | | | | • | • | | |
| 9f (3m) eight m | 67 | 149 | | • | | | | | | • | | | | | | • | | | • | |
| 9f (4f) nine f | 67 | 133 | • | | | | | | | • | | | | | | | • | • | | |
| 9f (5m/f) one m | 67 | 117 | | • | | | | • | | | | | | | | • | • | • | • | |
| 9f (6m) two f | 67 | 104 | • | | | | | | • | | | | | | | • | | | • | |
| 9f (7f) three m | 67 | 90 | | • | | | | | • | | | | | | | | • | • | | |
| 9f (8m) four f | 67 | 78 | | | | • | | • | | | | | | | | • | | | • | |
| 9f (9f) five m/f | 67 | 67 | • | | | | | | | | | • | | | | | • | • | | |

# PART II

# The Nine Numbers

# The Nine Numbers - Introduction

In this part, each of the nine numbers has its own chapter. Each chapter comprises a profile, derived from several sources, followed by a narrative.

The sources and implications of data in the profiles is as follows:

*Trigram:* symbolic calligraphy of the number as conceived originally by Oriental sages.

*Colour:* associated with Transformation Phase as agreed upon in *An Anthology of I Ching* and by Tibetan astrologer Sangye Wangchuk. The colour symbolizing this transformation can be used to enhance or to draw out this transformation in circumstances and settings.

*Element:* as conceived in Law of Five Transformations.

*Internal Representation:* from Law of Five Transformations and several volumes on Oriental Medicine.

*Physiognomy:* where the qualities of the Transformation Phase are perceived by others; from *An Anthology of I Ching.*

*Symbolized by:* what tradition claims as being the symbolic representations of the transformation. These animals can be used as empowerment animals or totems to invoke the energetics of the transformation.

*Primary Attribute:* based on trigram properties as described in the I Ching. This is a basic character quality.

*Family Member Type:* based on the I Ching and its interpretation of the interactions of different Trans-formation Phases as if in a family.

*Management Skills:* from the work of Warren Bellows and Nancy Post; how each transformation type best functions and interacts in groups.

*Occupations:* from *An Anthology of I Ching.*

*Illnesses:* from *An Anthology of I Ching* and other sources on Oriental medicine.

*Development Enhanced By:* from *An Anthology of I Ching* and Tibetan Astrologer Sangye Wangchuk.

*Tincture:* a herbal extract that enhances qualities of the trans-formation phase, as conceived by Rex Lassalle, DO. Herbal extracts, when taken in the proper doses as recommended by a herbalist can be used to deal with stress in a particular transformation or as a way of enhancing a particular transformation strength.

*Best Suited With:* best relationship possibilities as conceived in *Bai Hwa Zhong-guo Qi Xue Ming Li Ru Men* by Sinda Taguchi (see Chapter 13. Numbers in bold type (**1**) are the most auspicious. It has been my experience that this information is most useful for understanding communication styles as well as who it is easy or otherwise to communicate with. When it comes to using astrological data to choose a partner for life, my suggestion is to turn to the descriptions of the animal signs that belong to the Chinese zodiac.

*Directions to Travel:* from the *Bai*

*Hwa Zhong-guo Qi Xue Ming Li Ru Men* and John Mann and Stephen Gagne's *The Nine Ki Handbook*. Numbers here indicate wherever these numbers are situated on the Magic Square at the time one wants to travel. Numbers in bold type are the most auspicious.

*Cautiousness in Travelling:* from same sources as Directions to Travel. These are directions one should avoid or be cautious in travelling towards. Numbers in bold type indicate the most inauspicious directions. Note that the number of the profile being examined may be listed here. What this means is that when that number is in the House of Five (i.e. the centre) travel is not recommended at all.

The narratives have the following

pattern: General Information, Love Relationships, Business Relationships, Spiritual Matters and General Health Recommendations. This material comprises my own insights blended with the sources referred to in the text and the list of Further Reading.

As regards General Health Recommendations, generally speaking, if our life and lifestyle is more in line with the dynamics and recommendations listed for the year that we were born in, that is our adult natal year, we maintain relatively good health. When under stress, thus when our month or child natal month number is activated, we may need to pay closer attention to the general health recommendations as found in the month number narrative, especially if we are showing physical or emotional symptoms associated with our month (child natal) number. Once we have

followed the recommendations of the month number for some relative time period and our health is returning to 'normal', one should then return to recommendations indicated in the year or adult natal number material. Please be reminded that these recommendations are not prescriptive in nature and in no way should substitute for competent medical advice and supervision.

The final narrative in each number is a section on Personal Feng Shui Recommendations. In accordance with the Laws governing the Five Transformations (see the chapter on 'The Houses'), there are some transformations that are enhancing and supportive – those which a person might manage and utilize more easily – and others that are more challenging, hence more difficult to access and utilize. This section will look at the individual Nine Star Ki year numbers in relation to the various trigrams of the Bagua and their associated direction and properties. For each year number there will be sections on Sources of Support (including Notes of Caution), Challenging Regions of the Bagua and Qualities that are Useful in Mitigating the Challenges. Although some rudimentary Feng Shui suggestions may be given, the emphasis of these recommendations is on the necessary attitude for working successfully with the qualities that the given regions of the Bagua offer us. From a Nine Star Ki point of view, we should look beyond physical locality to the issues for success that are represented by the Bagua in a metaphoric way. Issues that are brought up and discussed in this respect will be of particular importance to the person whose natal year number is being addressed. Recommendations can then be extrapolated for working with the actual physical spaces in our lives in order to enhance our abilities to most effectively deal with these same issues. Those looking for specific cures are recommended to seek the advice of a qualified Feng Shui practitioner.

## OUR INTIMATE MANDALA

Between metaphors that are particularly useful to us and our actual physical surroundings, lies our own personal space. Treat yourself as the centre of your own intimate mandala, the centre of the universe from which you operate; you can visualize your spine and your vertical stance as representing the Zenith and Nadir, the coming together of heaven and earth, the Bagua region of Five or Tai Chi. In front of our spine is our heart, representative of fire or Li, the direction of the South. Behind us (such as the area of our kidneys) is the North or Kan. In this manner we can visualize all cardinal and ordinal points originating from ourselves. As you think of the regions of the Bagua and what they have to offer you in your process of self-actualization, scan your own body; focus on the right, left, front, back, the directions in between, above and below. Knowing what each of these directions represents, use your own psycho-physical manifestation as the bio-computer through which you seek answers to those areas of your life that are challenging you now. Find ways to enhance the success you are experiencing. In that way, the Bagua will become not only something that is out there, but something within and around us at all times. With this attitude, even if we look for additional Feng Shui cures for our circumstances, we stand a much better chance of finding those solutions that resonate best with who we truly are.

# Nine

## PROFILE

*Number*: 9

*Trigram*: ☲ Li (Clarity, the Fire)

*Colour*: Maroon (purple)

*Element*: Fire

*Internal representation*: Blood system, heart, small intestine, heart governor, triple heater, glandular system

*Physiognomy*: Eyes

*Symbolized by*: Pheasant, goldfish, crab, shrimp, oyster, turtle

*Primary attribute*: Clarity

*Family member type*: Middle daughter

*Management skills*:

YIN: Priority-Setting – selling priorities, marketing, sorting, problem solving, transforming, discriminating; and The Networker – team-building, socializing, customer relations, setting climates (the atmosphere)

YANG: The Coordinator – directing, controlling, cooperating, defining roles, conducting; and The Communicator – appreciating, internal communications, protecting, committing, creating trust, expressing, promoting

*Occupations*: Public servant, fundamentalist, writer, artist, artisan, optometrist, war correspondent, armourer, book dealer, beautician, publisher, diplomat, judge, barrister, politician, advertising agent, broker, fortune teller, horticulturist

*Illnesses*: Brain tumours, mental illnesses, heart ailments, blood disorders, fevers, eye diseases, glandular disorders, upper gastro-intestinal tract complaints

*Development enhanced by*: Being a light for self and others

*Tincture*: Nutmeg

*Best suited with*: 2,**3**,**4**,5,8

*Directions to travel*: 2,3,4,5,8 (best **2**)

*Cautiousness in travelling*: 1,6,7,9

---

## NARRATIVE

Nine is the most expansive of all the Nine Star Ki numbers, being at the beginning of the nine-year cycle as it spirals through time. This expansive quality has more to do with brilliance than all-pervasiveness. Along these lines, fire is associated with gestation in Five Transformation Theory, where what has been born is expanding and begins to be distin-guishable in its own right. No longer nascent or a bud, the initial brilliance of potential begins to shine forth.

Nine-fire people are the embodi-ment of brilliance. They are generally passionate, radiant in appearance and charged in their emotional ex-perience and expression. Thus like a star that is seen in the distance, a nine-fire person tends to be noticed.

If they walk into a crowded room, they are noticed almost immediately by those present. This is not only in terms of a relatively beautiful or handsome appearance; their word also has a strong impact on others. When grounded, they possess an unmatched clarity and brilliance in perception and expression. Because of this natural charisma in appearance and word, for a nine-fire person to remain balanced and sensitive to their environment, they must be conscious of their impact.

Their words are naturally impressive, even if there is no substance to them. Thus they could 'sell water by the river'. Inevitably they may mislead people at times. This is not because they consciously wish to deceive. On the contrary, nine-fire people tend to be very blunt and they cannot keep secrets. It is just that when caught in the limelight they get ungrounded and 'flamboyant'. Words can unwittingly slip out. This can make others around them cautious and even mistrusting of them. Being conscious of their appearance, as others around them are, they may have a tendency to draw conclusions on insufficient evidence, from appearances only.

Without fuel to burn, fire cannot exist. Thus, nine-fire people need to feel the support and care of those around them. At the same time, this does not mean they have close friends. Because of their charisma, they have many acquaintances. But friends come and go. Yet they are incredibly trusting of others to the point of being naïve at times.

Loyalty is an issue in their relationships, possibly because it is difficult for them to maintain lasting friendships. The nine-fire person cannot believe that people could have covert or ulterior motives. At times they may be asked or 'put up' to be the spokesperson for groups or causes. They are excellent in this role and will usually succeed in putting the point across. However, if challenged directly, the nine-fire person may retreat, looking for support from the crowd – only to find that no one is there. Even so, this person is very forgiving. The idea of bearing a grudge is a preposterous notion to them.

Life generally moves rather easily for a nine-fire person and because this is so for them, they assume that it is the same for others. Thus their expectation of others may be unrealistic. (They can also give an impression of having everything under control and thus find that when they

are in need, no one really is there to help because no one can believe that there could be a problem for them.) As life usually goes the way they want it to, they may live under the assumption that that is how it should be. If it doesn't there must be a problem 'out there'.

Nine-fires are not particularly competitive. They assume that they should win. While they hate to lose, the feeling of loss soon disappears as they move on to the next thing. Their natural tendency is to feel joyful and light-hearted about life. If placed under stress, or if this transformation is that of their natal month, the predominant negative emotional response will be one of anxiety. Because of their light-hearted quality and sense that life should move easily, when they experience the contrary or see the hardships of others, they will often express a genuine sadness.

## Love Relationships

Nine-fires are romantic by nature and express emotion quite easily. These traits plus their attractiveness makes them a flame around which many moths will gather. They are rarely without a partner but, at the same time, have to deal with the fact that they will naturally attract all sorts of people without initiating anything in particular. Thus they can be considered arrogant, fickle and teases. They may actually be dumbfounded by such accusations, as their naturally naïve character often makes them unconscious of their impact.

As a flame needs fuel to burn, so nine-fire people look to relationships with those more stable than themselves. The I Ching image for fire is expressed by the word 'clinging'. Thus nine-fire people may find themselves overly attached to those to whom they feel attracted. They can abandon themselves to a relationship, whether it be of short or long duration, and during that relationship they will be absolutely faithful – and expect the same from their partners. They may have fantasies of affairs, but that is usually as far as it goes. Although somewhat clinging, when a relationship is over for them, it's over. They will be sad, possibly anxious about what will happen next. But sooner or later another person will come along.

Although fire is considered a masculine notion in many systems of thought, Oriental systems classify it as female (yin) and the flaming expansive quality of this transforma-

tion phase makes a nine easier for women to handle as a natal year than for men. (This, however, may just be cultural, as physical and emotional expressiveness and passion are more 'acceptable' in women, as is the tendency to speak and act on feeling or intuition.)

## Business Relationships

A nine-fire person is a natural in positions of leadership, communication and selling. Leadership for a nine implies being a figurehead rather than a mastermind. Although not creative *per se,* they can create excitement around ideas and situations, and can act as catalysts. Their clarity and directness can also be quite disarming and useful in sorting out situations that are muddled in some way.

Because of their charisma and natural tendency to be in the lead, a nine-fire person may feel that anything they do is all right, and they therefore may have a tendency to jump the gun. Pointed in the desired direction, they will promote an idea or product successfully. They are excellent at making and developing contacts in a community or organization, and are therefore good at public relations. And within an organization, their passionate nature may express itself as a zeal that is very morale-building. They can value the team and appreciate relationships that make things work. At the same time, this does not mean that such a person would do well in a personnel position. To get involved on a deep level with fellow workers may have rewards for them on a personal basis, but in a professional setting it can be stultifying to the nine-fire's natural abilities. They are much better at bringing out and using the skills of others than dealing with personalities in the work environment.

They are only average in their financial abilities, and are not inclined to save. Their expenses therefore often match their incomes. Thus although adept at surviving, a nine-fire person is not someone an organization is advised to put in a position where conservation and development of finances is needed.

## Spiritual Matters

As fire lights up the dark, revealing what is present, so nine-fires have the potential for strong discriminating awareness. Their gift is being able to distinguish what is and is not meaningful. Rooted in earth and reaching towards heaven, they have a very direct approach to spiritual matters. Even the most profound or esoteric truths may be just obvious facts for them.

Thus nine-fires can be a light for themselves and those around them. What they need to guard against is being caught up in their emotions. They should attempt to temper their tendency to get caught up in mere appearances and allow their mind to settle upon what they are perceiving. Thus first impressions and a keen intuition can be backed by intellectual clarity.

## General Health Recommendations

Nine-fires should guard against overindulgence in various aspects of life. Under stress, especially if the nine-fire is the natal month, the natural joy that they exude may be transformed into an anxiety that overshadows them. This can have an adverse effect on the functioning of their upper gastro-intestinal tract, heart and glandular system. The yin-style personality expression of this would be slow laboured action and speech. The yang-style expression of anxiety would be the hysterical, constantly jabbering, nervously laughing personality.

A well-rounded vegetarian diet is recommended as saturated fats found in animal foods may contribute to heart and circulatory problems. Some white meats such as fish and poultry may be acceptable. Nine-fires would also do best to avoid hot spices. Stimulants such as coffee and alcohol are best avoided as they may weaken and irritate the upper gastro-intestinal tract.

Exercise should emphasize gentle, flowing motion. Tai Chi would be excellent, as would forms of exercise that involve stretching and joint movement. Joint movements especially enhance movement of blood and its reoxygenation.

## PERSONAL FENG SHUI RECOMMENDATIONS

### Sources of Support

Bagua regions of Chen ☳ (3) and Sun ☴ (4)

☳ *Regarding Chen*: Develop this area to show an honouring of ancestry and the sources of your inspiration. In doing so, your mind will be kept sharp, on the cutting edge. There arises an invisible quality of support that encourages spontaneous, quick thinking to bolster your generally magnetizing

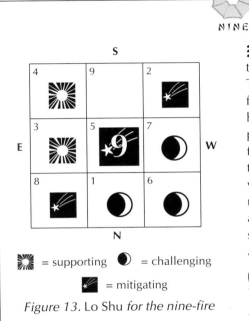

S

|   |   |   |
|---|---|---|
| 4 | 9 | 2 |
| 3 | 5 | 7 |
| 8 | 1 | 6 |

E ... W

N

= supporting   = challenging

= mitigating

*Figure 13.* Lo Shu *for the nine-fire*

≋ *Regarding Sun*: Allow this space to reflect your plans and dreams. These should not be mere flights of fantasy, but be based in clarity and honesty about whatever resources or potentials are available to you. In facing difficult situations it is useful to visualize what you want or how you want things to turn out. This region of the Bagua supports this approach. Place living plants in this space to indicate a rooted growth and the potential to flower.

! **Note of Caution**: These tree trigrams reflect inspiration and potential. They do not indicate or guarantee money in the bank. Non-attachment and patience need to be cultivated in order to utilize these regions of the Bagua effectively. Excessive attention to these areas may just flood you with too much to think about and

presence and enthusiasm. Build a shrine of acknowledgement or one to pray at. Arrange pictures, books, even sayings or art that reflect your honouring of this space and the resources it offers you.

complicate matters. By not paying enough attention to these areas your creativity will suffer as will your ability to sustain effort and enthusiasm. Be aware that you can only succeed on good looks and/or charisma for so long.

## Challenging Regions of the Bagua

Kan ☵ (1), Ch'ien ☰ (6), and ☱ Tui (7)

☵ *Regarding Kan*: This water trigram challenges you to be accountable. It requires you to understand your assumptions more deeply, to be clearer about your intentions, and inevitably your true life's calling. Acknowledging and working with the energetics of this space help you to be better prepared and less naïve, and/or react to situations based on anxiety, flamboyance

or your tendency to be whimsical. In the Bagua region of water itself as well as that space within the Bagua region of Li (9), balance your fire with water totems, symbols and colours. A goldfish aquarium is an excellent combination of these elements, as the goldfish is a fire totem. Be sure to keep the water in the tank very clean.

☰ *Regarding Ch'ien*: An excessive display of charisma or flamboyance – be it positive effusiveness or panic – can lead to a loss of conditional support and ineffective action with little true reward. In this region of the Bagua, you need to express the desire to be open and receptive to those whose words and assessments are based on historical data and knowledge of what has and has not worked in the past. Allow this to be the space from which you get feedback – and stop being so competitive! Perhaps your telephone, fax, or computer can go here. Make this a meeting place. Although such recommendations are generally true, the nine-fire who actually does this, with the correct attitude and intention, will find this region of the Bagua most supportive of their efforts.

☱ *Regarding Tui*: If you disregard support and are not open to assessment, you run the risk of losing what you have created and accumulated. This is a general issue for nine-fires (*see* the section on Business Matters). Don't always assume that everything will work out. This belief arises from your tendency to be naïve.

The space of Tui should be arranged to show that you truly cherish what you have accumulated. There should be qualities of light, order and the sense that what is in or an expression of this region of the Bagua is being properly preserved.

## Qualities That are Useful in Mitigating the Challenges to Ch'ien and Tui

Cultivate and work with the energetics of Ken (8, your convictions), Kun (2, working to transform your passions into compassion and a desire to serve higher principles) and Tai Chi, the centre (5, staying grounded and clear in your intention and purpose). Tai Chi or the Bagua region of 5 puts you in touch with the truth that your charisma and energetic ways cannot conceal. Relax in this truth and use these natural talents and inner resources with discriminating wisdom and compassion.

# Eight

PROFILE

*Number*: 8

*Trigram*: ☶ Ken (Keeping Still, the Mountain)

*Colour*: White

*Element*: Earth

*Internal representation*: Back, spleen, pancreas, stomach

*Physiognomy*: Hands

*Symbolized by*: Dog, bull, ox, leopard, mouse

*Primary attribute*: Keeping Still

*Family member type*: Youngest Son

*Management skills*: The Producer – distributing, nurturing, transporting, supporting, maintaining, delivering, producing, integrating, attention to detail

*Occupations*: Monk or nun, clergy, sculptor, service worker, police or civil service, bank teller, educator, beautician

*Illnesses*: Arthritis, fatigue, nasal difficulties, leg disorders, constipation, deep muscular pains, blood sugar imbalances, depression, feelings of hopelessness

*Development enhanced by*: Introspection and developing inner perception

*Tincture*: Cardamon

*Best suited with*: **9**,6,7

EIGHT

## NARRATIVE

This is the most yang of the earth element numbers and as such is ascribed such attributes as heaviness and stability, like a mountain. It represents the greatest solidification of matter in the maturation phase of Fire Transformation Theory. An eight-earth person accomplishes what they want through slow and persistent singleness of direction. The slow and methodical way in which they go about doing things can drive others to distraction. It can even seem that nothing is being accomplished. This is due to the fact that their action is deepening rather than spreading; they delve down into whatever it is that they are wanting to pursue. As a result their accomplishments are usually well founded.

At the same time, their meticulous attention to detail can foster a myopic tendency which leads them to get lost in detail, resulting in feelings of confusion and not being able to prioritize. Thus, while in moments of strength they seem confident, strong-willed, single-minded and perhaps even egotistical, there is a tendency to be indecisive, fragile, perhaps even timid at times of stress. When lost in the detail and depths of their investigation, they may act utterly helpless and need bolstering and stimulation from those around them in order to get their feet back on the ground.

An aspect of their single-minded focus is that they are loyal to others, to causes, or to whatever they see as significant in their lives. When balanced, this loyalty can create a tenacity which others may be shocked to see, as such people often appear calm and steady. Eight-earths are the most stubborn of the numbers and may even manifest extreme competitiveness when challenged. Such traits may also work against them if their loyalty leads them to abandon their better judgement and become involved in situations which they have not properly investigated. There is a tendency towards fanaticism.

An eight-earth is hard to read emotionally. In moments of elation or depression, their appearance can seem rather unchanged. They also conceal their strengths and weaknesses. Because of this unaffected surface, others often view eight-earth people as steady and reliable. Thus they often find themselves to be in the role of counsellor to others. They are naturally caring people who will go deeply into whatever it is others tell them. They must, therefore, develop detachment, otherwise they may find themselves involved more deeply in matters than is useful for them or the person who has come to them. They have a tendency to get over-involved and thus to worry about people and situations. This is especially true under stress.

Changes happen slowly on a mountain. Thus when it comes to decisions in their own lives, or in interactions with others, timing is something eight-earths need to address, as they have a tendency to be hesitant to the point of distraction. Generally they do not adapt well to changes they have not initiated themselves. This is not due to arrogance *per se,* but their manner of slow deliberation can lead others to conclude that the eight-earth is 'stuffy' or conservative.

## Love Relationships

As eight-earth people tend to treat all experiences as deep issues, so it is with their emotional and physical expression. In terms of sexuality, eights have a very strong and enduring sex drive, although they may not be overt in expressing it. Thus others may too quickly judge them as sexless or passionless, whereas in fact their sex drive is just very slow to rise and is something which they tend to keep private. Despite all their outer appearance of stoicism, the eight-earth is a sensitive person deep down, who can be hurt by the lack of under-standing others may have of how they operate in such matters.

A partner needs to be aware of the eight-earth person's sensitivity and reserve in matters of sexuality. If badgered too much, they will either not respond at all or display some outer affection of emotion out of a sense of duty rather than true feeling.

Once aroused, eight-earth people are single-minded. Once they find someone who stirs their interest, they will tirelessly pursue them. They do not 'shop around'. Yet they are not moralistic. It is as if in the interest of emotional economy they stick to those to whom they feel attracted. Thus they usually combine love and marriage well and enjoy establishing a home with all its daily affairs and routines. Women of this number enjoy the security of home life, but may worry excessively about mundane matters.

Men will see themselves as providers and protectors. However, they can also be chauvinistic, especially in the way they show disdain for women who do not interest them or meet their expectations. In such situations, an eight-earth man may be a gossip.

## Business Relationships

Generally eight-earth people are level-headed in business matters. They are not innovative, but once given an idea to pursue, they will work on the details intensely and create products of superior quality. They are usually diligent and demonstrate a pragmatic loyalty in working situations. They like to be acknowledged for what they do and feel slighted if their efforts go unnoticed. This does not mean, however, that they want to be put in the spotlight.

The eight-earth person is good as a distributor of information, goods, funds, etc. They can bring things together and keep movement going in a desired direction. They know what it takes to keep a staff team moving on a task. It is much better to keep them focused on tasks rather than personnel concerns, as they have a tendency to get over-involved in the lives of others. Under stress, they may exhibit an unhealthy co-dependency. It is advisable for eight-earth people to learn how to set boundaries.

As regards their personal finances, they are usually successful. They know how to get the most out of limited resources. This may be noticed particularly in younger people, and they get better at it over time. However, they are not ones to question closely about their financial affairs. They like to invest (especially in property), and may keep several bank accounts so that other people cannot work out their financial worth. In a business setting, they will be an asset, so long as they are told where to put money. If they are made a primary financial adviser or put in the position of directing where the money is to go they may make wild speculations or hold out until the 'big one' – whatever the 'big one' is conceived to be – comes along.

## Spiritual Matters

The eight-earth person's natural tendency towards stillness and constancy finds its highest expression in the creation of a peaceful yet deep spiritual life. These people need to work on understanding the workings and nature of the world around them – the process rather than the minute details,

They will find such spiritual contemplations easier in a clean, orderly environment. A shrine or altar which shows respect for earthly forces and elements is helpful for them. Such contemplations can ease their tendency towards making everything solid in their lives, including a notion of themselves, thus lightening their load. Spiritual life needn't be serious, intense and heavy – just well considered.

## General Health Recommendations

Because of their natural density (regardless of physical appearances) eight-earth people should avoid foods and lifestyles that create lethargy or may over-activate pancreatic functions. There is a natural tendency towards hypoglycaemia or diabetes, especially if this is the natal month number transformation, or if the person is placed under much stress. The psychological expression of this tendency is continual worry, depression, self-doubt and hopelessness. Foods that exacerbate the physiological and psychological tendencies are sugar, alcohol, cakes and pies. A diet of grains, beans, vegetables, fruits and some animal food is recommended. The emphasis in vegetables should be on mineral-rich sea vegetables in small quantities daily and on green leafy vegetables. Winter squash in season is also excellent.

Eight-earth people should do exercises that involve loosening, stretching and the movement of lymph. If their occupation involves sitting for considerable periods of time, they should pay particular attention to posture and take breaks where they can stretch and loosen their hips and neck muscles. Lighting in their work space should be full-spectrum and natural. Periodic Swedish-style or Tragering (lymphatic-type) massage is recommended.

## PERSONAL FENG SHUI RECOMMENDATIONS

### Sources of Support

The Bagua region of Li ☲ (9) and the allied regions of Kun ☷ (2) and Tai Chi ◐ (5)

☲ *Regarding Li*: This region of the Bagua provides you with the opportunity to lighten up and gain clarity. The 'exposure' implicit in Li helps you to see where you are stuck – regardless of whether you want to see it or not. When you are not able to get across what you mean, your plans or ambitions, the lightness of Li can prompt more sponta-

EIGHT

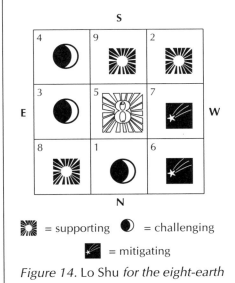

S

| 4 | 9 | 2 |
| 3 | 5 $8$ | 7 |
| 8 | 1 | 6 |

N

= supporting   = challenging

= mitigating

*Figure 14.* Lo Shu *for the eight-earth*

neous action and expression. By strengthening this region of the Bagua you will help to overcome the tendency of others to view you as distant.

With respect to the space of Li, be

daring! Arrange and decorate this region of the Bagua with rich tones and luxury. This is one region of the Bagua in which you should not be penny-pinching.

**! Note of Caution:** Even though you can be more extravagant here, do not abandon your attention to detail. Nine-fire energy can be magical in both a positive and a negative sense. In a negative sense it can be blinding. Couple this with your tendency to throw all caution to the wind and you may take ungrounded gambles. Step out, open up, but don't puff out your feathers! On the other hand, if you do not utilize or tap into this resource, you will lose the joy that serves to lighten your generally serious demeanour, thereby making you come across as stern, even heartless.

☵☵ *Regarding Kun*: As Ken is the yang expression of the earth transformation, Kun is the yin, more receptive aspect of earth. Even though you are loyal and caring, others may find you dry or believe you to be unfeeling. The Bagua region of Kun helps you to connect at a deeper, more emotional level with people. Sure, you don't want to wear your heart on your sleeve, but you do want people to know that you have a heart.

⦿ *Regarding Tai Chi*: Representing the vertical of the Zenith and Nadir, what Tai Chi offers you is a bit more detachment; a rope or hand to pull you out of the morass of detail you sometimes find yourself wallowing in. Tai Chi picks you up, helps you to reassess how you are, where you are and where you want to go. The colour gold that is associated with five-earth can be excellent in elevating you out of the drabness. As regards space, think of a nice gold carpet, gold figurines adorning the centre of your house or office. Perhaps try wearing gold-coloured clothes, such as a bright beret.

! **Note of Caution**: These earth Bagua regions act as allies. As such, there can be a tendency to mimic their qualities. However, such a tendency is usually corrected relatively quickly. Over-attentiveness to Kun may cause you to worry over and above your usual serious concern. A lack of attention to Kun will make you the pale man or woman in the grey suit. Over attention to Tai Chi will lead you to be more crude or harsh in your interactions. Lack of attention to Tai Chi will leave you feeling that you are stuck at the bottom of a very deep well with no ladder.

## Challenging Regions of the Bagua

Chen ☳ (3), Sun ☴ (4) and Kan ☵ (1)

☳ *Regarding Chen*: Being too pragmatic and sometimes rigidly loyal to principles, persons or situations even though all the evidence challenges you to reconsider your position can cut you off from new knowledge and opportunities. Not everything is concrete or tangible. This region of the Bagua demands that you go back to what originally inspired you! Honour that. Keep the space of Chen open and light. It may be a great space in which to exercise to shed built-up stress and/or a sense of stagnation. If you ignore this space, you may find that frustration builds up. This could lead you down into the depths as you feverishly try to hold on to what you really need to let go of, or lead you to explode and obliterate all that you have worked so hard for. The Bagua region of Chen reminds you that 'Form is emptiness and emptiness is form'.

☴ *Regarding Sun*: Whatever you hold in your hand, the potential for it originated in Sun. This region of the Bagua demands that you open your vision to greater possibilities than the ones you have limited yourself to thus far. Keep this region of the Bagua alive and growing. Come back to it. Bring to this space whatever you have created or have in mind. Single-pointedly focus and then allow your mind to expand into the larger picture. What have you excluded out of expediency and/or thrift? What more can you add to what you are doing? Here, what is grey and inert becomes colourful and alive. This region of the Bagua challenges your tendency to get stuck in convention. Step back and step out! Without such independence, you may end up strangling what you most cherish.

☵ *Regarding Kan*: In your effort to take care of all of the details and get tangible results, you may forget what your original intention and purpose were to start with. You may get results, but at what cost? And, have you considered the future repercussions? The Bagua region of Kan is to remind you of your life's flow and purpose. If we get too preoccupied solely with the end product, we may lose perspective as to how it fits in the overall scheme of things. In the water of Kan one finds the residues of what has gone before and what the potential for the future is. If this region of the Bagua is not honoured, then future growth is limited and we insensitively keep on with the status quo.

It is advisable to place running water into the Bagua region of Kan as well as the Kan region of Ken. This can include fountains and symbols of moving water as well as the totems and colours associated with water.

## Qualities that are Useful in Mitigating the Challenges to Kan

Cultivate and work with the energetics of Chi'en and Tui. With the Bagua region of Chi'en, try to remember who really cares and who really matters. Listen to your deeply caring side. And be prepared to accept feedback from those people or circumstances that reveal to you whether you are being true to yourself and your real priorities. As regards Tui, be willing to act kindly but accurately evaluate what you've achieved. In the energetic of Tui, you give yourself the opportunity to look closely at the fruits of your labours. Sit down and talk with friends about what you've done. What do they think? In honouring these two regions of the Bagua, you are asked to listen, receive, and relax. They help you to stay more in touch with your surroundings, allowing your gratitude and caring nature to become more evident to those around you. How can you use space and design to create a place in which you can receive and cultivate these qualities?

# Seven

## PROFILE

*Number*: 7

*Trigram*: ☱ Tui (Joyousness, the Lake)

*Colour*: Red

*Element*: Metal

*Internal representation*: Speech organs, lungs, large intestine, skin

*Physiognomy*: Mouth (lips)

*Symbolized by*: Sheep, birds, deer, elk, simians

*Primary attribute*: Joyousness (sense of ease)

*Family member type*: Youngest Daughter

*Management skills*: The Evaluator – performance evaluation, accounting, refining, evolving, managing change, comparing, contrasting, controlling quality, developing quality circles, terminating

*Occupations*: Public relations, entertainment industry, savings and loans worker, banker, publican, lecturer, dentist, food processing and distribution, spokesperson

*Illnesses*: Chest and breast difficulties, pelvic disorders, hip joint disorders, skull injuries, lung and large intestine imbalances, skin disorders

*Development enhanced by*: Recognition of spirituality and joy in giving to others

## SEVEN

*Tincture*: Mullein or raspberry

*Best suited with*: 2,5,8,1

*Directions to travel*: 6,2,8,1

*Cautiousness in travelling*: 3,4,7,9

---

## NARRATIVE

The metal or air element is associated with autumn – the time of harvest. It is also a time of changes and reflection.

Seven-metal people do experience a tremendous amount of actual change, especially in the early part of their lives. Along with the changes in their lives comes a keen sensitivity to those changes. They seem to possess an innate appreciation of the texture of life in all its dimensions and phases. Because of this sensitivity, they project an aura of knowing what is going on. Thus others are naturally attracted to them. They are people's people. Others may see the seven-metal person as someone who has everything under control. Some of this may be because of what the seven-metal has actually experienced. But because of the wide range of their experiences, they can draw inferences from and help others in circumstances they may know little or nothing about personally.

Other transformation phase people may go out of their way to look for experiences. But the seven-metal person is an accumulator. Changes and experiences readily come to them. They are not initiators, but harvesters of what the world offers to them. Thus they can develop a sense of entitlement, and others may view them as lazy. From the seven-metal person's point of view, however, they are just waiting for things to happen for them – which they usually do.

Because of the accumulating quality in their nature, the material world and possessions are usually no problem for these people. They may squander fortunes yet be able to generate funds whenever they need them. They are fond of jewellery. They are meticulous about their appearance; hair and clothes are arranged stylishly. They are keenly aware of aesthetics generally: fine art, decor, and such like. Yet with all this metal-like precision, there is usually one area in their life that is totally chaotic or a mess.

Seven-metal people are naturally reflective. They are excellent speakers and can captivate the people around them with the richness of the language they use. Although eloquent, this does not mean that they know what they are talking about or that what they are saying is true. They are interested more in appropriateness than accuracy. In personal relationships the purpose behind their white lies or approximate truths is not to deceive deliberately or to impress, but rather to avoid rocking the boat. Seven-metal people have a sense of insecurity which often leads them to speak or act in a way that will ensure that others remain their friends or at least are not offended. They abhor arguments and will go to almost any lengths to avoid offence. The advantage of this is that they make brilliant diplomats and can often resolve conflicts between other people or with someone close to them. They are generally 'up-beat' people and their optimism can be infectious. At the same time, this aura of confidence can in times of need put them in a position where the support they need is not forthcoming or is ineffective. They may be the object of other people's envy or jealousy.

While life in all its changes presents challenges to the seven-metal, to some extent they deal with these challenges by maintaining a strong bond with their past and their roots. They are romantic and at times nostalgic. This may operate as a means of buffering themselves from the full impact of events. Their 'work hard, play hard' philosophy of life keeps them in touch with their childlike nature. Thus they are loved by children. Their families are very important to them, yet there are times when their pleasure-seeking ways

lead them to be lax in attending to family responsibilities.

In general their relationships with others appear superficial. Their sharp, reflective minds make them aware of life's changes and the concerns that others may take to heart are, for the seven-metal, just signs of the times – something to be lived through. Thus the seven-metal may have a tendency to discount others' experiences, to gloss over rather than support others in dealing with their own processes.

## Love Relationships

Being nostalgic, easy-talking and generally attractive, seven-metal people easily attract partners. When they see someone they are attracted to, they can create situations in which it seems that the other is taking the initiative. They can control events while seemingly appearing as the victim of other people or of circumstances. In some instances this can manifest as passive aggression.

Seven-metals are very sensuous people. Making love must therefore be something like a fine art, where subtlety makes all the difference. Part of this comes from a desire to heighten their own pleasure and embellish their sense of self. But at the same time, they enjoy seeing their partner experience pleasure. Such an attitude usually arises from a sense of how things should be – what their notion of a *quality* relationship or encounter should be. Thus they may have a difficult time adapting to someone else's perception of what quality might be.

They cannot say no and may find themselves in situations which they come to realize are not to their liking.

In such circumstances, they may suddenly drop the relationship. This can happen repeatedly, partly because of their personal sense of aesthetics or because the relationship changes for them and the romance is gone. Thus sevens may find themselves going through many encounters and affairs, trying to recapture a feeling.

If they do marry – and many may choose not to – they should take their time selecting a partner. Using their keen senses and evaluative abilities, they should choose a long-term partner in a more mindful rather than sensuous frame of mind. Here, watching one's heart with one's head is good advice.

## Business Relationships

These are 'work hard, play hard' people. The seven-metal is not one to take work home. Work is work and home is home. When it's party time, no thought of work exists in the seven-metal's mind.

Seven-metals are not initiators. Nor are they particularly good at completing tasks. However, they are brilliant at evaluating processes, paying attention to quality, and are thus good at setting standards. Within a business venture they are agents of change. However, where others are involved they may appear to be lazy because of their 'wait and see' attitude. This attitude may, however, be an asset in that the seven-metal may be aware of subtle trends and patterns that are building to a maturing of events undetected by others around them. If others become irritated or impatient with this attitude and press too hard, the seven-metal may retreat to an even more distant (passive) position or just leave the situation altogether. As they are resourceful, they are generally confident that there is always someone out there looking for their talents.

Quality control and public relations are natural areas for the seven-metal. If an employee has to be fired or made redundant, their diplomatic ways and likeableness will probably smooth the process over for both sides. They are also excellent at running businesses that emphasize aesthetics, such as restaurants, art galleries or jewellery shops.

## Spiritual Matters

The I Ching trigram for the seven-metal is the Joyous Lake (Tui). Like a calm, cool lake it is characterized by a gentle calm exterior and a strong, deep interior.

Seven-metal people can appear calm on the surface and have the capacity to reflect anything that is around them. Because of this surface veneer, the depth of a seven-metal may remain hidden, even to themselves. They have a tendency to become preoccupied with what appears on the surface like being involved with a mirage. They may even recognize that there is more to what is going on than the surface appearance. Yet because they get caught up in the excitement of the experience as it appears, the deeper meanings of what is going on may elude them.

The more preoccupied they become in this way, the more it is like a lake that becomes turbulent. They then see only distortions and appear quite shallow. They may even be labelled as 'air heads' or as having a 'mind like a sieve'. This trend applies especially to the reactivated seven-metal child or to a seven-metal adult placed under extreme stress. In both cases, they can become 'experience junkies' – going after experiences just for the sake of having them.

Thus seven-metals need to be aware of addictive attitudes and cultivate time and space for quietness. Breathing-style meditations are useful to calm the mind and body. Once the lake is allowed to calm down, the reflection on the surface can then be contemplated and evaluated. Thus seven-metal people, when seeing things clearly, can bring up from their depths awareness and perceptions that may have been hidden from themselves and from others. Although they themselves may not recognize it at first, seven-metal people who give themselves time to drink from their own depths can experience a lasting sense of joy.

Meditation practices that have healing (for themselves and for others) as an emphasis are also recommended.

## General Health Recommendations

This element has as its primary organs and tissues the lungs, colon and skin. These three are vital in the mediating of change in our lives. As we change climate, environment or season, the skin acts as an external protective barrier, the colon as an internal one, and the lungs as a way of adjusting to the changes by modifying the respiratory input for the body. The impact on the skin, colon and lungs can be due to the physical changes in themselves, our

psychological or emotional response to the changes, or more likely both. The yang emotional imbalance a person may experience when under stress is rigid control; the yin imbalance is totally groundless and not able to get a grip on anything. Both arise out of clinging or attachment which is something the seven-metal person needs to address. The meditation processes recommended in the section on Spiritual Matters are useful for this.

As regards lungs, air quality is important. In addition to breathing exercises such as pranayama from the yoga tradition, air baths as recommended in Shizuko Yamamoto's *Barefoot Shiatsu* are helpful, as is scrubbing the skin with a stiff brush or loofa when bathing: stimulation of the skin benefits the lungs. (By the same token the use of poor-quality cosmetics and petrochemically based colognes and perfumes are injurious to the lungs and colon.) Exercises which encourage an evenness of breath such as Tai Chi and various martial arts are preferred to aerobic exercise where over-stimulation and forced or chaotic breathing may 'blow' the person out in the long run.

The quality of foods should be considered for lung, colon and skin health. Mucus-forming foods should be reduced or eliminated. Little or no dairy produce should be taken – depending of course on climatic considerations and personal constitution. Raw fruit should be reduced and replaced with cooked fruit. Moreover fruit mixtures such as fruit salad could prove detrimental.

More specifically for colon health, besides the above considerations, a diet rich in fibre is advised. Meats should be reduced and used as a complementary rather than a primary food. Old food that may have on its surface a high concentration of candida microbes and food that has lost its vitality due to refrigeration or freezing should be kept to a minimum. Care should be taken not to change the diet radically, too quickly or too often, as this will upset the intestinal flora and may lead to the rapid onset of disease.

Although all the recommendations made here are prudent for virtually every one of us, they are of especial importance to those who have a metal transformation phase as one of their natal influences.

Finally, seven-metals need to be sure to maintain some routine that provides them with enough stimulation to help in adapting to change.

There may be a tendency to be either very lazy or excessive, and such tendencies need to be seen clearly for what they are.

## PERSONAL FENG SHUI RECOMMENDATIONS

### Sources of Support

Bagua regions of Kun ☷ (2), Tai Chi ◐ (5), Ken ☶ (8) and Ch'ien ☰ (6)

☷ *Regarding Kun*: You can be cavalier, just allowing things to develop, for it is very likely that they will work out in your favour. Whilst you are quite likeable and don't like to put on airs, your nonchalance can make you seem above it all – a bit aloof. What Kun offers you is a sense of intimate connection. It allows you to touch and be touched. Develop this area to enhance a sense of nurturing

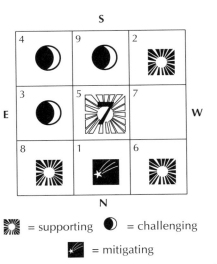

 = supporting ◐ = challenging
✦ = mitigating

*Figure 15.* Lo Shu *for the seven-metal*

and unconditional support for your ventures. Realize, though, that the peacefulness and receptivity of this region is backed by tenacity. As one of the most primal of the trigrams, developing this area in your life will give

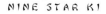
you a deep strength that is rooted in intimate connection and that will back up your luck. It will serve to humble you and soften any tendency towards a feeling of entitlement.

◯ *Regarding Tai Chi*: When you are balanced and focused, your timing is impeccable and the results of your actions natural and effortless. Keeping the Bagua region of Tai Chi (the centre) uncluttered will help you to maintain this quality. It will also help you to come back to your own centre if you should periodically lapse into inertia in the comfort that surrounds you.

☶ *Regarding Ken*: Sometimes your diplomatic ways make others uncertain as to where you really stand. Sometimes this may be what you want to portray; other times it may not. In either case, if you develop

the region of Ken as a place for contemplation and for the maturation of your inner strengths, it will give you the power of conviction, and this will, in turn, add force to the way you present yourself in the world. Developing this area will ensure that at least you know where you stand.

! *Note of Caution*: If there is too much focus in these earth areas, you may make whatever you do more cumbersome. It is worth keeping the balance between overkill and letting things run their course. You have strong evaluation skills. Take note of when you think enough is enough while working with these Bagua regions. Not every bottle meticulously arranged on the shelf needs to be dusted daily.

☰ *Regarding Ch'ien*: As the yang manifestation of metal, Ch'ien is an ally to Tui. As a support, Ch'ien can help you to be more critical in your choices and allegiances. As one of the more 'social' regions of the Bagua, Ch'ien helps you to prioritize and streamline your efforts and interactions with others.

**! Note of Caution:** Over-attentiveness to this region may subvert diplomacy, which for the most part serves you well. If you have enemies, look closely how you address this region of the Bagua in your life. On the other hand, if you disregard this region of the Bagua, you may find yourself lavishing your attention on anyone and everyone. Although this is noble in the highest sense, it can – in practical terms – waste a lot of time and energy. The great Tibetan master Gampopa once said that it is a sign of a superior man that he treats all with equanimity – yet still has a few good friends.

## Challenging regions of the Bagua
Li ☲ (9), Chen ☳ (3) and Sun ☴ (4)

☲ *Regarding Li:* So much of the success of seven-metal is about finesse and your ability to covertly influence what others do around you. Some may see this as your ability to empower others whilst others may see you as sneaky and manipulative.

Li is about exposure. Sure, you may enjoy the fame and notoriety this region of the Bagua gives you when you activate it. But it will also challenge you to be accountable. Probably what is most crucial for you is for you to be clear in your own mind about your real motives and what you are trying to accomplish. If you are really honest with yourself and stay attuned to the transparency Li provides in your ventures, then in all likelihood you will be more able to employ your diplomatic ways effectively to override any protests or objections.

Of all the transformations and trigrams, probably the most ostentatious are seven-metal and nine-fire. Therefore, when combined, the result can seem swollen and unnecessary. In order to cultivate this area, you need to stay present, focused and honest – *real*. Otherwise you will expose yourself to all sorts of criticism and scandal. If you take for granted the 'fame' this region of the Bagua can offer, remember the Oriental law: 'What has a front has a back'. By remembering this you can prevent all sorts of backfires and potential embarrassments.

**☶** *Regarding Chen:* The ease with which things come to you naturally may intoxicate you and make you forget the origins and sources of inspiration that have brought you your good fortune. Failure to honour this region of the Bagua may be the reason why some seven-metals see fortunes come and go. If you do not honour the way things arise and give them their due, why should you expect the rewards to keep rolling in? By strengthening Chen, you may find that the up-and-down nature of your success begins to settle down. To develop this region of the Bagua physically the emphasis should be spaciousness; light, airy, open.

**☴** *Regarding Sun:* Similar to Chen, the emphasis here is on expectations and the sense of entitlement seven-metals exhibit in having things come their way. With such an attitude, you run the risk of making too many assumptions and starving out what could potentially be yours in the future. As a reminder of what it takes to have fruit in your hand, planting a garden in the physical region of Sun and nurturing the little seedlings is an excellent way of reminding yourself what is involved in experiencing your enjoyment.

## Qualities that are Useful in Mitigating the Challenges to Chen and Sun

Between seven-metal and the tree trigrams of Chen and Sun is water or Kan (1). Going beyond the enjoyment of fruits, you need to remember that for there to be a future crop to enjoy, you need to apply your keen evaluative sense and reason. Has what you have received thus far been worth it? What are the positive qualities, the negative traits? What would you like to see in the future and how can you change things to bring about that result? The Bagua region of water or Kan is there to help you reassess the course of things as they have gone so far and to aid you in determining whether or not whatever you have received to date has served your life's course. For the Joyous Lake to remain clean, pure, and fresh, the streams feeding it must be able to pour liberally into it. Therefore actual running water around this region (rather than pictorial representations) is advantageous. Seven-metals are encouraged to take the time to retreat from their busy social schedules. Consider canoeing, maybe even white water rafting.

# Six

## PROFILE

*Number*: 6

*Trigram*: ☰ Ch'ien (Heaven, the Creative)

*Colour*: White

*Element*: Metal

*Internal representation*: Mind (pineal gland), lungs, large intestine, skin

*Physiognomy*: Skull, head

*Symbolized by*: Tiger, horse, lion

*Primary attribute*: Creative

*Family member type*: Father

*Management skills*: The Inspirer – equilibrating, inspiring, resonating, setting standards on ethics and task specification, balancing, receiving, moral leadership

*Occupations*: President, chairman, dictator, military commander, prime minister, king, government service, industrial machinery, lawyer, jeweller, salesman, priest, teacher, sports equipment salesman, psychiatrist, counsellor, campaigner, manager of transport-type venture

*Illnesses*: Lung ailments, swellings, migraines, skin disorders (acne), broken bones, heart ailments

*Development enhanced by*: Experience of oneness (universal brotherhood), working towards this

SIX

*Tincture*: Cubeb

*Best suited with*: 2,5,8,1

*Directions to travel*: 2,8,7,1

*Cautiousness in travelling*: 3,4,6,9

## NARRATIVE

This is the most yang of numbers according to the I Ching interpretation. Six-metal manifests full creative energy and thus six-metal people tend to be activators, people who accomplish things in all facets of their lives. The creative energy that they exude is not that of an innovator. Rather, they can take ideas from others and bring them into being.

Six-metal is also considered the primal father number. Consequently people of this number feel a tremendous sense of duty and responsibility. At an early age they demonstrate this in their family. They are often the child that watches over and takes care of their siblings. If they are younger and not made directly responsible for them in some way, the six-metal may spend time worrying about them. If a parent is missing from the family, six-metal children will often rise to the task of taking on the roles and responsibilities of the missing adult. Such care and concern can also extend to others in their lives. In fact, these are very moral and socially oriented people. They experience the world as having or needing order. This can make six-metals over-involved and somewhat tense – coiled for action.

They find it difficult to unwind or relax, unlike seven-metals. They have strong views and strong ideals and are quite willing to argue to get their point across, even if it involves going to excessive lengths to rationalize their position, views and actions. They do not take criticism well and may, especially under stress, exhibit a tendency to see the world in good/bad, black/white terms.

Six-metal people are very aware of their own weaknesses, but conceal them well out of fear of being exploited by others. On the other hand, this means that they can be overly self-critical and as a result sabotage their own efforts. They can then lapse into lethargy, blaming themselves for their predicament. In more extreme cases, they can become paralyzed by an overwhelming sense of guilt. However, such periods are relatively short in duration, and the six-metal then musters energy for the next conquest.

This self-critical attitude can be projected outward by six-metals, in which case they can be quite cutting towards others, expressing high expectations and being rather undiplomatic if they do not live up to their expectations or standards. Thus, six-metals must be aware of their power and influence over other people. If properly directed, the six-metal can become a shining example to others, with the capacity to encourage people towards heights they themselves may not have imagined they could attain.

The past plays a very important part in the lives of six-metal people. They try to keep lessons from the past in perspective while they build the present and plan for the future. At the same time, they are not the sort of people who reveal all their plans: they need to know that what is produced will have the marks of their authorship.

Six-metals work very hard and are achievement-oriented. Their motives may be either highly egotistical or highly altruistic. In either case, they accumulate power, wealth and status rather easily. In the process of acquiring such things, they may use those around them and thus may find themselves as social outcasts. However, if they focus their intentions on ideals that benefit others, they can be quite magnanimous. Their sense of caring and command over the world around them can lead them to be leaders in almost any field they choose. It all depends on their ideals and perspective. They can be great educators, company chairmen, religious leaders or tyrants. Their ability to command is natural and thus often carries with it an air of nobility and elegance. How these traits express themselves will be determined by the society or circle in which they find themselves.

## Love Relationships

Although the material and physical world is easy for the six-metal person to master, mastering their own emotional states in relationships is another matter. As family and social mores play a central role in their identity, being in a properly defined relationship is important to them. Along with this comes a very strong sex drive; the sex act itself is viewed in the light of morality and social order. Thus a six-metal person will tend to have strict definitions as to what is appropriate and not appropriate in a relationship and in sex: timing, place, act, and so forth. This means that there can be an over-emphasis on performance, with a resulting loss of spontaneity. If they are rigid in their views, they may seem over-confident, nonchalant, perhaps cavalier.

When under stress, men of this number (especially if it is their natal month number) may be either domineering or chauvinistic, or else may dominate the females in their lives by acting as though they were weak and needy. Not wishing to appear as failures, they may go to excessive lengths to perform duties and tasks which their partner requests or demands of them. They are also gullible and easily succumb to flattery. A woman of this number may be compelled to take on more family responsibilities than she is truly capable of handling, thus feeling over-burdened yet obliged to perform in that way.

Basically, a six-metal person seeks a deep and true relationship. And this does help them to feel that they have a proper place in the world. If this is achieved, then a six-metal becomes a devoted and awesome lover, provider or homemaker and family person.

## Business Relationships

As I have said, this person is not an innovator but an activator. Because they like to be part of or in charge of the established order, six-metal people do not look for ideas of change. But they do get things done.

Within a corporate setting, the six-metal person is difficult to give orders to. At the same time, they do not make the best of managers. If they can act on their own within a supportive setting, they can be an inspiration to others, providing they do not let success go to their heads. While they are strong-headed, they do not do well if they work in isolation or solitude. The stimulation from the outside provides the oil for their machinery to function.

Six-metals think big in financial terms. Value for money is something they understand well. Thus they are good at establishing compensation systems. Women of this number usually acquire wealth quite easily. Men of this number do well, providing they act under their own steam. Both men and women of this number handle money well, but there is a tendency to be tight-fisted. This does not mean that they are conservative; rather, they are accumulators. Generosity usually arises within them when they have a sense that they are benefiting the social order, the company or the community. And they like others around them to know that it is they who have been generous.

They are natural leaders – leaders in their field, leaders of others. No one is better at establishing order than a six-metal person. They do this especially well when it comes to setting standards in ethics and task specification, like a ship's captain getting his ship on course. In such situations, the six's natural brilliance shines forth. If placed under stress (or when the six is the natal month aspect), or where there is more disorder than anticipated, the commanding six may become excessively domineering, and this may in some cases turn into tyranny.

## Spiritual Matters

Six-metals have strong psychic abilities and intuitive awareness.

Coupled with this is a strong sense of morality and a need to be connected to society, the social structure and community mores. If dietary and lifestyle factors lead them to have an imbalanced yin condition, there may be an over-emphasis on psychic abilities. As the person becomes more ethereally oriented, focusing their attention on invisible or more subtle dimensions of reality, they become ungrounded and lose their practical sensibility and connection to the world around them. If factors make them more yang or tight, they may ignore their intuitive sensitivity and plunge into ardent dogmatism. It is only the balance between these two facets, and a lifestyle that supports it, which leads them deeper into their spiritual life. Six-metals are generally the most traditionally religious of the numbers. Balancing their intuition with their connection with society, the deeper intuitive knowledge that arises for them can become a wellspring from which they work in society towards peace and universal brotherhood.

Six-metals should make a point of acknowledging the importance of their environment and their ancestry. This serves as an inner and outer protection in their spiritual growth and expression.

## General Health Recommendations

These are people of strong constitution. They seldom become physically sick. However, as a result of their tendency towards pride, six-metals may push themselves to their limits too often. This can be the cause of a rapid onset of illness which is difficult to cure. Thus they should be wary of over-exertion and try to cultivate moderation in activities.

Like seven-metals, the health of their lungs, colon and skin is essential for their well-being. Six-metals may exhibit skin problems more than most and should be wary of suppressing symptoms as a solution when changes in diet and lifestyle are needed.

Mental tension and worry can play a major role in the sabotage of a six-metal's health. Thus they need to cultivate relaxation. Breathing exercises combined with observation of postural alignment are useful. Meditative processes that can be practised in a group will probably be more successful than solitary attempts at home. Yoga postures or exercise processes which turn the body upside down can also be useful in providing rich blood and oxygen to areas of the body that may be stagnant from tension and lack of activity. The health measures mentioned in the seven-metal chapter should also be considered.

Six-metals, more than most people, do not like to live within limits that they have not created themselves. Thus they must align themselves with whatever changes they need to make in order for such changes to be truly effective.

## PERSONAL FENG SHUI RECOMMENDATIONS

### Sources of Support

Bagua regions Kun ☷ (2), Tai Chi ◯ (5), Ken ☶ (8), and Tui ☱ (7)

☷ *Regarding Kun*: Here is the natural balance to your tendency to

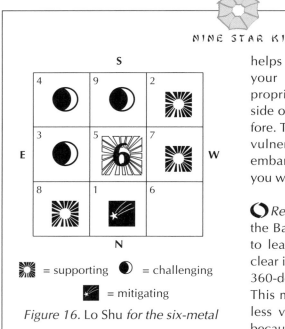

S

| 4 | 9 | 2 |
| 3 | 5 (6) | 7 |
| 8 | 1 | 6 |

E ... W

N

💥 = supporting   🌓 = challenging

⭐ = mitigating

*Figure 16.* Lo Shu *for the six-metal*

be emphatic and demanding. Kun puts you in touch with the unconditional and supports your need for building longer, more intimate relationships and alliances that will endure beyond the tasks at hand. It

helps you to cut through some of your stiffness and reliance on propriety, allowing the more caring side of your being to be come to the fore. This puts you in touch with your vulnerability, which can be a bit embarrassing – but probably serves you well.

🌑 *Regarding Tai Chi*: This region of the Bagua can reinforce your ability to lead. You should keep this area clear in order to be able to get a good 360-degree view of what is going on. This makes you more prepared and less vulnerable. At the same time, because Tai Chi is about good health through balance, you are able to be more realistic about what you want and expect, both from yourself and from everyone else. It also helps you to become a little more accepting of ambiguity, thus tempering your tendency towards trying to see everything as having a simple, clear-cut solution. This is a great antidote for the zealot and/or dictator in you.

☲ *Regarding Ken*: This region strengthens your resolve and can help you to build your confidence in a way that will not produce cockiness. Here you develop certainty about what you want and where you are going, even if this runs contrary to the views of the society and/or cultural milieu around you. It adds depth to your character and can help you be less fearful of showing a gentle side.

! *Note of Caution*: The six-metal person always needs to be aware of their contradictory tendencies towards dogmatism and pure intuitive awareness. The backing of Bagua regions that relate to earth transformation give you a grounding from which you can make your intuitive leaps. But don't take this support for granted. If you do, you may lapse into using this grounding as a justification for forcing things to happen in accordance with your will or wishes alone. Therefore, you are reminded to use your keen ability to assess what needs to be done and your higher sense of morality. If you use the earth regions of the Bagua wisely, you may become a benevolent strategist and commander.

☱ *Regarding Tui*: As the yin manifestation of metal, Tui is an ally of Ch'ien. This region of the Bagua offers a more general appreciation of the gifts in one's life and the tangible results of hard work. Sure, it is important to feel that what is in your life is meaningful, beneficial and righteous. But none of these reflect heartfelt appreciation and an attitude of honouring.

**! Note of Caution:** An excessive emphasis on Tui may heighten your sense of nostalgia and lead to greater regret and pain in the future caused by the inevitable change that all things go through. Not honouring the support of Tui can result in you seeming a steely materialist, measuring what is of value exclusively by monetary or socially acceptable standards rather than personal worth.

## Challenging Regions of the Bagua

Li ☲ (9), Chen ☳ (3) and Sun ☴ (4)

☲ *Regarding Li:* You have no problem with accountability. Still, you don't like having everyone know everything about who you are. Working with this region of the Bagua requires tact. Advertising, marketing, and getting yourself out and about – if that's what you want – all sound like good ways to promote what you want or who you are. But at the same time, with your assessment skills, you need to be able to predict or at least have a sense of what the outcome will be of any exposure you get. When confronted with the benefits and drawbacks of this region of the Bagua, you need to honestly ask yourself, 'Is it worth it?' If it is, go for it, but be prepared to have sound explanations for your actions and be willing to accept the bad with the good. The clairvoyant aspect of the nine-fire energetic coupled with the six-metal intuition can create a force that creates unbalanced situations – putting the cart before the horse. Cultivate a sense of humour. Otherwise you are going to take embarrassing moments as abject humiliation.

☳ *Regarding Chen*: If you are in touch with your intuitive side, then you will respect the magic inherent in this region of the Bagua. However, if you are too cocky and materialistic, you may degrade this region, seeing it as frivolous and pointless, and – as a result – suddenly find that inspiration disappears and the power of ancestry recedes, leaving you to soldier on regardless, becoming more bitter and self-important with every step. Along with the Bagua region itself, it is advisable to cultivate the three-tree region of the six-metal region of the Bagua with symbols and colours that

respect the sources of inspiration that have made possible your successes to date. (This can be achieved by locating the space associated with Chi'en (6), identifying the Chen (3) region of that space and honouring Chen accordingly.)

☴ *Regarding Sun*: Your insistence on results, and your desire to proclaim what you have, may not allow what is in the region of Sun to germinate, take root and flower. Rather than present the world with blooms and fruits, your impatience may only yield a crop of mere sprouts! Sometimes your notion as to what you want from a situation and its potentials can be too narrowly defined. Certainly, if you do not allow time and circumstances to unfold, you sell yourself short. Is control really that important? In this region of the Bagua, you need to be willing to tend to things like a wise elder cultivating a garden. In fact, plants that are meticulously watered and tended in this region are an excellent metaphor for the care and respect this area of the Bagua demands.

## Qualities that are Useful in Mitigating the Challenges to Chen and Sun

To develop a better relationship with the regions of Chen and Sun, pay particular attention to the region of Kan (1) generally and the Kan area of Ch'ien, Chen and Sun respectively. Doing so, you will help to lessen your dogmatic tendencies and open yourself up to a deeper understanding of whatever the invisible and less tangible offers you. Taking time to reflect, philosophical contemplation, going for a walk by a lake or relaxing in a hot tub are not wastes of time. The rewards you can receive by cultivating this calm dimension in your life, and these regions of the Bagua in general, can expand your scope and influence, perhaps even beyond your wildest dreams.

# Five

PROFILE

*Number*: 5

*Trigram*: ☷ Female trigram Kun (the Receptive) and Male trigram ☶ Ken (the Mountain)

*Colour*: Yellow

*Element*: Earth

*Internal representation*: Stomach, spleen, pancreas, lymphatics

*Physiognomy*: Hands and abdomen

*Symbolized by*: None

*Primary attribute*: Catalyst

*Family member type*: None

*Management skills*: The Consolidator catalyzing, leading, sorting, critiquing

*Occupations*: Politician, leader of enterprises, military or police officer, refuse collector, pawnshop owner, secondhand dealer, unskilled labourer

*Illnesses*: Have to do with excesses, infectious diseases, diarrhoea, circulatory problems, tumours, fever, immune-related diseases, blood sugar imbalances, depression, delusions, high blood pressure, heart disease, possibly gall bladder imbalances

*Development enhanced by*: Contemplation, listening

*Tincture*: Rosecan

*Best suited with*: 9,6,7

*Directions to travel*: 9,2,6,7          *Cautiousness in travelling*: 1,3,4

---

## NARRATIVE

Five-earth is the centre of the Magic Square. During a five-earth year, all the transformation phase energies are within their own houses. It is a time of great energy which demands intense reflection. It can also be a time when one feels very much on one's own.

Such characteristics are part of the five-earth person's nature. They are usually quite energetic. They share aspects with both the two-earth and the eight-earth, being caring individuals who have good insight. However, they can be a bit wishy-washy in their expression, becoming indecisive and thus unable to act on their insight. Put in the context of the maturation phase of the Five Transformations, five represents a point at which things are at their most dynamic in the maturation process, where the outer shell of appearance begins to fill in with substances for the first time.

Being in the centre of the Magic Square, the five-earth is like the hub in the centre of the spokes of a turning wheel. At the centre, they can act as a catalyst in the lives of others. They can be extraordinary problem-solvers and often find themselves as leaders, whether it be of a small group, a gang, an army, a nation or a religious order. They can weave order from disarray or come up with solutions for problems within groups. At the same time, a five-earth person can be a very needy individual. They often cannot use their talents to their own advantage. Being in the middle (or the leader), others may expect a five-earth to be more grounded, but in fact, such individuals generally feel as if the ground is moving under their feet constantly. Thus they have a strong longing to find a place or niche for themselves.

Being charismatic and often drawing attention to themselves unintentionally, they are often accused of being egocentric. This is not helped by the fact that the five-earth is rather blunt and stubborn, tends to be impatient, may complain a lot, and has a not-so-helpful tendency to mimic others. In moments of insecurity such traits may become more exaggerated as over-confidence and arrogance. At the root of their insecurity is self-doubt. In times of such self-doubt the healthy scepticism that a five-earth displays in order not to be taken in by others may turn into an unappealing cynicism which can make anyone or anything its target.

The five-earth is a complex personality – someone to be reckoned with. They find few close friends, but can cultivate enemies of greater or lesser intensity rather quickly. Though others may not be able to make sense of their actions and words, the balanced five-earth can be profoundly altruistic and have a deep compassionate heart – traits which will often go unnoticed by those around them.

A five-earth person's life is never uneventful. These people can either have exceptionally good fortune or experience a constant stream of disasters. In times of good fortune, they may become lackadaisical and as a result lose or spend it. If, on the other hand, circumstances are hard for them, they can be quite stoical and bear things that others would find difficult to endure. In such hardship, one will find a five-earth striving against the odds. Their desire for success is very strong. Their means to accomplish their ends are usually innovative. When out of balance this may manifest as impracticality. Having a strong sense that they are somehow on their own in the world, they do not bear criticism or even positive suggestions very well and will, consequently, learn from the 'school of hard knocks'.

As five is in the middle of the nine-year cycle, the expansive yin and contractive yang qualities are somewhat equal. Five-earth people therefore bear both male and female characteristics. This can manifest itself physically as an almost androgynous quality; the men of this number can be rather elegant if not beautiful while the women appear handsome. Within the personality there also exists almost a balance of traits that are classified as 'feminine' and 'masculine'. This can create an inner tension within the five-earth person. They may at times exhibit the keen observation yet superficial ways of the two-earth, while at others manifesting the penetrating insight and attention to detail of the eight-earth person. It all depends on circumstances. Extreme expressions of personality may also create confusion and tension for those around the five-earth person. Such versatility can, however, be an asset in that they are capable of handling diversity in a way that would leave others reeling. Consequently, five-earths tend to be quite unusual people with very interesting lives, people who are often the subject of other people's conversations.

## Love Relationships

There is a natural charisma that a five-earth person carries, leading them to find a partner easily. Both males and females of this number can be sexually irresistible to those around them. As regards sex itself, five-earths are the most physically focused of all the numbers. They love to make love, but equally love to see the pleasure they bring to their partners. Because they embrace extremes, partners may find that, at different times, they can either need to receive touch or stimulation or demand to be very physical with their partners. Unless they can maintain a balance within themselves, the intensity they exude coupled with their need or their imposing ways may lead partners to break off relations with them.

For a five-earth, 'variety is the spice of life', and they therefore have tendencies towards infidelity. This does not mean that they do not care for their partners or are fickle. In fact, they can feel within themselves deeply committed to one partner while they have various affairs on the side. Females of this number do this more out of a desire for more contact and more experiences; thus they often find themselves in 'love-triangle' difficulties. The men will be unfaithful to see if they are still attractive to others. Thus five-earth people are not particularly good at home-

making and usually find ways to recruit others to take on domestic responsibilities.

If a partner can tolerate their extremes in moods, needs and tendencies (usually towards infidelity), they will find a five-earth person passionate, caring and deeply committed. If they cannot and choose to leave, the five-earth will be truly saddened. But it won't be long before another person comes into their life.

## Business Relationships

The five-earth person could not be classified as the average worker. Some are so motivated that they rise to the top of their profession – and they are good at almost any profession they turn their minds to. Such people are extremely innovative and are excellent synthesizers of what to others would be discordant information. On the other hand, there are those five-earth people who are extremely lackadaisical or channel their more positive tendencies into destructive habits. Thus they can be the best or the worst at anything, depending on their motivation and the situations that circumstances offer them. The extremes that may be noted in different five-earth individuals may also be present in the same individual at different times. The high-flying five may have areas in their life that are not working at all. And it may even be that there are times when they are absolutely brilliant or absolutely helpless at the same task.

In terms of organizational skills, five-earths can seem to be rebellious. One can view them as 'problem' employees or choose to recognize their leadership and catalyzing abilities. While they are not particularly good at completing tasks, getting a five-earth person to spearhead a task force or to act as a spokesman for a project puts them in a position where their charisma and creative energies can come to the forefront. They will also exhibit caring and sharing qualities that can promote harmony within a group, with business partners or with new clients (whom they are good at impressing).

Five-earths have an unusual way of relating to money. While caring and generous to others in many ways, when it comes to money they can be misers. They hold on to their money tightly. As employees, these are people that may query their pay several times, asking where each pound has gone. More than others, they may communicate that somehow they have either been paid the wrong amount or that they should have more. Such attention to finances may lead an employer to view the five-earth as an excellent candidate to handle company money matters. However, where any corporate speculation is involved, employers should be warned that the five-earth, while never personally experiencing any grave financial hardship from which they cannot recover if they so choose, is not so fortunate with the money of others. When it comes to gambling or any financial speculation, five-earths will usually lose more than they gain.

## Spiritual Matters

Tibetan tradition views the five-earth person as religious by nature. There is a strong link between them and their ancestors and thus they should make a point of having the veneration of ancestors somehow included in the process of their spiritual life. Fives have very deep longings and needs when it comes to their spiritual life. Yet, because they are quick to think and act, the five-earth person has a tendency to miss the point if it is not obvious. To deepen their understanding, they must therefore practise listening and contemplation. Stillness is needed to balance their restless nature. As five-earths thrive with music around them, the use of bells, drums, ritual music and chanting are useful in nurturing their spiritual development. Such practices can prevent the five-earth from excessive self-involvement and concern.

The five-earth person is naturally altruistic, yet they may find that others dislike them for no apparent reason, other than the fact that they dislike fives just for being them-selves. Consequently, they should cultivate the virtues of patience and humility to soften their character.

## General Health Recommendations

Five-earth people are generally healthy. If their five is in the adult natal position, they should have a relatively strong immune system and can thus endure adverse environmental conditions and ward off sicknesses that others will be more easily prone to. However, if the five-earth is the child number or if five adults find them-selves placed in constantly stressful circumstances, their immunity could drop dramatically.

Five-earth people are prone to illnesses precipitated by going to one extreme or the other. On a physical level, the five-earth person may be very active or extremely inactive. When very active, they may exceed the limits of what their body can endure and may develop heart conditions as a consequence. If continuously underactive or if their over-activity leads them to 'crash', the resultant lethargy may lead to exhaustion and physically related depression.

On an emotional level, if their natural altruism lapses into a co-dependency marked by insecurity and constant preoccupation and worry, the five-earth may become hypercritical and negative (which could also be a source of ulcers). The more self-absorbed or withdrawn from the world a five becomes, the more likely they are to become so lackadaisical that they lose the initiative to respond to life's demands. Thus they may become increasingly doubtful of their own judgement,

lapsing into self-denigration and periods of depression.

Such physical and emotional tendencies, coupled with a diet high in stimulants, sugar and additives, as well as prescription and non-prescription mood-altering substances, may result in the diseases I have mentioned as well as hypoglycaemia, diabetes and chemical dependency. Moderation and balance are keys to a five-earth's continued health and well-being. A diet with few, if any, of the substances mentioned above is recommended. Moderate and above-average levels of exercise are recommended, especially those forms which activate the lymphatic system. Lengthy periods of sitting should be avoided. General Swedish-style massage is recommended periodically. Sleep and times for quality relaxation should be daily routines.

The challenge for a five-earth person is to realize that they possess the greatest of extremes on all levels of their being compared to other people. They have tremendous potential which if nurtured can create a life which is both rewarding for them and nurturing for others.

## PERSONAL FENG SHUI RECOMMENDATIONS

According to a conventional interpretation of the Bagua, unlike the other earth transformation numbers, the five-earth sits at the centre of the Bagua, which means that there is no ordinal or cardinal direction associated with it. However, if we look at the five-earth from a three-dimensional perspective, we can see that five-earth most aptly represents Zenith and Nadir, the positive and

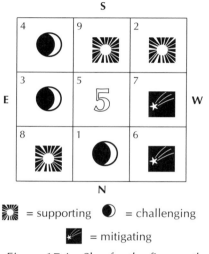

*Figure 17.* Lo Shu *for the five-earth*

negative polar axis around which all other directions emerge and revolve. Thus the polarity of opposites and the most basic representation of the inter-dependent nature of yin and yang give rise to the sheer raw power and intensity of the five. Like all other numbers and their transformations, five, although a balancing point in the expression of the transformation of earth, possesses some transformations that are either supportive of or challenging to the five-earth person. However, of all the numbers, the five-earth has the best opportunity to work constructively with even the most adverse of circumstances; but this does not mean that they always do, in which case a vacillation between success and disaster may be the rule. Such matters are truly in the hands of the five-earth person – which is probably why the *Mewa* tradition of Tibet extols the higher, more nobler qualities of the five-earth.

This being said, let's focus more specifically on the sources of support and challenges to five-earth.

## Sources of Support:

Bagua region of Li ☲ (9), Kun ☷ (2), and Ken ☶ (8)

☲ *Regarding Li*: Like five-earth, the region of Li (nine-fire) embodies charisma, but in a less bridled sense than would be the tendency of a five-earth person left to themselves. The activation of this region of the Bagua on the part of the five-earth will raise them up through the crowds and place them centre-stage in the public eye. If this is what you want, go for it.

! **Note of Caution**: When the sun shines, it shines on everything and everyone without distinction. It does not prefer one over the other – which is why it can be said that exposure more aptly describes the Bagua region of Li than does 'fame'. As a five-earth, you are turning up the volume when you activate this house. Yet, you sometimes vacillate. You may wish to retreat at times back into anonymity. Beware of the fact that once you have activated this house, in all likelihood you will not be able to retreat. If you attempt to do so, it could be perceived as being scandalous and do more damage to your efforts than if you had just left things alone in the first place. An over-emphasis of this Bagua region on your part will more than likely turn you into someone who gets up the noses of others. However, not using it at all or ineffectively will rob you of joy, and can still make people suspicious of you.

☷ *Regarding Kun*: With your complex personality that is caring, stoic and prone to mood swings, it is useful for you to seek an ally in the support of the region of Kun. It's not that you do not feel connected deeply to others, but that Kun helps you both to feel and to express the intimacy that allows others to perceive that you do really care and that you sometimes need care as well.

! **Note of Caution**: By over-emphasizing Kun, you may find yourself deeply embroiled in matters for which if anything goes wrong, you will be identified as the one to blame. By not accessing this region of the Bagua, you will find that all relationships remain conditional and that the thread of true lasting relationships eludes you.

☶ *Regarding Ken*: It is a basic fact that as a five, you will change what your interests are and what the course of your life is again and again. In this process, Ken ensures that you can focus and connect yourself to what is before you so that with each change, you carry a deeper knowledge. By simply cultivating this aspect of your being in accessing the Bagua region of Ken, you may even find that changes are about going deep rather than wide. This can benefit your commitment to careers, long term relationships and so on.

! **Note of Caution**: Too much emphasis on Ken brings the combination of your innate stoicism and the serious qualities of Ken to an almost monastic expression. If you want to create a granite wall around you, this is the way to go. On the other hand, by ignoring or not honouring Ken you invite more uncertainty and the possibility that things will come and go in your life in a dramatic, albeit whimsical, manner. The rub in this is that although you may seem to brush things off, such changes and the resulting uncertainty are really very painful for you and create much loneliness and self-doubt.

## Challenging Regions of the Bagua
Chen ☳ (3), Sun ☴ (4) and Kan ☵ (1)

☳ *Regarding Chen*: This region of the Bagua is most akin to your own nature. It is the invisible source of your most creative work and provides you with that innovative edge you sometime manifest in your unusual solutions to problems. In moments of insecurity and self-doubt, you may try to deny the contribution the energy of Chen provides you with in order to prove that you're solid, have both of your feet on the ground and don't believe in that sort of nonsense. What is interesting though, is that along with the inspiration of the ancestors comes their authority. Hence honouring them empowers you to affirm your own authority in a way that is dynamic and fluid rather than stiff and pretentious. Chen also demands that you abandon any self-image that defines you to yourself or others as being a 'slouch'.

☵ *Regarding Sun*: The tendency for you to lapse into materialism and hedonism is challenged by this region of the Bagua which warns you not to accept second best. There is so much more potential to work with. In this matter, it has to do with whether you can take this region of the Bagua seriously. If you do not, gird up your loins and be accepting of your lot. Also realize that such an attitude will create a situation where what you have will continually dissolve like sand through your fingers. To work actively and positively with this house ensures that there is more vitality and juiciness in what you create and manifest.

Do not let indifference and stoicism spoil what could be yours.

☵ *Regarding Kan*: Earth controls water. Unlike eight-earth's tendency towards over-seriousness and two-earth's co-dependency or obsession, in order to self-actualize the five-earth often has to overcome indifference or an attitude that is too accepting of keeping or viewing things in a way that locks them up in space and time. Many of these attitudes are an expression of the centrality of the five-earth and the sheer force of extremes in five-earth's being that make you think that you can tame forces or keep them at bay simply by hanging out, keeping inert, partying on …

The region of Kan has to do with the flow of life. To embrace the flow of life, we need to be willing to go deeper; to overcome resignation and jump into the stream so that we can feel or experience a more dynamic vision of what life can offer. The doorways to most rooms being usually identified as being the region of Kan or water, symbolically provide the portal through which we can encounter future possibilities and step upon the path of our life's true direction. The five-earth person needs to be more conscious of where they are headed and where they actually want to go. This is extremely challenging for the five-earth, who is so good at catalyzing the life of others, often by giving them that little

extra push. For themselves, however, they can often feel like there is no way to get from A to B. Therefore, they resign themselves to hanging out in A.

Earth can absorb water and turn things into mud. Seeing this tendency, each doorway, each entrance, should be arranged or decorated in a way that whispers possibility. A courtyard or living space with a central fountain may push the five-earth off the spot they may feel glued to and remind them of the flow in their life.

## Qualities that are Useful in Mitigating the Challenges to Kan

Sometimes we need to be reminded about what we have in order for us to rekindle a sense of appreciation. If we feel stuck and don't know which way to turn or how to direct our energy, a condition more frequently experienced by the five-earth person than others, the best regions of the Bagua to work with are Tui (7) and Ch'ien (6). In Tui, we can come to see the fruits of our actions thus far. This can stop the five-earth from focusing on what they don't have, which can lead them into inertia and increased uncertainty and resignation. Activating Ch'ien means turning to friends for practical help and guidance. This may feel awkward. After all, five-earths are usually in charge or are the caregivers themselves. But strengthening the Bagua region of Six or Ch'ien can be like going to the bank. No matter how small your account, you are not really bankrupt or unworthy of a loan. Activating this region, you may bring forth people and resources in your life that can help you back on your feet. If things are not so dire, activating this region of the Bagua can give you the support to see more clearly what you have gained thus far that can be used as a foundation for making one more positive step in your destiny.

# Four

### PROFILE

*Number*: 4

*Trigram*: ☴ Sun (Wind, the Gentle/Penetrating)

*Colour*: Green

*Element*: Tree

*Internal representation*: Nervous system, breathing system (diaphragmatic muscles), gall bladder

*Physiognomy*: Legs, (noticeable eyes – hypnotic)

*Symbolized by*: Cock, chicken, crane, snake, earthworm, unicorn

*Primary attribute*: Penetration

*Family member type*: Eldest Daughter

*Management skills*: The Decision-Maker – making decisions, individuating, clarifying, scheduling, initiating conflict, structuring, timekeeping

*Occupations*: Removals industry, shipping, building, furniture construction, advertising, travel agent, business person, meditator, guide, communications industry, teacher, public relations, master of ceremonies, manufacture and/or selling of wood and/or rope and associated products

Illnesses: Colds, hyperactivity, intestinal upsets, gall bladder ailments, connective tissue problems

*Development enhanced by*:
Reflection, concentration, penetration

*Tincture*: Goldenseal

*Best suited with*: 1,9

*Directions to travel*: 9,1,3

*Cautiousness in travelling*: 2,4,6,7,8

---

# NARRATIVE

Four-tree is the yin or more expansive of the two numbers representing the tree transformation. The tree transformation is also referred to as the space transformation. Both names represent aspects of qualities that both four- and three-tree people exhibit. (For brevity's sake, we shall just refer to the transformation as 'tree'.)

The tree element is symbolic of spring, where fine young shoots break through the ground in an attempt to assert themselves in their environment. There is a sense of freshness, uncertainty and vulnera-

bility in the air that can manifest as an irritable quality.

Four-tree people demonstrate these spring-like qualities. Like young shoots struggling to survive, they want to make it, to be someone. They are independent and determined. However, their determination, which is often expressed by a veneer of toughness, conceals a soft, vulnerable interior. Four-trees are truly ground-breakers: discovering, coming up with new ideas, seeing things as if for the first time. There can be a sense of innocence and wonderment with such people that is reflected in their eyes. In fact, inter-action with the world for a four-tree focuses around vision and being able to see things clearly. It is important for a four-tree to make eye contact in order to feel that they are communi-cating with others. However, their gaze can be quite mesmerizing, as their eyes are deep and hauntingly intense. (Others may find such a gaze intimidating, and may even think that the four-tree is acting as a tempter or temptress. However, there is usually nothing special behind the four-tree's gaze that would bespeak treachery. Of course, such a person usually discovers early on the power of their gaze and will use it to be convincing or to get their own way.)

Although four-trees can see situa-tions in a clear way and possess a high degree of common sense, this does not mean that they necessarily have vast experience or a deep knowledge to back up their percep-tions. They are excellent generalists who easily pick up a lot of informa-tion just on first impression, as if they had a sixth sense for general tones and feelings. But, because of this impressionability, they may overlook the details or inner workings of cir-cumstances – especially when the circumstances are not quite as straightforward as they seem. Thus fours can become confused by com-plexities and may project on to such situations all sorts of notions which have little to do with their original perceptions. They may confound their own common sense. And, because they possess a sense of natural maturity of being, others are often convinced by whatever the four-tree says. The four-tree may even know that what they are imparting to others is not exactly right, but it is almost as if the ripening of their perceptions – seeing clearly upon reflection – has not caught up with their mouths.

Fortunately, because they are so sensitive to their environment and the people around them, they never push a hard line and therefore usually try to find some delicate way of bringing things around into a more realistic perspective. Too often, however, they don't get a chance to accomplish this because others have already departed before they can overcome their own insecurities and be more straightforward. This hesitancy and 'beating around the bush' style means the four-tree is often misunderstood. They also cannot keep secrets, especially other people's secrets and they are therefore accused, and rightly so, of breaking confidentiality.

Like the elemental quality of space, the four-tree is an open field for impressions to pour on to. They always have many ideas which appear to them mentally as visual images. Yet when it comes to action, they can only handle one idea at a time. Give a four-tree person too much to do and they will panic or constantly chop and change so that nothing gets done. The more complex the situation, the more likely it is that they will lose their natural perspective and hence their sense of priorities. In fact, priorities for a four-tree are not necessarily determined by what is needed or a desired outcome. Rather, priorities emerge from an intuitive compassion and a sense of the right timing of events.

Timing is very important to the

four-tree person. They are, in fact, the most time conscious of all the numbers. Essentially all things have time frames for them and when dealing with a four-tree it is quite useful to spell things out in time frames. When timing is disrupted the four-tree can become frantic and act in a thoroughly confused and disoriented manner. Also, when placed under stress, four-trees lose their ability to estimate realistic times for plans or events. In such circumstances, they usually put things off to the last moment, and are thus often labelled procrastinators. When this occurs, they can genuinely believe that they have allowed enough time for things to take place. They often cannot see that their abhorrence of detail has slowed up timely decisions and that their hesitation and worry actually creates such a predicament.

Thus they find themselves living life at a somewhat hectic, jerky pace. Their lives can be filled with constant ups and downs, but the four-tree's attitude generally remains positive. If an idea, notion or situation comes crashing down, there are dozens of others to take their place.

The tree or space transformation has inherent within it the quality of independence. Like the young shoot that breaks the ground, the four-tree person wants very much to emerge and establish their own identity. Yet, like the young shoot, the four-tree person is highly vulnerable to the environment and conditions need to be right for them to succeed in their efforts. As the young shoot needs sufficient water, quality soil, warmth, sunlight and air, so the four-tree needs support for their efforts towards independence. They need to consider and be mindful of their environment and respect the circumstances and people around them who make it possible for them to succeed.

In times when they are uncertain of their strengths, four-trees may abdicate self-control to an authority that appears to be supportive and stronger and more competent than themselves. They then become blindly obedient. Such obedience, however, is usually conditional. In the safety of such support they can once again come to feel confident of their own abilities, at which point it is not uncommon for the four-tree to be back-biting and a rumour monger towards those whom they previously relied on for support.

Because of this obvious symbiotic relationship with their environment and the people around them, people usually have something to say about the four-tree. Thus they may be the subject of gossip. Being forward-moving, however, four-tree people are not likely to be bothered by this. They delicately move through life always discovering, always striving.

## Love Relationships

The four-tree is a strong believer in 'true love'. They are the innocents who have romantic notions about the right person, the right relationship and perfect timing. They are therefore very naïve. Yet this naïvety coupled with their emotional maturity, physical expressiveness and deep alluring eyes makes the four-tree person the object of attraction for others.

Although attractive to many people, the four-tree strives to be selective about whom they become involved with. Because of their natural vulnerability, they are rather guarded about conveying their true feelings. When involved with someone, their strong romantic ideals may lead them to project on to a partner all sorts of attributes that have little or nothing to do with who the partner really is. Gradually they may come to see things as they really are, but not before they and their partners have gone through several misunderstandings.

Four-tree people are looking for a deep relationship. Yet it is not uncommon for them to be attracted to people because of their power or influence, rather than because of their character. In such circumstances, they may only wake up to the fact that it was not the person, but the money or status that attracted them after they have become deeply committed.

Nevertheless, because they are generally loyal people, when a rela-tionship is not working out the four is willing to wait for things to come around and improve. A four needs to put effort into communicating more with their partner to clear up confu-sions. If they do not and the relation-ship worsens, the strain may lead the four-tree to become uncharacteristi-cally aggressive and cavalier. They may have several extra-marital relations or affairs which to them are of little significance. For them it is just a matter of waiting until the relationship they are in works out, or else until the 'right' person finally comes along.

This is a challenging area in the four-tree's life.

## Business Relationships

These are people who do best when employed by someone else. A four-tree will be loyal and productive for an employer to whom they can look up and by whom they feel supported.

Given an idea to explore, the four-tree can run with it, probably farther than anyone else can take it. They have a keen sense of what will and won't work, although working out exactly *how* is not their forte. If such ideas are just their own creation and are not receiving the support of others, the four-tree may take things in too rash or impetuous a direction. However, in the right supportive environment, where they are being encouraged and valued, four-tree people's intuitions about ideas and situations should be trusted. They are efficient and know how to enhance the efficiency of others.

Four-tree people are generally good at clarifying situations, using their common-sense approach to reduce things to simple units to work with. However, if the situation demands increased complexity or there are a lot of undertones or hidden agendas, one can almost see a fog descend over their eyes; their natural common sense is then clouded in a layer of total bewilderment. When this occurs, the four's vagueness, indecision or inaction is not really a ploy to shirk responsibility. Rather, they are simply overwhelmed. A lightening of their load will once again allow their natural abilities to shine forth. A simple way to by-pass this stress response is for the four-tree to develop decision-making tools, instruments, or processes. Whatever device they come up with will probably be all-encompassing.

As regards relationships within a business, the four is generally likeable and sociable, even though they may be the brunt of much office gossip.

Because they have a quality of being able to approach issues with sensitivity, they are quite skilled at resolving conflict within an organization.

It is best not to put too much financial responsibility in the hands of a four adult or four child whose adult natal number cannot hold the four quality in check. (Seven- or six-metal to four-tree is advised.) Fours generally have a tendency to part with money easily, and may be convinced by others to invest unwisely.

## Spiritual Matters

The four-tree person needs to balance their generalist tendencies with penetration. From the space quality of their transformation phase, it is as if, hovering in space, they get a good sense of what is going on, but need to linger a bit longer, to relax and allow their vision to deepen beyond first impressions. From the tree quality of their transformation phase, they possess a natural irritability which wants to push ahead to the next thing; thus what is present around them is felt, but somewhat blurred. If their spatial quality is enhanced and they can take the time to gain a proper perspective, their actions are magnetizing and rich. Patience needs to be cultivated. This can be a potent antidote to their tendency to be bored or frustrated.

For such people 'cleanliness is next to godliness' is an important dictum to live by. Four-tree people need to take care of their own cleanliness and the cleanliness of their environment to create a serene atmosphere. A serene atmosphere can create more space and less frenetic churning in their lives. They can then have the proper time and space to penetrate deeper into life's mysteries and thus cultivate an inner strength that can prevent their sensitive, vulnerable nature from being overwhelmed or sidetracked.

It is wise for a four-tree to seek out a teacher that they feel kinship with. Meditations where movement is involved, such as yoga or Tai Chi would be advantageous.

## General Health Recommendations

Depending on the nature of the stress in a four-tree's life, the insecurity and vulnerability they manifest when imbalanced can produce either a totally flat effect, lacking energy, or a body that is tight and rigid (character-ized by clenched teeth, with jaw and mouth disease symptoms, and clenched fists with resulting tenden-cies towards arthritic processes and connective tissue damage). In either case, the root emotional cause is usually frustration and anger. Other possible ailments are indicated in the profile.

A person with tree/space as one of their numbers needs to maintain a healthy level of physical activity. Forms of exercise that activate the musculature and especially the legs are recommended – jogging, brisk walking, swimming, cycling, and any sport that involves running. Four-trees may also have a tendency towards visual difficulties. Right-left brain exercises and therapeutic light apparatuses (like the Downing 'Lumatron', a light-emitting instru-ment which facilitates the transmis-sion of the full field of the visible light spectrum to the brain via the eyes) are useful, as well as conventional eye exercises.

As regards diet, a four-tree person may be over-fond of flour, oily foods and dairy products high in saturated fats, such as ice cream and sharper cheeses. These should be kept to a minimum as they aggravate the liver and gall bladder. Foods that are high in sodium or potassium (such as snack foods, nightshade vegetables and tropical fruits) should also be avoided, as they can inhibit (in the case of high sodium) or overstimulate (in the case of high potassium) healthy muscular discharge. Calcium-rich foods such as sea vegetables and dark green leafy vegetables are helpful in the diet. Alcoholic beverages should either not be consumed or kept to a minimum as they may increase the tree/space person's general sense of irritation to a point where violence is possible.

A four-tree should avoid being exposed to easterly winds, especially in spring. During such times the torso and throat should be well covered. Massage processes such as shiatsu and sports massage are helpful, as are isometrics. With a proper healthy balance in diet, exercise and relaxation, four-trees can maintain a strong, active physical life with a mental clarity that can give them a zest for living, learning and just being.

## PERSONAL FENG SHUI RECOMMENDATIONS

### Sources of Support

Bagua regions of Kan ☵ (1) and Chen ☳ (3)

☵ *Regarding Kan*: The waters of Kan contain the essence of all that has

143

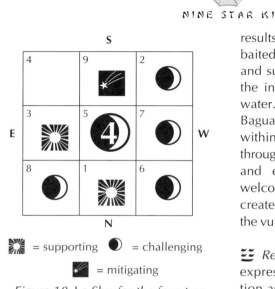

S

| 4 | 9 | 2 |
| 3 | 5 | 7 |
| 8 | 1 | 6 |

E ... W

N

= supporting   = challenging

= mitigating

*Figure 18.* Lo Shu *for the four-tree*

come before and reveals in its movement and direction the most efficacious path to embark upon. Therefore that which will keep you in touch with your potential does not involve looking forward to distant

results, or baiting yourself (or being baited by others) with material gain and success, but means tapping into the invisible, subtle, fluid quality of water. Honouring this region of the Bagua generally and the water region within the Bagua region of four itself through the use of colour and symbol, and establishing an ambience of welcome and openness will help to create a greater sense of certainty for the vulnerable four-tree.

≋ *Regarding Chen*: This is the Yang expression of the same transformation as four-tree. Through accessing this region of the Bagua your tendency towards relying on generalities and lapsing into somewhat fuzzy visions of what is possible will receive an infusion of inspiration that can clarify your vision and encourage you to use ancestry and the sources of inspiration for more independent action.

**! Note of Caution:** With regard to Kan, becoming fixated or obsessed with your direction could lead you to become excessively cautious. A type of myopia may set in, in which case you can become blinded to the potential right before your eyes.

As regards Chen, sometimes an infusion of energy from this region can increase confusion, especially if you try to do too much. Enjoy the enthusiasm and energy you receive from Chen, but keep your singular focus; take one thing at a time.

## Challenging Regions of the Bagua

Ch'ien ☰ (6), Tui ☱ (7), Kun ☷ (2), Tai Chi ◐ (5), and Ken ☶ (8)

☰ *Regarding Ch'ien*: With all the potential they possess, four-trees can find themselves dreaming of what they *could* do and can be very difficult to pin down as regards commitments and time frames. In these matters, the conditional support Ch'ien offers is accountability. By giving this region of the Bagua its due and cultivating friends and allies, you create the energy to be on top of things and maintain your focus. If you do not honour it, Ch'ien can leave you feeling oppressed and defensive. This can express itself in your losing the vitality and joy of your dreams and feeling as if every action, move or product you have the potential to manifest is being dissected, analyzed or quantified. Is the bottom line getting to you?

☱ *Regarding Tui*: The softer, more yin side of metal, Tui can be the region of the Bagua which helps you to realize your dreams. The edge on this Metal transformation, however, is that whereas tree-beings dream of possibilities that may or may not amount to anything tangible, the Bagua region of Tui encourages your evaluative skills and helps you to be more honest and real about what you can actually achieve. But remember not to throw out your other seemingly impractical schemes and visions. Save them. Let them ferment. What is impractical today may be possible tomorrow.

☷ *Regarding Kun*: Relationships are important to four-trees, but so is independence – especially independence that entails freedom of thought. Unlike three-trees who are more fierce as regards their independence in general, as a four-tree you like relationships, but these need to encompass honour and respect for your ideals and dreams. In fact, what is difficult for a four-tree in relationships is their insistence on holding onto romantic ideals of what relationship is itself about. These ideals may be very limited in their scope and thus, in matters of friendship and long-term relationship, the four-tree may find it difficult to recognize or appreciate intimacy or unconditional love.

◐ *Regarding Tai Chi*: Although the motto 'Cleanliness is next to Godliness' is worth heeding, the four-tree must be sure to maintain constant vigilance to work with and see the benefits of this recommendation. It is not that they do not value cleanliness or order as a balancing or grounding force. It just doesn't impress them as a priority worth focusing on unless it serves them at a given moment or as a last resort. This inconsistency in honouring of the space of Tai Chi creates vacillation in the success for the four-tree's efforts in accomplishing and staying with a task.

☲ *Regarding Ken:* Lingering in romantic notions and/or not going beyond generalities to the finer details, the four-tree may take lightly the conviction that is the hallmark of this region of the Bagua. For sure, the light-hearted, spacious quality of the four-tree character and its ways may seem more appealing than the practical (and at times over-serious ) quality inherent in this yang aspect of the earth transformation. However, in not honouring this region of the Bagua properly, the plans and ideals of the four-tree may not be well conceived and thought through, the result being

little long-term benefit. Penetrating insight is the quality that the four-tree generally needs to cultivate. Ken calls us to work with commitment on deepening our relationships to our inner selves and others, and pursuing the higher goals of our dreams. But sometimes the constraining nature of this region is an affront to the independence so sought after and valued by the four-tree.

## Qualities that are Useful in Mitigating the Challenges to all Earth Transformations
(Kun, Tai Chi and Ken)

Bringing dreams and visions of the tree transformations through to becoming tangible realities, the function of the earth transformation regions of the Bagua requires the use of fire transformation and its region of the Bagua (ie 9 or Li). We go from the unborn and etheric (space/tree) to the vibrational (fire) into the tangible (earth).

Thus to counter the ways in which you may get caught up in the non-tangible and procrastinate to the point at which whatever you achieve is only brought about through last-minute haste and pressure, the Bagua region of Li can be activated. By activating Li, you become exposed to a larger vision. It also makes you more direct in your communication. If you say more about what you want, in all probability you will get faster, more timely feedback from others. Whether it be a relationship or a building project, if you hold onto ideals but don't spell out to others what you have in mind, you won't even give people the opportunity to respond, let alone allow them to come close to meeting your ideals. Therefore the exposure of Li, although perhaps daunting, may actually serve your dreams more than you had ever imagined possible. Are you ready for this, or do you want to wait to think about it until you absolutely have to give in? And remember, if you want to activate this region of the Bagua, really go to town. What would you place in your ideal Li region of the Bagua – a plush maroon sofa and love seat on which to share your visions with friends whilst a warm fire burns in the fireplace?

# Three

### PROFILE

*Number*: 3

*Trigram*: ☳ Chen (Thunder, the Arousing)

*Colour*: Indigo (jade green)

*Element*: Tree

*Internal representation*: Liver, feet, musculature, connective tissue

*Physiognomy*: Vocal system

*Symbolized by*: Eagle, dragon, swallow, cicada

*Primary attribute*: Arousing

*Family member type*: Eldest Son

*Management skills*: The Planner – planning, mapping, defining borders, adapting, visualizing, brainstorming, recognizing, organizing, environmental scanning

*Occupations*: Prince, innovator, inventor, constructor, television industry, munitions, engineer, musician, sportsman, surgeon, teacher, writer, speaker

*Illnesses*: Ulcers, tumours, liver diseases, foot ailments, disorders of the nervous system, phobias, hysteria, muscular disorders, vision disturbances, throat ailments

*Development enhanced by*: External and internal growth (maturation)

*Tincture*: Saffron

*Best suited with*: 1,9

*Directions to travel*: 9,1,4

*Cautiousness in travelling*: 2,3,6, 7,8

---

## NARRATIVE

As four-tree is the yin expression of the tree/space transformation, where the shoots of spring are just breaking the ground, so three-tree is the more yang expression where the shoots have established themselves in a way that proclaims that spring is really here.

And so it is that three-tree people are bold, if not brash. They are optimistic and garrulous, which is often interpreted by others as being idealistic and foolish. A three-tree person has a tremendous amount of energy and is generally a self-starter. Their minds are very quick and as a result, they may have a tendency to jump the gun. This may take the form of starting a project too soon or with a zeal that often dwindles as completion draws near. The process of doing is more important than the process of completing. On the other hand, just as there are plants that shoot up and mature quickly, but are so fragile that they wither with the heat of summer, so it is with the three-tree person. Their energy and brashness conceal a very delicate sensitivity. Thus there are moments when the three-tree spontaneously creates something which is precious for the moment, but soon fades. Such efforts may go unnoticed by others, as they may be overwhelmed with the three-tree's overall energetic outpouring and intensity.

Three-tree people are 'ideas' people. They love to brainstorm and can usually come up with totally fresh ways of looking at things. They see things in their minds and may thus have the capacity to be visionary. They are creative but usually create in spontaneous ways, without plans. Some of their projects can therefore be total flops. Yet this doesn't daunt the three as there are plenty more ideas to pursue. Unlike the four-tree who has many ideas but must do things one at a time, the three-tree person also has many ideas but likes to do a lot of things all at once.

To an outsider, the manner in which a three-tree sets to work may seem aimless and inefficient. There may not be any detectable order in which things are done. They may start one project, then stop it to go to another one, going on and on like that. The unbalanced, stressed three-tree may over-extend this process so that very little is accomplished. On the other hand, if the three-tree's energy is focused, an outsider may suddenly observe that several tasks are completed all at once.

It helps a three-tree to stay more on target if time frames and priorities are established. Long and complicated tasks are generally frustrating for a three-tree unless approached in a way that gives them a sense of time, priority, *and* the mental space in which to be able to do it. After giving them instructions, it's best to leave them alone to get on with it. However, there will be times when the three-tree just can't seem to pull it together because their mind is filled with too many considerations.

Three-trees are quite likeable, but they can also be overwhelming. Their moods or feelings are easily projected into the space around them, which can be either a delight or absolutely stifling to the people around them, depending on circumstances. In general, there is an intensity about them, whether it be positive or negative. They can be quite rude, or shock people with what they say. This is partly due to the fact that three-trees talk as they think and often formulate their ideas as the environment and the people around them allow. Thus they themselves may not even know exactly what they are thinking at any time, and may be quite contradictory in what they say. It all depends on where they are in the formulation process. They should pause to reflect and respond. Threes tend to be quick talkers who in their efforts to straighten out the messages they have given may inadvertently confuse people more. The three-tree can also have the unfortunate habit of finishing sentences for others as they talk.

As spring reflects growth that has not yet matured, so the three-tree person is constantly on the move. They want to act as if they've got everything under control when it isn't quite true. They don't like admitting to defeat or shortcomings. They are generally the most vain of all the numbers and are very conscious of their physical presentation. Because of this and because of the fact that their movement is fluid and often sensual, young girls who have a three either in the child or in the adult natal position often find themselves being rigidly controlled by their parents. Mothers may be envious of their alluring physicality. Fathers may be harsh or cruel. Although I have no statistics, many women whom I have interviewed who have a three in their Nine Ki numbers have experienced sexual abuse at an early age.

Three-trees either thirst for or are thrust into independence at an early age. Their success in life's pursuits can be meteoric. Of all the numbers, three-trees learn best and accomplish most from their own efforts. They are ambitious and may push things to the limits. When in balance, they have the ability to know when to stop. However, their aims can be tainted with an egotistical pursuit of pleasure and success that can manipulate or disregard the needs of others. When under stress, three-trees may ignore their environment and disregard feedback from those around them. Thus, as quickly as they have gained success, they could squander it.

Three-trees are advised to make efforts to get a handle on and master their talents at an early age, lest they endanger their stability in later years.

Frustration is an emotional tendency a three-tree needs to be aware of. If put under stress, which can happen quite easily as they are so independent and don't like to feel challenged or incompetent in some way, their frustration can launch them into fully fledged anger. They can throw tantrums and are the loudest in vocal expression of all the numbers. However, like distant thunder, there is no real danger when they are this way. They usually cool down of their own accord. If confronted by a stronger adversary, the loud, brash three may become conciliatory. Basically they don't want to be hurt or disfigured.

This also partially helps to account for their tendency to flatter.

Sometimes it is to protect themselves; at other times, they can do it just to get their own way. The three-tree may have to deal with fallout from their brazen actions and talk, as others may not be as likely to forgive and forget as they are. Because they are action-oriented and visibly seen to be doing something, they are usually blamed when things go wrong in matters that involve them. Blame is something threes will find hard to escape, even in relation to people that they help.

## Love Relationships

The three-tree person wants to be in a relationship in which they can be intensely involved and still maintain their independence. Because of these two factors, they may have many love affairs, but will usually marry at an early age. If they do not marry at an early age, it will be because of their many ambitions. In relating to a three-tree, a partner must be aware that their intensity may be equally expressed in other endeavours, though not necessarily other partners.

Their own physical appearance is very important, as is that of their partner. The men of this number are vain and the women jealous of other women's looks. For a three-tree, physicality and the tactile aspects of sexuality are foremost. Such people can literally feel starved if not touched. At the same time, because of their intensity, a three-tree person may find that their strong passions are difficult to contain and thus may wilfully suppress their sexual and emotional desires. This can have a debilitating effect on a physical and emotional level. The men may become distant and aloof or aggressive, depending on the context. The women may view their lives as dull and there is a tendency towards female reproductive tract problems. Because of their intensity and the internal struggle that it produces, balance within a relationship constantly changes, somewhat dramatically.

On the whole, if allowed to express their free-spirited and playful nature, a three-tree can be a vibrant and exciting partner. And if the other partner can accommodate such dynamism and the space a three often needs within a relationship, they may find underneath all the motion and activity a very sensitive and loving individual.

## Business Relationships

If one looks at the list of professions in the profile, one notes that they are occupations for independent thinkers,

doers or people in the spotlight. Three-tree people do not make good organization people, unless, of course, the organization is theirs.

If they are in an organization three-trees are best suited to positions where they can brainstorm and are given a free rein to run with their creativity. As three-tree is also classified as a space transformation, one may see that their perceptions come from a panoramic vision of situations which makes them excellent strategists. At the same time, they are probably not the ones to carry out the strategy. To put such plans and authority into the hands of a three is to risk endless sidetracks. They are not economical, and may therefore expend a lot of time and energy in different directions from those originally requested. That is why it is best if they are given time frames and priorities with some designated diversionary tasks in order to satisfy their need to spread out. At the same time, another aspect of their panoramic vision is that they are keenly aware of the work environment. So if there is a need to know what the ambiance of the work space is, their perceptions can be trusted.

If a three person is put in a situation where people of higher or more powerful rank try to use their position or put pressure on them, one of several things is likely to happen: they may throw some form of tantrum; they may look for a direct confrontation, or they may just totally withdraw from the scene, which could include walking out. Their independence is that important.

A three-tree person needs to work hard at holding on to financial resources. They may earn a lot, but they also spend a lot. They enjoy pleasures, but they also find it important to give others a good time. Thus they can be generous to a fault. Because of this, placing them in a financial role or in a personnel position that requires strict adherence to prescribed policies would create untold stress in their lives.

## Spiritual Matters

The main issues in the spiritual life of a three-tree are maturation and grounding. They have a naturally spacious quality to their being, along with an intensity which can at times manifest as chaos.

As their power of seeing is so vivid, any spiritual practices that involve visualization are excellent as a way of providing them with a focus and grounding. At the same time, because of their spacious quality, they can relate to meditations like those of Zen, that emphasize the insubstantial nature of phenomena. The use of sacred sound or mantra is beneficial for them and others as it can channel the tremendous energy they carry in their vocal system. Meditative practices and disciplines that have as their focus purification will also help the three-tree to ground and clarify their actions, speech and mental patterns.

What a three-tree must guard against in considering these practices is to be constantly chopping, changing and mixing them up. The three's interest is so wide that rather than going deep and experience fruition, they may spread themselves too thinly to accomplish much in any particular direction. If they allow themselves to go deeper, threes will be able to develop their mystical nature, the primary strength in their spiritual life.

## General Health Recommendations

Three-tree people are perhaps the most agile of all the nine numbers. There is a fine relationship between their musculature and their nervous system which allows for precision, speed and grace. Thus it is that these people need to maintain a healthy level of exercise, but also need to balance this with processes of deep relaxation. Over-exertion and under-exertion can have a notable negative effect on their musculature and nervous system. There is a tendency towards sprains, muscular and connective tissue strain and damage, joint difficulties and (more nerve-related) paralysis.

The organs of the body associated with the tree/space transformation are the liver and the gall bladder. Care should be taken not to burden these organs with excess food in general and, more particularly, with foods high in oils, fats or flour products, dairy produce, alcohol, and psychoactive drugs, prescription or otherwise. Smoking cigarettes and marijuana smoking would be especially ill-advised.

Like the muscles and other organs of the body, the liver needs to be stimulated *and* allowed to rest. Three-tree people must therefore be conscious of the need for adequate rest to allow their livers to regenerate and build quality blood for the body. Late night or a nocturnal occupation is not recommended for such people. Other tree-related imbalances are listed in the profile. Of special note is the fact that as three-trees are generally overactive mentally, there is a tendency towards mental tension when under stress which can lead to various emotional and mental problems. More than likely, this will express itself in overt or repressed frustration and anger. Thus self-reflective meditation and relaxation techniques will not only help the three-tree's physical wellbeing, but also their mental and emotional state.

Like the four-tree person, a three-tree benefits from isometric and stretching forms of exercise. Yoga and other techniques that emphasize balance are also helpful. Progressive relaxation, autogenic training and self-hypnosis are just some of the relaxation techniques that benefit the three-tree. A diet light in animal foods and rich in complex carbohydrates, fruits and vegetables (especially greens) is recommended. Like the four-tree, a three should keep covered on windy days, especially when the wind blows from the east.

## PERSONAL FENG SHUI RECOMMENDATIONS

### Sources of Support:

Bagua regions of Kan ☵ (1) and Sun ☴ (4)

☵ *Regarding Kan*: The dynamic force from which the creativity of Chen spontaneously arises does have a source – perhaps as invisible and elusive as itself. That source is Kan. As the Bagua region of Kan is about the flow of life at the most basic of levels, honouring and working with Kan reminds the three-tree of their own purpose and provides the fluid nourishment that keeps the creativity of the three-tree moving forward.

The imagery of fountains, lakes, or waterfalls placed in the water region of the Bagua region of Chen as well

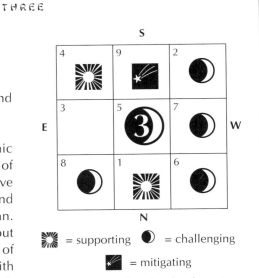

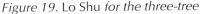

*Figure 19.* Lo Shu *for the three-tree*

as the Bagua region of Kan itself, is actually quite settling for visually-oriented three-trees, offering them a sense of direction and honouring all that has gone before.

☲ *Regarding Sun*: Working with the more yin aspect of the tree transformation by giving attention to this region of the Bagua will help you to move beyond the realm of abstract ideas into a more focused vision of what those ideas are actually capable of manifesting. The emphasis here is not on the finished product (that having more to do with earth energetics), but rather a general sense of the product or desired outcome. If nothing else, this yin aspect of tree helps the three-tree to be a bit more sensitive to input from others and to be more aware of the need to convey their somewhat grandiose visions in ways that are more digestible to others.

!*Note of Caution*: With respect to Kan, an over-emphasis on this region may cause the three-tree to find themselves less communicative, almost speechless, when trying to convey what they can see or envision. Not enough attention to this region may lose the three-tree their inspiration and result in what they want or envision becoming so intangible as to be almost completely unrealistic. A balance between these two extremes is struck by having respect for silent openess as a portal through which your spontaneous visions can arise.

With regards to Sun, there is a value in the gentle focus that gives you a more general appreciation of what is possible to create. At the same time, you should guard against lapsing into a fuzziness that takes the edge off of your creative drive. You should always feel a little – perhaps even a lot – ahead of your time. When your timing is off, look closely at the Bagua region of Sun. Patience with a bit of an edge is the rule. Drive on, but periodically check your speed.

## Challenging Regions of the Bagua

Chi'en ☰ (6), Tui ☱ (7) and the Earth transformations of Kun ☷ (2), Tai Chi ◐(5) and Ken ☶ (8)

☰ *Regarding Chi'en:* Independence at all costs makes you sometimes appear an untouchable autocrat. The Bagua region of Chi'en reminds you that you are not operating in a vacuum. If you are unwilling to heed this reminder from those who – in the long run – may be your greatest allies in bringing things in your life to fruition, you may find yourself standing on stage with nothing to show. An honouring of present allies and conditional support through a respectful development of this region of the Bagua is advised.

☱ *Regarding Tui:* Constantly in a state of creating more and more, sometimes you forget to slow down and smell the roses. It is important for the three-tree to take time, to be able to stand witness to the magnificence of their creation. Thus cultivation and appreciation of this region of the Bagua gives you a sense of gentlenesss and time for reflection. If you do not honour this region, you may later regret precious moments lost and tangible feedback which may be just the nurturing and information you need for future inspiration.

☷ *Regarding Kun:* Too much insistence on independence and revelling in the sheer force of the avalanche of your endlessly creative mind may make you insensitive to nurturing relationships and the care that each of us needs to receive to a greater or lesser degree throughout our lives. Can you just sit in a room with loved ones, enjoying the moment without planning and scheming for the future? Give people a break. Listen! Be receptive to what unconditional love can offer you. Cultivate this region of the Bagua as if you were building the perfect womb for yourself and others. Can you accept cosiness now and then? Possibly what makes you shy away from intimacy is that, in truth, the belly of the dragon is very tender.

*Regarding Tai Chi*: Soaring through space, even the dragon sometimes needs to touch down, take a moment's rest, get centred and refocus on a rallying point. Beware of your tendency to keep moving, creating and doing until moving, creating, and doing become a dizzying habit rather than a spacious display of your innate creativity. Much more than uncluttered space, you need to create an earthy warmth in tone, colour and presentation in this region of the Bagua. To be sure, as this region of the Bagua is Zenith and Nadir, it is important to feel openness from above as well as below. Consider a skylight in this region of the Bagua.

*Regarding Ken*: What are you committed to? Without taking time to contemplate and refocus on what the point of it all is, you may find yourself drifting from one thing to another, caught in the intensity of whatever your mind is dealing with now. You may convince yourself that this is 'freedom'. But, in the long run, such freedom without conviction will just dissipate your energy in more directions than is useful and leave you feeling hollow. The intensity of this region of the Bagua may seem boring, perhaps stifling. Remember, you may never do anything in a linear rational manner. However, you can work with the energetics of Ken to periodically remind and recommit yourself to your original vision and intent. In doing so, what you manifest will exude a heightened quality of excellence and power.

## Qualities that are Useful in Mitigating the Challenges to the Earth Transformations

To work more effectively with the earth-transformation regions of the Bagua, you need to be willing to share your vision with joy and lightness, rather than with a whip or laser. One aspect of exposure in the Bagua region of Li (9) is networking. To effectively capitalize on exposure and reach out to others, the three-tree needs to cultivate and access the warmth and joy of Li and be willing to bring these qualities into the earth-transformation dimensions of their life. Linger with people. Spend more times spelling out what you want – what your visions are. In doing so you will cultivate deeper relationships and demonstrate your commitments. If the signs of success that arise from the Bagua regions of the earth transformations are not manifesting in your life, return to Li and cultivate it again. You cannot just drop pearls of inspiration and then disappear back into the ethers. Revisit Li one more time. Cultivate it some more. Then, if necessary, do it again.

# Two

PROFILE

*Number*: 2

*Trigram*: ☷ Kun (Earth, the Receptive)

*Colour*: Black

*Element*: Earth

*Internal representation*: Stomach, spleen, lower half of body, flesh

*Physiognomy*: Abdomen

*Symbolized by*: Cow, mare, ant

*Primary attribute*: Receptive

*Family member type*: Mother

*Management skills*: Manager, Supporter – sustaining, supporting, stabilizing, holding, retaining, assimilating, anchoring, centring

*Occupations*: Wise woman, Shamaness, matriarch, union member, mother, obstetrician, doctor, antique and curio dealer, nurse, gardener, grocer, supermarket and bakery help, civil engineer, farmer

*Illnesses*: Skin disorders, blood disorders, goitre, tongue and throat symptoms, digestive tract ailments, congestion, blood sugar imbalances, depression, sense of being overwhelmed

*Development enhanced by*: Philanthropy, receptiveness, altruistic offering of service

164

*Tincture*: Dandelion

*Best suited with*: 9,6,7

*Directions to travel*: 6,7,9,8

*Cautiousness in travelling*: 1,2,3,4

## NARRATIVE

In Appendix 2, I explain how each number in succession, from greatest to smallest, represents an increasingly contracting (yang) force in the space-time continuum. Thus, as the cycle of years moves from nine to one (see Figure 37, page 305), people experience an increased sense of speed and intensity in their lives. (It is also true that as the number nine year comes round again, people will, in general, experience more ease.) Interestingly enough, as if to counter-balance this effect, one of the primary characteristics of two-earth is that it is the most receptive (yin) of all the nine numbers.

To clarify this seeming paradox in terms of the maturation process of which it is part in the Five Transformation Theory, it is almost as if whatever has budded (tree transformation) and blossomed (fire transformation) begins to take on its first appearance as a mature entity. This is a bold step in the cycle from creation to dissolution. It is no surprise therefore that two-earth people exhibit the qualities of tenaciousness and strong will (even stubbornness), yet also mildness, kindness and gentleness. They manifest both the yang intensity and the yin receptivity of the time.

Two-earth is considered the primal mother number (as six-metal is the

primal father number). As such, whether male or female, there is a distinctly feminine quality to this person's way of being. They feel an intimate connection with their environment and strive to maintain order in whatever they are involved in. They can be somewhat old-fashioned and conservative in their endeavours and are workers rather than innovators.

Being caring and hard-working, if a two-earth throws a party, they are very concerned about how things look and feel for others. They will try to maintain the right atmosphere for their guests, and will busily flit around making sure that their guests are having a good time and have enough to eat and drink. In such circumstances (and also more generally) they may appear as social butterflies, somewhat superficial in their brief encounters with those they feel they are attending to. However, ask a two-earth how such a party or event went and they will be able to tell you what was going on with each and every person with whom they had contact. Their powers of observation can be exceedingly keen. Unlike the caring quality inherent in the other earth numbers, five and eight, the two-earth's care focuses on a general sense of well-being rather than the specific issues and problems in other people's lives. Thus their attention and caring tends to be more unconditional and constant.

Although one could call a two-earth person more of a generalist as regards their observation and learning, they do like to take note of the details. They can be as interested in the operations of a machine as they are in the dynamics of a relationship. At the same time, the details don't actually matter to them very much, even though they may exhibit an obsessive interest in them. It's as though they are hungry for as much as they can know of what is happening, but really only want to get the general drift of things. Others may consider this to be superficial. Twos learn quickly and forget quickly, but ever so much want to be helpful and a part of whatever is going on. For a two-earth anything worth doing is worth doing *now.*

A two-earth's energies are best focused when they are part of some larger plan or part of a group. They are not leaders but joiners, and they remain faithful to any group they join. They are not initiators or self-starters, but given a task, they will go at it with a tenacity not seen in the other numbers. Like a good mother, they will care for and look after the tasks and needs of the group, even in the face of great difficulties. If left to their own devices, they get bored and are somewhat at a loss for a sense of purpose.

Although best within a group, two-earths need overt acknowledgement of their achievements. Whatever they are doing, they want to let others know how it is going. If some level of acknowledgement is not forthcoming, they are thrown back upon themselves and become self-doubting. They may be envious of the attention others receive and, as a result, may be quite callous, if not vicious, towards such people. Two-earths usually make it harder on themselves in this respect in that they like to associate either with people older than themselves or with people that they rate as 'somebody'. Thus they may also exhibit a tendency to try to fit in by putting on airs. In the long run, such behaviour has an undermining effect on them, making them retreat to safer, more secure ground. Thus, in times of personal stress, a two-earth may prefer to stick to what they know rather than venture out and risk failure. Such periods are short-lived, however, they can easily let go of their envy, pull themselves up and go in search of another task or group into which they can pour their energy.

## Love Relationships

The primary emphasis in a love relationship for a two-earth person is to be able to lavish their care and love on others. Such an attitude naturally attracts people to them. However, their willingness to display such care and affection may at times be interpreted as a sexual invitation, especially if the two-earth is female. This is not necessarily the case. Two-earths do enjoy sexual involvement, but it is just one of the many ways they employ to demonstrate their care for their partners. The men of this number are generally liked by women because of their care and consideration. The women of this number will usually be drawn to men who are strong, athletic and in some way powerful. When she finds the man of her liking, a two-earth woman will be fairly direct in letting him know. If a man in whom she has no interest approaches her, she will set him straight in an instant.

Two-earths get into trouble in relationships when they display their tendency to be obsessive over the details of their partner's life. They may also try to be everyone and everything for their partner. In such a case, sex may become a dutiful act, performed to please. Thus a two-earth needs to be able to distinguish between devotion and co-dependence. If they do not assess this periodically, they run the risk of their partner feeling suffocated by their affections and attentions.

In general, this is a person who will be a devoted and faithful partner, whose unconditional love and caring can be both moving and inspiring both to their partner and to others around them. Still, they are well-advised to watch their obsessive tendencies, as well as over-reliance on their partner. Both of those tendencies may lead to unexpected separation.

## Business Relationships

This is a person who cares. As part of a group or organization two-earths will immerse themselves in the tasks, functions and relationships. They like to be a part of the team. Organizations in which they work best are public or service-oriented. They may also be found in volunteer positions. Fields of work and positions that will create stress for them are those that are scientific or technical in nature, as the precision that is demanded can be mentally and physically taxing on the two-earth.

As part of a team, in the role of a supporter rather than a director, the two-earth person will avidly dive into tasks and will work consistently until they are completed. They have a sense of how systems work and can develop routines to keep things moving along. But they will need direction. Don't assume that when they say they understand they really do. A well laid-out plan is useful for the two-earth to have in front of them. With good supervision and support from fellow workers, the two-earth will create products of superior quality.

On a personal level, a happy, purposeful two-earth person creates bonds and a sense of caring. Their team spirit can be contagious and they are skilled at teaching others what needs to be done. Problems arise when, out of a sense of insecurity or jealousy, they create rivalries. When balanced, however, the two-earth wants to be involved with the team and with fellow workers. They will probably find themselves listening to co-workers' problems and concerns. They therefore do not do well in a supervisory capacity. The idea of having to hire, fire, or judge others is contrary to their unconditional caring nature. Put a two-earth person in such a position and you will have a person that may appear to be doing the task at hand, as they do want to please those in authority. But in doing so, they may be experiencing endless worry, sleepless nights and self-doubt.

As regards finances, two-earths are frugal and tend to accumulate steadily. They do not speculate. Thus they can be good at watching and balancing the books. On a personal level, however, they may find that when touched by someone else's need they are over-generous and thus place themselves in financial difficulties. Still, little harm comes from such generosity. Money may come to them in unexpected ways. A two-earth's financial practices may be less extreme than the five-earth's – more modestly fortunate or unfortunate.

## Spiritual Matters

Service to others is the trademark of two-earth people. And to clarify this virtue so that it arises more out of altruism, the two-earth needs to address any self-doubt or sense of deep sadness that they may be harbouring. These two factors, if allowed to cloud the two-earth's world view, may create cynicism, jealousy or even contempt of others. Thus they need to work on cultivating greater confidence in themselves.

To do this, a two-earth should find others who have committed themselves to the spiritual values and path they wish to tread. Because of their devotional nature and team mentality, they can be examples of spiritual or religious discipline, but they need to know the difference between faith and blind adherence.

Compassion is strong with such people, yet they need to be able to distinguish between true compassion and 'idiot compassion' or co-dependence. Rather than just giving because they want to or think they should, a two-earth must pay more attention to the real needs of others so that they can truly benefit the people they are serving. If they do not give this more thought, they may find that they are rebuffed more than appreciated for what they do.

Self-empowerment practices and meditations are advised. The use of music and chanting would be useful. If they can overcome doubt and become confident in their service and compassion, the unconditional nature of the two-earth can be a powerful force in clearing away obstacles in life for themselves and the people around them.

## General Health Recommendations

Two-earth people have a difficult time accepting that they need to be pro-active in their health. With so many others in need they may feel that they have no time to pay attention to themselves, and may feel they do not deserve other people's interest in their health. They may even go so far as to refuse help. But two-earth people must come to realize (usually with help from kind yet persistent friends), that they can best serve noble causes if they take care of themselves. Usually a two-earth will reluctantly give in to such logic, but once they have given in, they are quick to feel the benefits of a pro-active health programme.

Most two-earth people will tend to be plump rather than slender. Food and earthy sustenance may be of either constant or little interest to such folk. Thus they may be gourmands and eat excessively, or they may eat very little, but make poor choices in what they eat. Of the foods they are attracted to when out of balance energetically, it is such things as sugars and other refined foods, alcohol and stimulants such as caffeine that they will indulge in excessively. Such foods are difficult for them to metabolize. Hypoglycaemia, blood sugar imbalances and problems related to bad dietary habits can lead to blood and lymph disorders. If the two-earth is over-extended emotionally by becoming over-involved in other people's problems, self-doubt, deep sadness and possible depression will ensue. Add to this a diet that is stressful and the two-earth can suffer even more depression, fatigue and immune-related diseases.

Two-earth people need to eat sensibly, particularly avoiding refined carbohydrate, alcoholic beverages, caffeinated drinks and 'junk food'. They need to exercise and stay active. Exercise processes that particularly facilitate blood and lymphatic cleansing are recommended. Mini-trampolines and inversion machines are useful devices for the two-earth. They would also benefit from the occasional Swedish or lymphatic style of massage. If they are to get involved in processes of relaxation or meditation, it is best that they incorporate meaningful thoughts and prayers that allow them to feel that the quiet moments they take to recharge themselves also benefit others.

## PERSONAL FENG SHUI RECOMMENDATIONS

### Sources of Support

Bagua regions of Li ☲ (9), Tai Chi ◯ (5) and Ken ☶ (8)

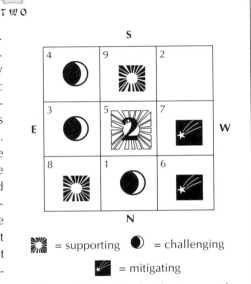

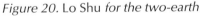 = supporting ◖ = challenging

= mitigating

*Figure 20.* Lo Shu *for the two-earth*

☲ *Regarding Li*: It's so easy for you to be self-sacrificing, a willing friend, an exemplary helper. The clarity in the exposure of Li gives you an ability to utilize your care and concern more precisely. And although

173

you do not necessarily seek the limelight, recognition for your efforts is always appreciated and – in fact – spurs you on. Thus tapping into and accentuating the Bagua region of Li makes your efforts stand out. It can also bolster your will when you need to set limits.

!Note of Caution: Exposure and fame are always double-edged. Relying on it too strongly, you may develop a heightened sense of your importance. What comes with this is a flamboyance that can make you oblivious to an increased level of naïvety. You then become a target for those who see you as a soft heart or an easy mark. In not utilizing the support offered by the resources of Li, you may find that without the infusion of joy and energy Li offers, you will feel more in the trenches –

overlooked and taken advantage of. The volatility of Li always demands seeking a middle way. Discernment is the issue.

○ *Regarding Tai Chi*: The support of Tai Chi for Kun is found in the detachment it encourages. All of the earth transformation regions and their qualities have something to do with nurturing. In the case of five-earth, this region of the Bagua allows you to pull yourself back and take a look at what is happening from a distance. This does not divorce you from situations, but gives you the room to know how best to utilize your energy without over-extending yourself or expecting too much of yourself and not enough of others. For Kun, the healthiness Tai Chi encourages is the overcoming of co-dependency and learning how to nurture yourself.

Once you truly master that, you have endless resources and boundless compassion.

! Note of Caution: If Tai Chi is over-emphasized, you may lose the emotional quality, the intimacy that allows others to feel close and comfortable with you. To not value Tai Chi – the centre of who you are – enough means chaos will ensue and you will spend your time trying to rescue lost causes. Life becomes a complicated, gooey mess. Cleaning up this region to keep it open is critical.

☲☲ *Regarding Ken*: This yang aspect of the earth transformation encourages you beyond emotionality to develop a conviction that sees things and works with things as they are. If you are going to continue extending yourself to others, to work, to causes, to the

Beloved, the contemplation inherent in this region of the Bagua provides you with a deeper knowledge and reinforces your resolve.

! Note of Caution: Paying excess attention to Ken can exacerbate your tendency towards being obsessional, worried, intense. Not honouring this region and the support it can give you leads to fuzzy motives, and a scattered approach that can dissipate your energy and leave others wondering if you really know what you are doing. You may then come across as shallow or superficial.

## Challenging Regions of the Bagua

Chen ☳ (3), Sun ☴ (4) and Kan ☵ (1)

☳ *Regarding Chen*: It is a natural inclination to find yourself easily

175

absorbed with problems, worries and concerns. The weight of matters can take on a tangible, palpable quality that leads you to experience self-doubt, even depression. Chen challenges you to step back, to lift your gaze from the path before you and look up into the heavens. It reminds you to tap into whatever inspires you and gives you the invisible spark you need to be upright – your own person – as you work on behalf of others. Thus as tree-transformation people need to recognize their rootedness to earth, earth people need to stay in touch with the invisible and inspirational. Without it, a two-earth's world becomes increasingly solid and unconditional care and compassion, syrupy. In the long run, this may lead you to become frustrated and bring out the vixen in your nature. Along with honouring and working

with colours, symbols and archetypes in the Bagua region of Chen, it is advisable to make a special place of the sub-region of Chen within the Bagua region of Kun, itself.

☳ *Regarding Sun*: Given their tendency to over-extend themselves, it is extremely helpful for two-earths to be reminded of their personal potentials as well as the potentials of the circumstances they may find themselves in. Without such a reminder, they may become forlorn and feel a sense of emotional bankruptcy. More things or tangible material comforts are not going to allay these feelings as much as a message of upliftment from this yin manifestation of tree in the Bagua. By not honouring this region of the Bagua, opportunities may be lost as your ability to perceive the resources available to you becomes increasingly distorted. In the Bagua region of Sun, focus on colour and light. Place objects in this space that symbolize the potentials you feel the need to tap into to do your work. In that space, breathe in the energy of these symbols and vision them working through you.

☵ *Regarding Kan*: Although you may act somewhat superficial in your social mannerisms, much of this is to distract others from being too aware of your keen observation of and care for them. Unconditional care and love is a hallmark feature of the two-earth character as they self-actualize. Yet whilst you can easily care deeply and can get yourself into a state with your cares and worries, this may not serve the deeper purpose and course of your life. Thus you may shy away from or treat glibly your overall purpose and direction. Indeed, it is

noble and good to be unconditionally caring of others and more than likely this will be an intrinsic part of your path. However, is there a way to focus this and direct it in a way that serves to move you forward in the course of your life?

In attending to or being distracted by the details and the crisis or concern before you, the larger picture may elude you. The result is the coming together of earth and water, creating mud – and being stuck in it. You must come to understand that putting yourself first at times – especially when it comes to acknowledging and aligning yourself to the flow of your life – will actually streamline and provide you with more resources for benefitting others. You can manifest all the power and care of an Earth Mother without being anyone's door mat. Are you willing to give it a try?

## Qualities that are Useful in Mitigating the Challenges to Kan

Cultivate the qualities in the Bagua regions of Ch'ien and Tui. The Bagua region of Ch'ien gives you the support and encouragement from those whose interests may be conditional but which, nonetheless, are similar to yours. They may even provide you with a history or context in which to assess what you need to do in life or a given situation and whether the efforts expended are really benefitting anyone. The reality of this region of the Bagua and what it represents for you in your life may seem a bit too clear cut, even sharp, but sometimes to move forward and align ourselves to our true direction, we need to extricate ourselves from circumstances that are nothing more than side-shows and distractions.

Tui, being the Yin manifestation of the Metal transformation, provides you with a space in which you can look upon the fruits of your endeavours. This evokes your evaluative abilities and encourages gentle honesty. What has worked well? What has not? With that which has not, perhaps a sense of regret, a desire to go back and do it differently, may be just the encouragement you need to let go and make changes that ensure better results for the future.

# One

PROFILE

*Number*: 1

*Trigram*: ☵ K'an (Water, the Abysmal)

*Colour*: White

*Element*: Water

*Internal representation*: Kidneys, bladder, sex organs, bones, nervous system

*Physiognomy*: Ear

*Symbolized by*: Pig, rat, fox, bat

*Primary attribute*: Hardship, danger

*Family member type*: Middle Son

*Management skills*:

YIN: The Allocator – containing, setting limits, storing, allocating resources, delineating boundaries, managing resources

YANG: The Motivator – generating, regulating, motivating, energizing, providing direction, reflecting, risk-analysis

*Occupations*: Social worker, printing and dyeing, fishing industry, chemist, massage therapist, philosopher, writer, dairy worker, oilman, restaurant owner, waiter, bartender, lawyer, maintenance person

*Illnesses*: Kidney ailments, earache, venereal disease, melancholia, abnormal menses, haemorrhoids, neurasthenia, paranoia

*Development enhanced by*: Baptism, purification practices

*Tincture*: Skullcap

*Best suited with*: 6,7,3,4

*Directions to travel*: 6,7,3,4

*Cautiousness in travelling*: 1,2,8,9

---

## NARRATIVE

One-water represents the end of the nine-year descending spiral through time. The word 'spiral' is used here rather than 'cycle' because it points to the fact that while the energetics of what comes around through time bear similar characteristics and appear the same, history does not in fact repeat itself. Something new is always added, albeit in keeping with the dynamics of the transformations present. A cycle is a closed circuit. A spiral is open-ended, but moves in a cycle-like path.

The water transformation phase is associated with winter. What has been created, developed and matured now experiences its own dissolution. Winter is a time of year when life recedes deep into the ground, and movement is subtle, if present at all, while the thaw of spring is awaited.

Thus the one-water is a deep-thinking person who is rather enigmatic. There is a quality of solitude that pervades their being. In social situations, usually to ease those around them, they may appear chatty and superficial. They will generally not say what is on their minds as their natural brilliance takes them to deeper and more subtle levels than they expect others to be able to understand. Although generally correct in this assumption, it nevertheless needs close scrutiny, as this attitude can lead them to be opinionated and contemptuous of others. The enigmatic aura that they project even while in conversation can make others feel a bit uncertain as to what the one-water is really about. People may try to be liked by one-waters for fear of becoming the subject of their disdain. Thus, one-water people need to be more skilful with, and develop more equanimity about, their opinions, lest they be viewed as bigots.

Because they keep their deepest thoughts and plans to themselves, one-water people's actions will often seem abrupt and sudden, even though they have been planning things for some time. Ask a one-water person a question that involves consideration and you may have to wait some time before the answer bobs to the surface. Ironically, although deep-thinking, if they are put into a position where what is going on is not known or familiar to them and they have not been able to formulate their opinions clearly, one-water people may find themselves swept along by the momentum of the situation. Thus, they can fall prey to a herd or mob mentality, something they will tend to regret deeply once they have a chance to settle down and be more reflective. Their natural wilfulness is so intense that in such circumstances, having made a sudden change of direction, the one-water finds it difficult to maintain equilibrium.

Although water has its own inherent properties, its location, force and movement is dependent upon the circumstances around it. Thus a one-water displays a fluid adaptability. Regardless of the circumstances, a one-water can fit in and play the part, and will usually do so whether they like it or not. When their attention and personal involvement is demanded in situations not to their liking, they will reluctantly perform as required, lying and flattering if necessary just to keep things superficially satisfactory.

Because they are sensitive to the effects of their environment and circumstances, and because of their natural fluidity, one-waters usually experience life as somewhat constrained but always changing. They need to strive hard to know themselves because their life experience is constantly shifting. Their superficial ways conceal a deeper desire to come to terms with the significance of all the happenings in their life. They need to develop and maintain a well-defined detachment to accomplish this. Their insights can be furthered by paying more attention to what others have to say, something which does not come easily to them. If they cannot come around to a more detached view of life, they will constantly experience upset and every change will be viewed as one more hardship to endure.

The one-water person may appear as sad or meekly reserved. Yet they have a thirst for life and living. They appear drab or rather colourless, particularly in their dress but they actually enjoy being colourful and can bring up from their depths a vivaciousness which is absolutely magnetizing. Although they can be disdainful of others and appear judgemental or withdrawn on social occasions, still the experience of being at such a gathering means a lot to them at a deeper level. For, although one-waters like solitude, they do not like to be excluded or isolated. If a one-water can draw up and project even a glimpse of joy in a situation, not only will this bring delight to others, but as it is reflected back to them, it will begin to permeate more of their experiences.

The fluidity of a one-water will create a life that is varied and challenging. These people will usually find that their circumstances change a lot. Family, finances and overall security continually change for them and if they resist or deny such change, freezing up rather than 'going with the flow', they risk creating unnecessary stress for themselves. One-waters may also find themselves moving or travelling frequently in their lifetime. It is only natural for such people to be cautious in their undertakings, in a sense trying to stem the tide of the ebb and flow in their life. To resist or deny such change and movement, however, will create in them a fear of life that can be paralysing and cause stress and dis-ease.

## Love Relationships

Although one-water people enjoy solitude, they want to feel free to choose to be alone. Thus there is no contradiction in the fact that they may like companionship. However, companionship to them is not necessarily defined as doing something with their partner. The companion to a one-water needs to be like a vessel or a cup. The cup contains, but is not a part of, the water. Thus, the one-water's partner must get used to the idea that they are with but not necessarily a part of the one-water's life.

This does not mean that such a person should feel discounted or any less significant in the one-water person's life. One-waters are not people to choose partners lightly. They ask questions, check attributes, reflect deeply about the person they are considering as a partner. Once committed, they settle in and hold on. They may, on the surface, act unperturbed or nonchalant, but underneath they possess a love which runs deep.

If the involvement is sexual, the bond between one-waters and their partners is even more powerful as the exchange of sexual energy is one of the primary ways in which one-waters learn more about themselves and deepen their spirituality. Because of this, there may be a tendency to over-emphasize sex in their lives, either by minimizing or exaggerating its importance. If they are sexually rebuffed or disappointed, one-waters may rigidly abstain from sexual involvement. On the other hand, they may have such a strong sex drive that their passions are animalistic. The men of this number may act like gigolos, while the women maintain an entourage of several lovers or conjure ways of experiencing sexual pleasure. Because a one-water's experience of sexuality runs so deep, and as sexual identity and security are often major issues in the lives of other people, a one-water's personal knowledge and expertise in this area of life makes them good as counsellors for both men and women.

A lesson one-waters should learn in their love relationships is detachment. Once involved, especially sexually, one-water people can be extremely possessive. As a result, they may not only lose their own sense of self-identity, but also sacrifice or neglect other important relationships in their lives. They also have a tendency to be excessively lavish with money and gifts and thus can heedlessly squander whatever savings they have accumulated. Such behaviour often comes about when the one-water fears being abandoned.

One-waters must come to terms with the fact that their need for solitude is best satisfied when they recognize how companionship can create the support necessary for that need to be met. Being more verbal in communicating their appreciation and love for their partner will not only create a greater sense of closeness, but will also possibly alleviate their tendency to cling. If such issues are not addressed, one-

waters and their partners may be locked in a relationship for years; the one-waters feeling isolated and mis-understood, their partners feeling trapped.

## Business Relationships

Because they are cautious and thoughtful about matters that are important to them, one-water people are excellent in roles that require clear, succinct communication within an organization. They can often paraphrase a vast array of verbiage into a form that just makes the point. However, they can go too far in this respect, cutting back excessively and then expecting people to understand complex concepts with just a few words. In such instances, the enigmatic or cryptic response the one-water person gives may seem

very powerful, but what exactly is meant is not clear to anyone but themselves. It is therefore important for them to be receptive enough to be able to elaborate when necessary, and to do so in a way which does not convey disdain.

The one-water person is not a team player in the sense that a two-earth is. They are loners, but generally rely on having some context in which they can operate independently. Consequently, they are excellent at setting limits and establishing boundaries within an organizational structure.

As water nourishes most of what exists on this planet, so it is that one-water people nourish the organizations of which they are part. They energize situations and help keep staff moving. Thus they may be useful in management positions or in some capacity that involves estab-

lishing the direction of a plan. They are excellent in developing mission statements and mapping out the interconnections of all the various sub-components of a situation. This does not mean, however, that the one-water person should be viewed as an administrator, for detail can be quite tedious for such people. They are not good at looking for new ideas, but rather for new connections in what is already in place.

Nor are one-waters suited to positions where they are actively involved in the completion of tasks as a primary responsibility. Their forte is reflecting upon what has gone before and bringing their deep insights to bear on the present so that plans for the future may be steered in more meaningful directions. It must be borne in mind, however, that for them meaningfulness will not be determined by other people or by an organization, but by their own experiences. If one-waters find what they are involved with meaningless, they are likely to drop their involvement or just leave. What a one-water needs to guard against is over-reacting in these situations. There are times when they worry too much about things and take tasks or situations to unnecessary depths.

One-water people also do not handle positions which involve heavy physical labour very well, either because they are too frail or sensitive, or because they find such work unacceptable. Of course they will do the work if necessary, but they will somehow convey to those around them that it is not to their liking.

Financially, a one-water has neither excessively good nor excessively bad fortune. They don't amass much wealth personally, but they get by. In a business context, especially, where risks are involved and the competition is slick, it is best not to have a one-water involved in transactions as they can easily be swindled. They have a tendency to be impressed by big displays of power and money. This is especially true if the person they are negotiating with is of the opposite sex. At the same time, where resources other than money are involved, their cautiousness allows them to apportion those resources so as to sustain them in the long term. They are generally conscious of their own limitations.

## Spiritual Matters

Because of their deep-thinking nature, it is meaning that plays a central role in the one-water's spiritual life. Life's events come fast and furious to them and it is a

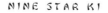

challenge in their life to learn and let go, almost simultaneously.

To be present and relax into the moment as it is, a one-water needs to go through a baptism or purification process – to clean things up and not hold on. Humour is an attribute to cultivate as it is too easy for one-waters to find themselves being too serious about the significance of things and holding on to matters and issues in their life unnecessarily. As they let go more and 'go with the flow', their insights become easier to communicate.

One-water people, because of their depth and sensitivity, have an innate sense of the human condition, Although they can appear conde-scending to others, much of this behaviour comes from almost caring too much for people. With more detachment, this way of being can be transformed into an active compas-sion, and will be like soothing waters for those to whom they turn their attention.

Relaxation and silent meditation are helpful. Having bowls of water on a shrine or altar is grounding, also the use of sound, especially crystal bowls or chimes. Meditation on compassion should be emphasized. As sexuality can be an important factor in spiritual development, one-waters who have practised various purifications and spiritual disciplines may wish to investigate the Tao of Love or consult an authentic master regarding tantric sexual practice.

## General Health Recommendations

One-water people must learn to take care of their bladder-kidney energy, along with associated tissues, structures and functions, like the skeletal structure and the reproductive system (see profile). Such people are more prone to problems with sexual organs. Women may have gynaecological difficulties, irregular menses, etc., while men may have prostate problems, and possibly impotence at times.

These are people who need to take care not to get too cold. Adequate warmth around the stomach, middle and lower back and ears is recommended. Such people need to keep good-quality water and salt as basics in their food preparation. Salt-covered snacks and the salting of foods at the table are not recommended. Nor should food be too hot or too cold. Macrobiotic food preparation and observances should be investigated.

Because of their sensitivity, one-water people are prone to nervous irritation, which usually expresses itself as fear, even paranoia when under extreme duress. A stressed one-water may express a timidity that makes them immobile or rigid, like ice. This can, in turn, have negative effects on all the physiological aspects mentioned earlier. Progressive relaxation can be useful to this person, as is soothing asynchronous music which allows the mind to settle. A one-water would also benefit from right and left brain exercises. Such practices and observances are useful to the one-water over their lifetime as unbridled tension and stress may lead them to become senile in later years.

Exercise should be aimed at keeping the skeletal system flexible, especially the spine. Yoga would be an excellent choice as would swimming, preferably in salt water or pools that use ozone or oyster shell for purification rather than chlorine.

## PERSONAL FENG SHUI RECOMMENDATIONS

### Sources of Support

Bagua regions of Ch'ien ☰ (6) and Tui ☱ (7)

☰ *Regarding Ch'ien*: Although solitude provides you with quiet nurturing that fuels your deep insights, you prefer not to be isolated. In truth, in friendship and conditional support as exemplified by the Bagua region of Ch'ien, you are provided with a context – the kind of well-defined, tangible background support that allows you to trust your depths and to surface with something of

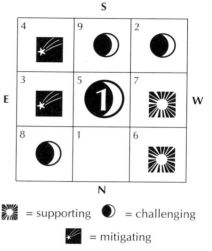

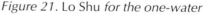

= supporting ☽ = challenging

= mitigating

*Figure 21.* Lo Shu *for the one-water*

value to share. Thus your philosophical musings and glimpses into what has gone before and what is to be has a firm foundation. With the aid of Ch'ien what you manifest is reliable, practical and more accessible.

≋ *Regarding Tui*: The enigmatic loner in you finds in Tui the opportunity to savour and enjoy what you have created thus far. Think of projects, creations, your children. How have these moulded your character, contributed to your outlook, fuelled you to have the courage to change and move in new directions? Your abilities to foresee the future and what is possible needs to be grounded in an appreciation of what has gone before. In Tui there is expressed a gentle, reflective demeanour that rounds out your understandings and that can give them mood and texture.

! **Note of Caution**: What has been created and the tangible nature of conditional friends and their support may cause you to abdicate your own power and succumb to timidity. True, you need the support of this region of the Bagua to succeed, but do not become awe-struck by the display of these metal transformations. Remember, you need quiet and solitude in order to develop yourself and the insights that will serve you in the future. To over emphasize the importance of Ch'ien and Tui can lead to a more shallow, less fulfilled life. Conversely, to not acknowledge their importance enough is to run the risk of becoming more isolated, inaccessible and unaccountable. It is advised that in both of these metal regions that the one-water region of both Ch'ien and Tui be made open and clear. You need to be able to enter into and leave clearly and cleanly.

## Challenging Regions of the Bagua
Kun ☷ (2), Tai Chi ⚪(5), Ken ☶ (8) and Li ☲ (9)

☷ *Regarding Kun*: In the inherent struggle one-waters go through, it can be that in order to get the solitude you crave, you will need to divorce yourself from attachments to friends, family or whatever. Whilst this is understandable, it can, at times, seem abrupt and hurtful to those around you. Whereas Ch'ien is about conditional friendship and support, Kun emphasizes the intimate nature of relating. Thus it is from the Bagua region of Kun that one-waters are reminded not to throw the baby out with the bath water, that without intimacy, the insights and the life it leads them to develop will feel empty of juice. An analogy is the difference between mountain-fed spring and distilled water. One is life-giving and energy-providing. The other is just water.

In the region of Kun and wherever you retreat to, it is valuable to adorn these places with colours, tones and symbols that remind you of intimacy and of the connection to what you cherish and gives you life.

⚪*Regarding Tai Chi*: Through caution or timidity a one-water may not allow their qualities to shine forth. There is great value in solitude and there are times when, in order to strengthen our resources, times of retreat are absolutely necessary. In this instance, caution is well heeded. But, if the time and need for caution and solitude are over, then the qualities developed may not serve anyone and could, in fact, be destroyed from the stagnation that comes from being idle.

Tai Chi is about healthiness; developing the resourcefulness of knowing how to extend to others and take care of oneself. It is about balance. The Bagua region of Tai Chi demands that the one-water pay attention to all aspects of life – for there is not one aspect of life that does not benefit from receiving water, albeit in varying degrees. The open space of Tai Chi provides a conduit through which water can flow to wherever it is needed. If blocked or cluttered, water stagnates in pools or meanders and may even get dissipated in a host of directions without necessarily benefiting any of them.

☶ *Regarding Ken*: More specific than Tai Chi, which concerns itself with overall benefits, Ken places on one-water the responsibility to consider circumstances carefully, to prioritize and make commitments. This is a weighty task and can cause the greatest feeling of oppression for the one-water. Still, if there is a tangible contribution a one-water can make, there must be resolve and a willingness to direct efforts. What is painful for the water person is the knowledge that to do so, there must be sacrifices along the way – the repercussions of which they well understand.

Thus, in this region of the Bagua, gently flowing warm waters may soften the situation. A hot tub, mineral bath, the gentle flow of water over stones in a fountain – all of these water touches may help in the region of Ken. And, after a time of contemplation or meditation, settle back with a hot cup of tea.

☲ *Regarding Li*: In your appreciation for depth and solitude, the exposure

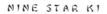

and/or fame as expressed in the Bagua region of Li can seem superficial and beside the point. Beyond these feelings, however, can be the timidity – even fear – of being drawn out to the light. After all, you like to be discreet and selective about whom you offer what. To expose yourself to the light and heat of Li can build up a pressure inside you and a fear that all you have worked for could just go up like a cloud of vapour. But, your drowning of the flame of Li, whilst protecting you and your plans for the present, may destroy any tangible rewards and joy you could receive in the future. The situation is volatile and intense, but do you really want to remain a church mouse?

## Qualities that are Useful in Mitigating the Challenges to Li

Using the tree regions of the Bagua of Chen (3) and Sun (4) can mitigate the relationship you have with Li.

In Chen, you find sources of inspiration in ideas and examples of how others before you have stepped forward. Even though you have your own path to go on, it's reassuring to see how others have proceeded. And from this, ideas will come forth – as if out of the blue. Consider this region of the Bagua in your surroundings. This is an excellent area in which to spend time visualizing, brainstorming and developing a bit more boldness to step forward. Make it like a well-watered, rich green pasture that you can stand in, breathe, and stretch – stretch beyond what you have limited yourself to thus far.

The Bagua region of Sun should be like the perennial carrot dangled before the eyes as a way to create incentive. Deep down you know what potentials are available for future developments and possibilities. Although intangible, try to see these developments and possibilities as clearly as you can. What symbols, qualities, or objects can you place in this region of the Bagua to spur you on? Now, focus on one thing, one goal. See it as clearly as is possible. Having a narrower focus will make stepping forth and utilizing the resourcefulness of Li less daunting.

# Evaluating Number Combinations

# The Houses

As I said in Part I, both the natal month and the natal year numbers will migrate to different houses in the Magic Square over time. Since each number represents a particular transformation phase, as does each house, there is a mix of qualities which can be complementary, supportive, confrontative or conflicting in nature. Thus we go through our lives learning to adjust to ever-changing circumstances which have, at the same time, a certain level of regularity or order. As we become familiar with our experiences in each one of the houses and

| SE | S | SW |
|---|---|---|
| House of<br>4<br>TREE | House of<br>9<br>FIRE | House of<br>2<br>EARTH |
| House of<br>3<br>TREE | House of<br>5<br>EARTH | House of<br>7<br>METAL |
| House of<br>8<br>EARTH | House of<br>1<br>WATER | House of<br>6<br>METAL |
| NE | N | NW |

*Figure 22. The Magic Square showing the houses and their transformation phases*

begin to pay more attention to where our natal numbers are in time, we have the advantage of knowing to some extent what to expect, and can modify our behaviour and interactions accordingly.

Besides the knowledge we gain from understanding transformation and elemental mixes, the houses are also used for directionology. For although our natal numbers migrate, the houses remain stationary; as do the compass directions they represent. As this volume is not about directionology or systems of geomancy, only general recommendations as to adverse and positive directions for travel are listed in the profile. Briefly, if a number is positive for a person, wherever that number is on the Magic Square will be a positive direction for that person to travel at that time. The exception to this is when either the natal month or the natal year number is in the House of Five. At such times, travelling is generally not recommended.

Other adverse conditions include when one is travelling towards or away from one's natal numbers ( for example, if you are a four-tree and you are travelling east when your four is in the House of Three (east) or seven (west)), or when the number five is in the centre of the magic square. In such times, precaution and self-preparation are advised. Remember, though, that in life, we sometimes need to move or travel in such ways – it may be unavoidable. Therefore, one should learn not to become paralyzed with fear about travelling in these directions, but to adapt and prepare for the possible challenges which may arise. In this way, we will develop greater resourcefulness.

For the purpose of prediction, a person studying Nine Star Ki should try to familiarize themselves with the impact the houses have on their natal month and year numbers. *In particular, one should pay attention to the house that the child number was in at the time of birth and the House of Five, which is where the adult number always resides at the time of birth.*

Thus it is important for everyone to understand the House of Five, as it impacts on all adult natal number potentials. It will, therefore, be discussed first. All other house numbers will then be discussed briefly, including a general way of viewing the transformation mixes that occur as the child numbers occupy a given house at birth. House descriptions are dynamic, describing what one may experience as one's numbers pass through them. As regards one's natal month number, the impact of the given house it resided in at the time of birth will be more of a constant or pervasive factor in one's life, during childhood and especially when under stress. Descriptions will be metaphoric in the sense that they will use the Five Transformations concepts of mother–son, the cycle of regeneration and the ko or cycle of control, and present them in a psychological format. Such patterns and mixes are subtle, yet significant in our relationships in the world, so I would recommend you to delve deeper into Five Transformations theory for greater understanding and appreciation.

## THE HOUSE OF FIVE

The House of Five is depicted as a house of danger, of alluring powers and upheavals. It is also considered a house in which either very fortunate or very unfortunate circumstances can arise. Looked at with a greater introspection, the energetics that we are presented with when our natal numbers occupy the House of Five are more appropriately viewed as karmic reckoning: what has been sown over time is reaped now. This can be positive or negative, but is usually a very accurate fruition of what has gone before, particularly over the previous eight years.

At the time of our birth, the number of the year (and month, if our natal month number is the same as our natal year number) in which we were born resides in the House of Five. On a basic energetic level, this will mean that we must understand what the mix is between the transformation phase of our natal year (or month) and the earth quality of the House of Five. The House of Five in itself, however, is representative of a precarious balance between expanding and contracting forces. On a personal level, this means that the characteristics of the number residing in the House of Five will present themselves in the broadest possible way, even to extremes – from the most altruistic behaviour to the most egocentric. From a more balanced perspective, what is being addressed here is how one learns to be out in the world and, at the same time, take care of oneself.

We need to balance self-nurturing with service to others and the world around us in order to develop our adult natal potentials fully. The service we render to others depends on the varying characteristics of the natal numbers. Nurturing has to do with recognizing what it is that we need to take care of ourselves so that our service to others does not become crippling. We do not need to balance service and nurturing evenly. It is more a question of being mature and sensitive enough to know what our potentials are and how to maximize them. An ability to be introspective is necessary if self-nurturing is not to become self-indulgence and service is not to become martyrdom. When a person knows what balance is right for them, they are self-actualizing. As they self-actualize, a true altruism naturally emerges that is enlivening for all concerned.

When a person is actualizing their adult natal number potentials in their life, they may tend to express some of the characteristics of the House of Five. Thus the manner in which a person acts may be misconstrued as arrogant and self-centred or timid and self-effacing. Such an erroneous view has something to do with projection; their success reflects back to others the struggle they themselves experience.

Every nine years, when the current year puts all numbers back into the configuration they were in at our birth, we come face to face with what our potentials are and the developments of the previous eight years as measured against them. We can see how we have done and how we are doing. Are we taking care of out needs? Do we feel empowered in our interactions in the world? If we have been careless in our relationships and interactions, there is a strong likelihood that we will have to face that fact at this time. If we have been working towards a greater integration of our needs and potentials, our work will come to fruition at this time.

In either case, during the time when our natal year comes back into the House of Five, it is best to reflect, assess, accept and plan for the future based on what we have gleaned from our experiences and where we now want to go in our lives. This is not a year for action, however, and travelling or making any radical shifts in what we are doing is ill-advised, However, because it is such a challenging time, it can be quite difficult to face oneself truthfully. There may even be a tendency to become frenetically busy, as if wriggling in the energetics of the time. Nevertheless, the best thing one can

do is to be mindful and allow oneself to relax into the experience of being with oneself. In quietness and reflection, one can then lay plans or try to project where one wants to be in the next nine years and what one needs to reach those goals. Such plans will then be activated in the following year. To attempt to initiate new projects or ideas at this time is ill-advised.

It must be remembered that while we have a dominant natal month and year number, we possess within our make-up aspects of all nine numbers in varying degrees. As all numbers migrate over time and must thus pass through the House of Five, there will be times when the different aspects of our being need to be more carefully scrutinized. Next to our natal year, our natal month number will be the most significant in the House of Five. During those times we may find that childhood issues are confronted, as well as how well we have overcome various levels of co-dependence on the world. As with the natal year, it is wise to take some time to reflect quietly on those aspects of our lives. Like the natal year number, when the natal month number resides in the House of Five, one should plan but not initiate changes. Also, travelling may cause stress and imbalances that take a long time to overcome.

Apart from the migration of numbers into the House of Five on a yearly basis, they also migrate monthly. Within each year, therefore, our natal month and year numbers will also enter the House of Five, and at these times it is best to stay put and reflect upon the issues that our numbers bring up for us.

During the times when our natal year or month enter the House of Five, especially in the cycle of nine years, our health is more greatly challenged. *The Anthology of I Ching* suggests that it is a time when we should be alert to digestive difficulties, heart complaints, immune-related diseases, even cerebral haemorrhages.[6] One possible explanation for this is that during such times we may become destabilized as we are asked to come to grips with ourselves emotionally.

## The Five Year in the House of Five

Every nine years the five year enters its own house. Historically, such years are challenging times. The years 1914 and 1941 saw the world massively preoccupied with war. In the recent history of the United States, the Korean War was in 1950 and the Tet

Offensive in Vietnam was in 1968. The beginning of 1986 was heralded by the explosion of the space shuttle Challenger. Others may wish to investigate the history of other countries to see whether the five year has produced major events that shaped or were an expression of the times.

What is significant on a personal level is that all numbers reside in their own houses, that is three sits in the House of Three, six in the House of Six, and so on. Consequently, what each of us experience is our own primal forces in their most dynamic or raw state. In particular, both our adult and our child natal number qualities become accentuated. Thus it is made painfully clear how we are handling these aspects of our lives, as well as all the qualities that make up our character from the other numbers. It is a time when we can feel rather alone.

Therefore a sense of separation between individuals, cultures, societies and nations can become exaggerated. A five month can create a similar effect, but not as dramatically or with as much force as the five year. Such a year can be as potent, as regards self-examination and transformation, as when our own natal year or month is in the House of Five, if not more so.

Such times demand stillness and reflection if we are to work with them successfully. Unfortunately the rawness of the times may invoke tendencies to project and needlessly initiate turmoil and conflict. Perhaps if the energetics of these times are understood more clearly, individuals and nations will be able to examine things more closely, review actions and plan ways of overcoming rather than creating division. It is a potent time to come up with new strategies and solutions to old problems as well as focusing on aspirations for the future.

## THE OTHER HOUSES: SOME GENERAL GUIDELINES

Before looking more specifically at the other houses and their energetics, there are some general guidelines that are useful for further interpretations. These guidelines are based on principles from the Law of Five Trans-formations; the mother–son relation-ships, and the cycle of ko or energetic controls. Naboru Muramoto's *Healing Ourselves* is, once again, an excellent source for studying these concepts further.

The mother–son relationship has to do with how one transformation or element feeds and nurtures another. Each transformation will be the child of one transformation and the mother of another. Thus:

tree/space (3,4) is the child of water (1) and
tree/space (3,4) is the mother of fire (9);
fire (9) is the child of tree/space (3,4) and
fire (9) is the mother of earth (2,5,8);
earth (2,5,8) is the child of fire (9) and
earth (2,5,8) is the mother of metal/air (6,7);
metal/air (6,7) is the child of earth (2,5,8) and
metal/air (6,7) is the mother of water (1);
water (1) is the child of metal/air (6,7) and
water (1) is the mother of tree/space (3,4).

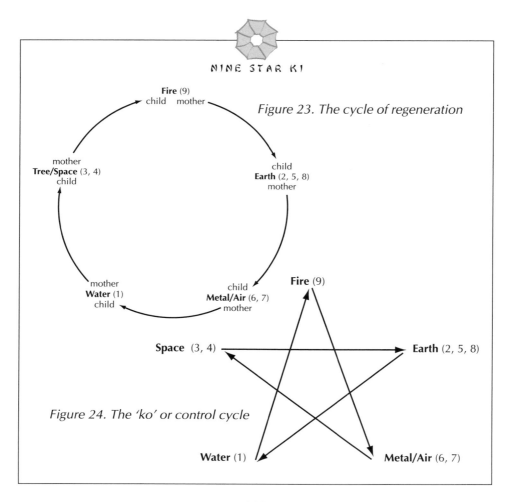

NINE STAR KI

**Fire** (9)
child    mother

*Figure 23. The cycle of regeneration*

mother
**Tree/Space** (3, 4)
child

child
**Earth** (2, 5, 8)
mother

mother
**Water** (1)
child

child
**Metal/Air** (6, 7)
mother

**Fire** (9)

**Space** (3, 4)

**Earth** (2, 5, 8)

*Figure 24. The 'ko' or control cycle*

**Water** (1)

**Metal/Air** (6, 7)

Traditionally, the ko cycle goes by various names, including the 'cycle of death' or 'control cycle'. These names highlight qualities inherent in the cycle, demonstrating the dynamic tension between the transformations, yet they also put this dynamic in a negative light. I prefer to call it the cycle of dynamic transformation. That being said, let us explore the traditional implications of the laws that govern this cycle. As things move towards death, their path of deterioration is in a certain progression through the Five Transformations. The cycle is also a cycle of control, for when any particular transformation is radically excessive or deficient in the balance of healthy life forms, this has a direct effect on another transformation. The relationship between transformations and the transformations they control are as follows:

| | | |
|---|---|---|
| tree/space (3,4) | controls | earth (2,5,8) |
| earth (2,5,8) | " | water (1) |
| water (1) | " | fire (9) |
| fire (9) | " | metal/air (6,7) |
| metal/air | " | tree/space (3,4) |

The beneficial aspect to the ko cycle resides in a dynamic tension between controlling and controlled transformation, the results of which can be rapid growth and unexpected development and the control of excesses in the controlled transformation. Unless the child or natal month number is the same as the adult natal year number, it will reside in one of the other eight houses in the Magic Square. To find the house that the child number resides in refer to the Universal Chart that has the adult natal year number that you are looking at in the centre

(House of Five). Depending on the relationship of the natal month transformation and the transformation of the house that it resides in at the time of birth, a person will experience their childhood, periods of dependency, and stress in particular ways that have to do with the mix of these two transformations. There are two aspects of this mix. On a basic level, there are the factors of the mother–son and ko cycle in the Law of Five Transformations that will be the source of *general attitudes.* On a subtler level, there will be the actual qualities of the transformations/ elements involved that create the *character* or the way in which these general attitudes are projected from a personality. As regards the actual transformations/elements involved, what one will also observe is that before the stress and imbalance patterns of the

natal month transformation emerge, the physiological and psychological characteristics inherent in the particular house that it resides in will be activated.

For example, let us assume that a 4 adult, 9 child is experiencing stress. As the 9 child resides in the House of One-Water, such a person will probably experience the fear and cautiousness of the water transformation and possibly even manifest such stress symptoms as low back pain, prostate or genital/urinary tract problems before experiencing the anxiety characteristic of a nine-fire.

Thus experiencing the characteristics or symptoms of the house that the child natal number resides in can be a useful way of recognizing that one is entering into a stress mode, or that childhood or dependency patterns have been activated. Therefore, when examining the characteristics of the child natal month transformation, you need to consider the house that the child natal month number resides in.

This of course requires some degree of finesse in understanding Five Transformation theory. However, when it comes to the more basic attitudes the person will be experiencing, there are some useful metaphors regarding houses, mother–son relationship and control cycle patterns that can be used as rules of thumb before deeper investigation.

Apart from the impact that the House of Five has on our adult natal number at the time of birth, there are basically six ways described further on in this chapter, in which the mother–son relationship and the ko cycle reveal themselves in the relationship between the child month natal number and the house that it resides in at the time of birth.

There are two ways in which you can find out which house the child natal number resides in at the time of birth. First, use the calculation methods recommended in Part I. Find the Universal Chart that has the required natal year number in the centre (the House of Five). On that chart, look for the natal month number. It will be in a particular house, the number of which you can identify by referring to the Magic Square at the beginning of this chapter (Figure 22). Figure 10 and the accompanying example on page 38 will give you an idea of how to do it.

The second method involves calculating the natal year and month numbers and then finding that combination on the Easy Reference Table (Figure 12, page 54). This table will also show you in which of the six

ways the natal month numbers and the houses relate to each other, so making it easier for you to go directly to the most relevant relationship on the pages that follow. Of course, you could also go through the six descriptions and locate the particular month and house configurations you are looking for by scanning the combination listings provided.

In the headings that follow, the numbers in parentheses are the child natal month numbers and the numbers spelled out are the houses.

*When the child natal number is the mother to the transformation of the house that it resides in*: (3) nine, (4) nine, (9) two, (9) five, (9) eight ,(2) six, (2) seven, (5) six, (5) seven, (8) six, (8) seven, (6) one, (7) one, (1) three, (1) four

When the mother comes to visit the son, she usually has opinions about how he is living. When a person has a child natal number that is the mother to the transformation of the house that the child number resides in, they will usually be over-vigilant, preoccupied with their surroundings, and more opinionated than people with other configurations. Such people need to be aware of their over-critical predisposition. Their expectations may be higher than those around them, as may be their levels of elation or disappointment.

*When the child natal number is the son to the transformation of the house that it resides in*: (3) one, (4) one, (9) three, (9) four, (2) nine, (5) nine, (8) nine, (6) two, (6) five, (6) eight, (7) two, (7) five, (7) eight, (1) six, (1) seven

Here is a situation where a person may have difficulty breaking from their dependency and childhood patterns. In this particular configuration, it is as if the child does not have enough inner strength to move out of the house. Thus in childhood or when under stress, such a person may feel complacent about their situation. They may complain about life's experiences, yet have little motivation to take any concrete steps towards changing things. At times others may want to shake such a person up, a desire which in many cases is appropriate, as these people have a limited view of their potential.

*When the child natal number is in the house of the transformation it controls*:
(3) two, (3) five, (3) eight, (4) two, (4) five, (4) eight, (9) six, (9) seven, (2) one, (5) one, (8) one, (6) three, (6) four, (7) three, (7) four, (1) nine

When an element is out of balance dramatically, it has a stifling effect on the transformation that it controls. However in this particular situation there is a more unfamiliar dynamic Here the transformation that would normally be in control is being contained by the transformation it controls.

Metaphorically speaking, the child is living in a house where it is being constrained, almost against its will or natural tendencies. The result is a person who in childhood, or under stress when the child natal number is activated, tends to be rebellious or explosive. There is a constant urge to assert themselves in order to shed their feelings of being trapped. Thus the abruptness or emotional response this person has when confronted with unpleasant experiences has more to do with internal psychological mechanisms than a clear response to outside stimulation; hence the response can be disproportionate to what the situation actually warrants. A person who understands this aspect of themselves is less likely to blame or alienate others at such moments.

*When the child natal number is in the house of the transformation by which it is controlled*: (3) six, (3) seven, (4) six, (4) seven, (9) one, (2) three, (2) four, (5) three, (5) four, (8) three, (8) four, (6) nine, (7) nine, (1) two, (1) five, (1) eight

Here is a situation where the child, or person in stress feels rightly controlled. There is a tendency towards resigna-

tion, a feeling of 'This is how it is and why should it be any different?' This should not be viewed as compla-cency, however, as when the child natal number resides in the mother's house. Here, there can be more of a sense of resentment, as well as a strong desire to break free. Whereas the child residing in the mother's house may need some prodding, the person in this situation needs support as they strive to overcome impossibility' thinking

*When the child natal number and the adult natal year number are the same*: 1 (1), 2 (2), 3 (3), 4 (4), 5 (5), 6 (6), 7 (7), 8 (8), 9 (9)

Here is a situation where, at the time of birth, the child and adult number both reside in the House of Five. Regardless of the transformation of the number, therefore, the energetics of five-earth and the House of Five must be viewed as strong factors in the person's life.

The lives of such individuals seem constant. Whereas for others, at the end of the second cycle of nine or when there is a move towards greater independence, the experience is one of making a shift from one energetic to another, there is no such transition here. Life just goes on feeling the way it always has been. Thus childhood patterns are carried over into adult life. Dealing with authority may be like dealing with one's mother and father. Because one transformation only is represented there is seemingly no contrast in experience. Thus it can be difficult for such a person to understand someone else's point of view, or to conceive of someone experiencing life in any other way than the way they themselves experi-ence it. Thus such people can be stubborn and seemingly arrogant.

This configuration also means that their strengths are their weaknesses. Because of the strong House of Five dominance they can be uncertain about themselves and overdo things. If they remain balanced however, they will have all the positive qualities of the transformation plus the energy of the five-earth house.

On the physical level, it is more than likely that such a person will be hypoglycaemic. The dietary guidance and stress management techniques recommended for their particular transformation should be used. Psychoactive substances can be par-ticularly injurious to such people.

*When the child natal number resides in the house that is the same as its own transformation, but not the same as its adult natal number:* (2) five, (2) eight, (3) four, (4) three, (5) two, (5) eight, (6) seven, (7) six, (8) two, (8) five

Because the energetic of the house is a more yin or yang aspect of the same transformation as the child natal month number, a person might experience a sense of wholeness from this combination. Such a person may have a generally relaxed demeanour – they may even appear to be masterful when handling stress. Rather than trying to change situations if they are not in keeping with what they want, such people may be more willing to work with things as they are. They may, however, also exhibit a tendency towards complacency.

It is only because we are focusing on the relationship between the child natal number and the houses that the more challenging aspects of these relationships are being looked at. Such challenges should not be viewed as either good or bad. Rather, when in childhood, or later when stress re-evokes childhood patterns, the struggle from dependence and co-dependency towards independence must take into account the house and the house/natal number factor. This is also true for the natal year number, but in the case of the child natal month number, there is more of a sense of history to work through.

Looked at more objectively, each house has the potential to support growth and maturation. As a number migrates into a particular house it becomes a matter of seizing the moment, taking from the situation what it offers. From the child natal month perspective, such a situation offers us the opportunity to loosen our fixation on the limitations we are experiencing.

Now let us look at the remainder of the houses more closely.

## HOUSE OF SIX-METAL

This is a house where things move forward in your life. There is a sense of being in control of situations. Your past efforts pay off as things come together during this time. At the same time, the resulting harvest can lead you to be arrogant and cast an aura of entitlement. Thus you can be pushy, argumentative and self-righteous. You must learn the difference between manifesting your capabilities in a direct and forthright manner and just plain showing off.

Generally, your physical condition will be strong and active in this house, but there are precautions to take. Be wary of accidents while in some form of transport. Moving accidents can lead to injuries to the head or nerves. Excess heat should be avoided. Watch closely any injuries to the chest region, the brain and the bones. On an emotional level, there may be a tendency to cling rigidly to ideas, even in the face of information that proves that they are inaccurate or inappropriate. The kind of pushy behaviour mentioned above may be symptomatic of that tendency.

The numbers 9, 4, and 3 should be especially mindful when occupying this house.

## HOUSE OF SEVEN-METAL

There is a sense of ease in this house. It is a time of fruition where what comes to one seemingly involves no effort. Yet what is taking place is not happenstance, but the direct result of previous effort. To think differently, kick back and act frivolously at this time is to risk losing as much as one stands to gain.

Thus the challenge of the times is to be wary of becoming intoxicated by good fortune, on a personal, material or financial level. Enjoy, but maintain balance. Sloppiness in action will lead to misunderstandings. You may find that artistic and aesthetic appreciation is heightened at this time, but this may lead you to be seduced by appearances. The handling of money and property (including possibilities and deals) needs more care. Attraction between men and women here may lead to affairs, but will not necessarily have any lasting value. It is a good time to be more mindful of assessing your circumstances and possibly creating a new order in your life.

People with the numbers, 4, 3 and 9 will find this house challenging. Generally, those visiting this house should be mindful of injuries to the mouth, respiratory tract and bone fractures resulting from accidents. On an emotional level, there is a tendency to lose focus and become caught up in romantic notions not grounded in reality.

## HOUSE OF EIGHT-EARTH

This is a house of inner depth. Stillness is the sign of the times. A person whose natal numbers are in the house may feel bogged down, and may therefore project a lot, appearing pushy and obstinate. The reason may be that they want to see things happen around them, because little may be happening for them personally. Others may find the person uncharacteristically cool or reserved.

Rather than fight the stillness, it is best to go with the energetics of the times and to be willing to look deep and honestly within yourself. If you do this you will be able to look into depths perhaps previously unnoticed or difficult to tap. For those whose numbers control or are controlled by eight-earth (1, 3 and 4), there may arise a keener sense of stagnation, frustration or hopelessness as they enter and occupy this house. A change of direction may occur as old patterns are looked at with more honesty. Ceremony will give way to sincerity.

Circulatory, joint and bone problems may arise at this time. Moreover, other people may inflict injuries on you because they don't understand your internal quietness and uncharacteristic stubborness.

## HOUSE OF NINE-FIRE

Fire lights things up. It reveals. Consequently, this is a time of fame and fortune, where what you have done receives public attention. It may also be that what you wish to conceal is also revealed. Thus it can be a time of embarrassment to those whose dealings with others, with society or with the law, may be less than honest. Criminal proceedings may occur at this time.

On a personal level, you may find that a new sphere of friends and contacts arises while old ones disappear. Some of these changes are a natural progression. Some may lead you not to treat seriously or with care the connections and friends you already have. Thus discernment is advised and flamboyance is to be guarded against.

Water (one) and metal/air (six, seven) people will especially feel the 'heat' and must watch, more carefully than others whose numbers enter this house, for illnesses arising from fire energetics. Fevers, burns, irritation of the eyes, circulatory problems and epidemic-type illnesses need to be guarded against.

There is a general sense of light-ness at this time which may become ungrounded. Loss of balance may give rise to hysteria or anxiety. A fire can only remain alight if one is prudent with fuel. Beware of over-extending yourself.

## HOUSE OF ONE-WATER

This is the house of winter and the north. It is a dark period where there is little movement on the surface. Caution is needed during these times and excessive activity can result in accidents and rapid dissipation of energy. When visiting this house, it is best to be quiet and reflective. Meditation, time for personal reflec-tion, research into the deeper matters of life, will create a stronger knowledge base from which to act. Finances may be difficult at these times and one must be conservative with outlays. This is not a time to be innovative. Wait until you move out of this house before embarking on new ideas and ventures. There may be unexpected expenses.

On a personal level, you may find that friends and associates appear to keep their distance. This is because, when you are experiencing the House of One, you are less expressive, probably more enigmatic, and thus leave people feeling somewhat uncertain of their relationship to you. There is nevertheless a strong intuitive sense operating at these times, and thus the nuances of relationships are seen more clearly. If stress arises, this intuition may become hypersensitivity, in which case a person in this house

may develop some fear, even paranoia, about getting close to others.

Illnesses that have to do with fluids of the body – blood, lymph, water, semen – and their associated organs should be guarded against with appropriate preventive measures. It is also best to be wary of hazards from liquids in the environment, like poor-quality water, overconsumption of alcohol, floods or toxic waste. The numbers 9, 2 and 5 should be particularly mindful at these times.

## HOUSE OF TWO-EARTH

This is a time when not much of significance happens, and any efforts to make things happen will usually result in negative outcomes and reactions from others. You can stick to the mundane with moderate success at such times. However, with greater plans or ideas, you should accumulate rather than initiate. You can accumulate money, resources, allies, etc. in preparation for a new venture, but don't start just yet.

Beware of excessive banter and boasting about what you can do. During this time people occupying this house may appear uncharacteristically superficial. This could put off needed allies.

On an emotional level, a person whose natal numbers are in this house may experience a general state of worry that pervades many areas of their life. They may also find themselves over-involved in the concerns of others. As regards health, physical problems with lymphatics and other aspects of the earth element need to be guarded against. People with

natal numbers 1, 3 and 4 should be generally more conscious of these effects when in the House of Two.

## HOUSE OF THREE-TREE/SPACE

 This house possesses the power and energy of spring. Ideas come flooding in and with them the energy to begin undertakings of grand proportions. In this house, people find their creativity stimulated. However, there can be an accompanying lack of groundedness. Because the mind is so active, small but necessary details in projects may be overlooked. Consequently, although great things are possible, so are dismal failures.

When a person's natal numbers visit this house, there is a desire to get on and do things. If stifled or thwarted, frustration may ensue with a greater likelihood of outbursts of anger. Even the calmest person may find themselves breaking out at this time, and vocal expression tends to be louder and more direct than usual. Physical activity and expression increase.

Because of this increased expression, there may be an imbalance involving the nervous system and tree/space-related organs and tissues (such as the liver, gall bladder, muscles and connective tissue) if preventive measures are not taken. You should remain physically active, watch your consumption of oil, flour products and animal food, and guard against exposure to easterly winds. Earth (2, 5, 8) and metal/air (6, 7) people should be particularly mindful.

## HOUSE OF FOUR-TREE/SPACE

 This is a time when one sees tangible results in what one has previously initiated. Most affairs and dealings in your life will go smoothly. Because of this, you can focus more, become more contemplative, and act when the timing makes action appropriate. There is, however, the tree/space tendency towards impetuosity. You should guard against this as it is unnecessary and may, in fact, undermine possible accomplishments, rather like pulling a plant out of the ground to see how it is growing. Using the vision of tree/space energy, one can steer things in the best direction. Thus the formula for getting things done should be look, think, then act.

Communication skills are enhanced at this time and the use of

voice and media can be quite effective. Just don't lead people on. There is
a natural maturity of outlook here, and
anything to the contrary has more to
do with self-sabotage and confusion
than with outside influences.

Imbalances that may arise during
this time are paralysis and digestive
and respiratory tract ailments. You
should be mindful of the same
aspects of lifestyle as mentioned
in the description of the House of
Three-Tree/Space, paying particular
attention to keeping the throat
and chest warm and away from
draughts. Earth (2, 5, 8) and metal/air
(6, 7) people are more susceptible to
the imbalances inherent in this house.

# The Adult and Child Numbers Together

Broadly speaking, the adult natal year number expresses itself as positive potential. Traits of growth and self-actualization in the physical, mental and spiritual dimensions of our lives are associated with this number. If such traits or potentials are not visible or expressed in a person's way of being, it is likely that there is either a self-limiting factor or some outside influence impinging on them. This would also account for any imbalances or illness associated with the particular natal year number.

The child natal month number also expresses potentials, but because it is by nature more dependent on environment and circumstances than the natal year, there is a greater tendency to weaknesses, imbalances and general stress symptoms. It may be that a person is living out of their natal month number experience in terms of relationships, jobs, preferences and responsibilities. They may function well in all these circumstances and arenas, but not without risking a greater tendency to stress and related imbalances in their lives.

This does not imply that the child number influence is to be ignored and only the natal year number enhanced. In fact, where the natal month number shows its greatest usefulness is in the way we learn to promote self-nurturing. Direction and action are best served by living from the natal year experience while nurturing is best served by understanding the interaction between both the child month and the adult year natal number energetics. It is important to understand this interaction if you truly want to create a life that is balanced, meaningful and satisfying.

Like the general guidelines presented for the transformation interactions that occur when the child natal month number resides in a certain house, there are similar guidelines for the transformation interactions between child and adult natal numbers. These guidelines are useful irrespective of the more particular elemental mix. Of course, for deeper insights the reader is advised to study the various dimensions of Five Transformations Theory.

Muramoto's book *Healing Ourselves* is once again recommended for those wishing to study these concepts further, as are the Nine Star Ki books by Takashi Yoshikawa and Michio Kushi listed in the Further Reading section. A unique aspect of *Nine Star Ki*, however, is that the dimensions of Nine Star Ki that we are discussing at present are more thoroughly presented here than in any other book the author has been able to find.

Once again it is the mother–son and ko cycle principles within the

Law of Five Transformations that are at work here. (See Figures 23 and 24.) The key words in the descriptions that follow are *support, control* and *same as.* The child natal number can support the adult natal number (e.g. 9(3)) or vice versa (e.g. 3(9)). (Note that the adult natal number is always *outside* the parentheses and the child number *inside* them.) The child number can also control the adult number (4(7)) or vice versa (7(4)). There are also combinations in which the transformations of the child and adult natal numbers are the same (e.g. 2(8)). If the two numbers are identical (4(4), 2(2) etc.), the previous chapter shows how they both reside in and are impacted by the House of Five (see page 214).

To discover which description fits the birth-date you have chosen to look at, you can either scan the descriptions below for the number combination you are looking for or refer to the Easy Reference Table (Figure 12, page 54). However, as you become more familiar with the Law of Five Transformations, you will be able to find the most relevant descriptions relatively easily.

*When the child natal number transformation supports the adult natal number transformation*: 9(3), 9(4), 2(9), 5(9), 8(9), 6(2), 6(5), 6(8), 7(2), 7(5), 7(8), 1(6), 1(7), 3(1), 4(1)

In this situation, there is a natural transition from childhood to adulthood. The child, in the mother position of the mother–son law of acupuncture theory, nurtures the adult transformation; thus the person does not have a sense of trauma about what life offers them. Even as

an adult, the child qualities exhibited or indulged in usually help to enhance the adult expression. Consequently, even the stresses and imbalances that arise from the child natal month transformation are taken in their stride and the lessons to be learned from such experiences are more fully integrated than in any of the other child-adult configurations.

*When the adult natal number transformation supports the child natal number transformation*: 3(9), 4(9), 9(2), 9(5), 9(8), 2(6), 2(7), 5(6), 5(7), 8(6), 8(7), 6(1), 7(1), 1(3), 1(4)

As in the previous description, there is a sense of ease or compatibility between adult and child experience. In the previous example, the child was supportive of the adult. Here it is the other way round. Thus a person with this configuration may find that they are expressing their natal year potential when suddenly their more child natal month patterns begin to emerge into interactions. They may as a result become demanding or pushy in situations in which they originally had a clearer perspective. In such circumstances, some form of supportive confrontation is usually needed to bring the person to their senses; this can be from within themselves or from someone else. In either case, there is not much tension or strain involved in re-establishing a more balanced and harmonious interaction.

*When the adult natal number transformation controls the child natal number transformation*: 3(2), 3(5), 3(8), 4(2), 4(8), 9(6), 9(7), 2(1), 5(1), 8(1), 6(3), 6(4), 7(3), 7(4), 1(9)

Here is a situation where the person exhibits a tremendous amount of self-control. Like a superego, the adult natal transformation acts as a reminder to the child natal transformation of a higher order of things – not literally higher, but in the sense of being looked at by oneself from a different, more independent perspective. This may curb impulsiveness but it can also result in a person overlooking or considering unimportant many childhood nurturing needs. Thus they may be highly self-repressive and are often loners.

At an early age, they may be considered good children as their self-monitoring keeps them in line. They tend to be rather self-critical and are better at admonishing themselves than anyone else in their lives could be. Unless their parents possess an adult or child number that is the same as their adult natal number, they will have little impact in disciplining them. In fact, if they are admonished by someone else, it is almost as if insult has been added to injury. They usually know when they are out of line.

Such a number configuration could lead to problems in situations where there is a hierarchy or authority structure to be related to. Two opposing tendencies could arise: total compliance or total defiance.

*When the child natal number transformation controls the adult natal number transformation*: 2(3), 2(4), 5(3), 5(4), 8(3), 8(4), 1(2), 1(5), 1(8), 9(1), 6(9), 7(9), 3(6), 3(7), 4(6), 4(7)

In such configurations, there is a tendency towards impetuous behaviour. Here is a situation where a person's adult potentials and their ability to deal with situations are constantly being challenged by childhood patterns and responses. Independence and assertiveness are challenged by constant reminders of their limitations, conditions and habitual patterns. A person may thus give up their ideals, procrastinate, abdicate responsibility or blame others. There is a resulting tendency towards conscious or unconscious manipulation in relationships with others.

In such a situation, you should try to determine what the actual nurturing needs of the child natal month expression are. By acknowledging these needs and trying to meet them, you can lighten the pressures or control on the adult number transformation, thus allowing the adult expression to arise more freely.

*When the child and adult natal numbers share the same transformation but are different in their number: 2(5), 2(8), 3(4), 4(3), 5(2), 5(8), 6(7), 7(6), 8(2), 8(5)*

Many of the characteristics of the same adult and child number, as explained in the previous chapter, apply here. However, because there is a numerical variation, the yin and yang aspects are also represented. Thus the person has greater physical resilience and emotional perspective and flexibility than the double-numbered person – that is, a person whose adult natal year and child natal month numbers are the same. The personality is more well rounded from the standpoint of one transformation. In a sense, such people could be considered archetypes of the transformation that their numbers represent. They can thus exude a confidence not seen in double-numbered combinations.

## GENDER ENERGETICS AND THE ADULT/CHILD CONFIGURATION

As stated previously, in the cycle of nine numbers, there are those with a more contractive nature and those with a more expansive nature. This applies in the annual, monthly and daily cycles. Throughout Oriental thought, contractive and expansive qualities have been metaphorically referred to in gender terms. The more yang or contractive numbers are thus referred to as being masculine in nature, while the more yin or expansive numbers are referred to as being feminine in nature. In Nine Star Ki, 2, 4, 7 and 9 are considered feminine, while 1, 3, 6 and 8 are considered masculine. The number 5 is considered either masculine or feminine. (In the work of Rex Lassalle, the number 5 is ascribed the gender of the person concerned, as well as the attributes of a two-earth if the person is female, or eight-earth if the person is male. At the same time, it is my experience that while this is true, one will also find that the person will exhibit opposite gender and earth number tendencies as well as tendencies distinctive to five-earth natal energetics. Thus when a five is a part of a person's Nine Star Ki chart, it is important to examine two, five- and eight-earth characteristics as well as masculine and feminine tendencies and the various gender energetic configurations as described below.)

For example, for a person born on

13 April 1946, the natal year number is 9 and the month is 3. The configuration would be written as 9(3) eight. If we take into consideration the gender of the natal year and month numbers, the same configuration would be written as 9*f* (3*m*) eight*m, f* standing for female and *m* for male.

Although the gender typology would not change for the numbers, Gagne and Mann, in their *Nine Ki Handbook,* note that the impact of the gender of the numbers does differ depending on whether the person is male or female. In the example given above, if the person being considered is female, then the female attribute of 9 is considered the same as her gender, whereas the male aspect of 3 is considered opposite to her gender. If the person were male, the opposite would be the case; 9 would be opposite his gender, while 3 would be the same. When 5 is either the adult or the child number, it should be considered both masculine and feminine at the start. One can then look at the masculine–feminine configurations to see which is best suited to the character of the person being evaluated.

For example, let us assume John is a 6 natal year with a 5 natal month. Six is masculine and 5 can be either feminine or masculine. Thus John's gender energetic configuration could be male–female or male–male. In the typology being used, this would make John a same–opposite or same–same. John would therefore read the material for both to see which one he identifies with most. And, because of the extreme nature of the number 5, it could also be that in some circumstances he feels one way and in others he feels the other way.

Gagne and Mann use this 'same' and 'opposite' concept in the development of their four basic gender configurations: same/same, same/opposite, opposite/same and opposite/ opposite. Especially in relation to other people, the configuration of the gender energetics can have a noted impact. Because Gagne and Mann's method of presenting these configurations works so well. I have – with thanks to Stephen Gagne – elected to keep to their format. A brief description of each configuration follows.

When looking at these descriptions it is important to view genders from a polarity rather than a dualistic, either/or, perspective. The fact of the matter is that we embody both. The dominance of the force of one gender at the time of birth (as yin and yang are never equal) leads to the formation and experience of the particular gender that we are. At the same time, to become a 'whole' person, we must learn to integrate the male and female aspects of our being.

SAME/SAME: *Males that are* 1(1), 1(3), 1(6), 1(8), 3(1), 3(3), 3(6), 3(8), 6(1), 6(3), 6(6), 6(8), 8(1), 8(3), 8(6), 8(8). *Females that are* 2(2), 2(4), 2(7), 2(9), 4(2), 4(4), 4(7), 4(9), 7(2), 7(4), 7(7), 7(9), 9(2), 9(4),9(7), 9(9)

These are people that are confident in their gender identity and expression. Consequently, they rarely have any conflict within themselves as regards self-expression. They relate easily with both males and females.

Because they are strongly influenced by their own gender energetics, they often find it difficult to empathize with the opposite sex. They will also idealize the opposite sex, and people of the opposite sex may have difficulty living up to the same/same's expectations. As they expect a relationship to go the way they want it to, they do not catch on quickly when relationships are going awry. Thus they may hold on to relationships and go on in dysfunctional ways longer than is useful to either partner. If they are not in a long-standing relationship, they may have several casual relationships (either in sequence or at once) while waiting for their ideal to appear. At the same time, they may remain aloof. In terms of sexual activity, they can remain abstinent for long periods (and thus easily adapt to a monastic life) or just enjoy sexuality in a more playful way.

These people rarely have problems with their reproductive systems. Their sexual potency is strong.

SAME/OPPOSITE: *Males that are* 1(2), 1(4), 1(7), 1(9), 3(2), 3(4), 3(7), 3(9), 6(2), 6(4), 6(7), 6(9), 8(2), 8(4), 8(7), 8(9). *Females that are* 2(1), 2(3), 2(6), 2(8), 4(1), 4(3), 4(6), 4(8), 7(1), 7(3), 7(6), 7(8), 9(1), 9(3), 9(6), 9(8)

These people have their own gender in the natal year position and the opposite gender in the natal month position. This configuration gives them a positive self-image. They have the confidence and depth of their own gender in their self-expressive aspect (natal year) and a direct experience of the opposite polarity or gender in their conditional aspect. As they are in touch with both aspects of their being in a way that evokes ease in their being, they can usually empathize with both men and women. Such people make excellent counsellors and confidants to the opposite sex, who usually find it easy to relate to the same/opposite. Same/opposites may even prefer to have more friends of the opposite sex, which may arouse jealousy and concern in their own partners or the partners of their friends. However, they are rarely flirtatious – just more relaxed around the opposite sex.

Under stress, same/opposites may find that their generally relaxed manner gives way to a sense of unease and insecurity. Self-doubt and gender insecurity can lead to periods of emotional (and sexual) repression or misgivings.

OPPOSITE/SAME: *Males that are* 2(1), 2(3), 2(6), 2(8), 4(1), 4(3), 4(6), 4(8), 7(1), 7(3), 7(6), 7(8), 9(1), 9(3), 9(6), 9(8). *Females that are* 1(2), 1(4), 1(7), 1(9), 3(2), 3(4), 3(7), 3(9), 6(2), 6(4), 6(7), 6(9), 8(2), 8(4), 8(7), 8(9)

These people are somewhat self-conscious of their gender identity. They tend to act characteristically masculine or feminine in accordance with stereotypes and images. However, when challenged, they become confronted with a basic insecurity and can experience much self-doubt.

Because their adult natal number is opposite to their own gender, the opposite/same has a deep understanding of the opposite sex. They can be excellent at objectively viewing another person's situation or predicament. However, they easily get caught up in their own feelings, the stereotypes and the social standards around them. They long for deep relationships and must come to terms with the fact that when they do not find them, it has more to do with their own inner tensions than the inadequacies of others. Also, the bravado with which they act in times of self-doubt can be a factor that inhibits authentic contact with others.

OPPOSITE/OPPOSITE: *Males that are* 2(2), 2(4), 2(7), 2(9), 4(2), 4(4), 4(7), 4(9), 7(2), 7(4), 7(7), 7(9), 9(2), 9(4), 9(7), 9(9). Females that are 1(1), 1(3), 1(6), 1(8), 3(1), 3(3), 3(6), 3(8), 6(1), 6(3), 6(6), 6(8), 8(1), 8(3), 8(6), 8(8)

These are people who lack the strength of their own gender energetics. Because of this, there is a certain level of constant discomfort in their being. Life always seems a challenge

to an opposite/opposite. There is a sense of struggle about life and what it offers. Thus these people are usually extremely wilful. They get on and do things and project a confidence which comes from their constant feeling that they have to keep their chin up and push on in life.

Because their gender identity is based on the strength of the opposite gender energetic, the opposite sex plays the role of antagonist in their lives. Because of their personal sense of command, the opposite/opposite may create a persona which is alluring, intense and possibly confusing to those attracted to them. What often happens in this situation and in others where the opposite/opposite has dealings with the opposite sex, is that they may create tensions, misunderstandings and conflict. In an

236

attempt to temper the strength of the opposite gender in their personality, the opposite/ opposite may project outward and see all faults and sources of aggravation as arising from the opposite sex. (From a psychoanalytical point of view, it may even be that this projection creates a feeling of lack of support from the parent opposite their own gender – daughter to father, son to mother – thus creating a state of mind in later life where detachment from parental influences or images becomes problematic.) They tend to belittle or exploit the opposite sex in personal relationships. This accounts for a tendency to go to extremes in sexual relationships where they can be either resolutely abstinent or totally hedonistic. The experience of sex can play an inordinately important role as a reference point in a relationship, yet at the same time, be devoid of any personal experience of pleasure or satisfaction. On a physical level, the opposite/opposite energetic can lead to chronic or continuous imbalances and disease of the reproductive tract.

Such people usually find that they can relax more in the presence of their own gender. As they look to role models of their own gender they may also idealize the lives of those they look up to or wish to emulate. With all the discomfort and inner tension they may experience, the opposite/opposite's 'life-as-a-challenge' mentality makes them exceedingly hard working and dedicated to whatever causes, endeavours or missions they set their minds to. Thus they are an inspiration to those around them. As such they often become leaders with devoted followers.

**Please note** that with respect to the number 5, because of its androgynous qualities, it is possible for the person to have a five year or month fall into several categories.

When five is the year number for a man, if his month number is masculine (1, 3, 5, 6 or 8), his chart can be read as a same/same or opposite/same. If he has a female month number (2, 4, 5, 7 or 9), his chart can be read as same/opposite or opposite/opposite.

When five is the year number for a woman, if she has a masculine month number (1, 3, 5, 6 or 8), her configuration can be read as same/opposite or opposite/opposite. If she has a female month number (2, 4, 5, 7 or 9), her chart can be read as same/same or opposite/same.

When five is the month number of a man, if his year number is masculine (1, 3, 5, 6 or 8), the configuration of his chart can be read as same/same or same/opposite. If his year number is feminine (2, 4, 5, 7 or 9), his chart can be read as opposite/same or opposite/opposite.

When five is the month number for a woman, if her year number is masculine (1, 3, 5, 6 or 8), her chart can be read as opposite/same or opposite/opposite. If her year number is feminine (2, 4, 5, 7 or 9), her chart can be read as same/same or same/opposite.

It should be noted that the combination of a 5 year with a 5 month (5(5)) figures in all categories. This accounts for the chameleon quality of these individuals, their ability to mimic others and their tendency to express the widest array of emotional responses to life.

# The Dynamics of Relationships

When one looks at relationships in the context of the I Ching, the medical system of acupuncture and the laws of nature as conceived in the Law of Five Transformations, one is addressing our basic inter-connectedness with the world.

In the realm of personal and professional relationships, therefore, there is no judgement on any relationship – it is not good or bad. It is just a matter of understanding how elements or transformations interact. Some interactions flow; others create challenges, blockages etc. To say that one situation or interaction is better than another is to miss the point. Relationships do not need to be serene to be meaningful and a source of support and growth for the persons concerned. In fact, as the transformations are stimulated and activated in accordance with the seasons, the years and changing circumstances, one will not find a relationship which can be defined in one given way as if static.

In no way does such a statement

contradict the notion that there are fundamental energetic interactions which do persist over time. By analogy, an apple is an apple all the time. However, there are phases in the life of an apple that are harder and softer, sweeter and more sour, etc. Thus, while seeing that we have an apple in front of us, the qualities of that apple will vary according to where it is in its life cycle. Indeed, our relationship to the apple will vary depending on what our preferences are and the state of the apple. Relationships between humans are no different, and they need to be viewed dynamically. Viewed dynamically, the way in which we relate changes in accordance with what aspects of ourselves are being activated at any given time as a result of circumstances, both internal and external. From this point of view, one can say that all relationships are workable. What makes them unworkable is our fixation with outcomes.

Four points need to be made with regard to the way in which a relationship can be facilitated. First, what makes a relationship workable is our willingness to face ourselves and be true to who we are. Secondly, when we do this we come to realize that all beings are striving for the same things we strive for and that, thirdly, there are differences of approach, according to personal strengths, weaknesses and circumstances. Lastly, all relationships die in the wake of assumptions made by the partners, and any relationship can survive, flourish and thrive in an atmosphere of openness, humour and love.

Nine Star Ki is invaluable in

helping us to get in touch with our basic, conditioned nature with all its strengths and weaknesses. With a self-assessment that is based on elemental/transformational factors rather than cultural stereotypes or ideals we can more creatively and accurately develop our skills and potentials. Becoming more honest and familiar with ourselves on such a level, we learn to relax with who we are. We learn to become friends with ourselves. This is, in fact, the first and necessary step towards being able to extend friendship to others and relate in an authentic way.

Knowing ourselves better in a positive way, we next need to be able to appreciate and relate to others as they are. Generally, one needs an attitude of openness, humour and love, as mentioned above. In themselves, these three can help to cut through almost any situation. At the same time, often because of our perceptions and pro- jections, our relationships can remain bogged down in confusion with the resulting misunderstandings. In such situations, the Ki can be a way of tapping into how such confusion and misunderstanding arise by examining the general qualities, in particular the psycholog- ical predispositions inherent in the various transformations dominant in the make-up of the persons concerned.

Up until this point, we have been addressing the elemental/transforma- tional mixes that create styles of relating for any individual. It is now time to demonstrate how this same model can be used to analyze styles of interaction between individuals.

## PERCEPTION

It is commonly recognized in various schools of psychology that our view of the world is based on our experience of it. It is also becoming increasingly clear in psychology that the events in our lives are not meaningful in themselves. What gives them meaning is our perceptions, reactions and responses, which build upon each other, layer after layer. Much of the material presented thus far has been about ways in which each transformation phase influences our perceptions, reactions and responses. It has also been stressed how the natal year and natal month transformations form a constitutional core from which our world is experienced.

We are born with a particular natal adult year and natal child month. In the year we are born, our natal year number occupies the House of Five and our natal month occupies whichever house it reaches in the movement of numbers through time and space. This is not only true of our own numbers. It also means that all numbers are in a particular position based on the given year. Except in a five-earth year, the numbers do not occupy their own houses. Thus each number's transformation will possess qualities based on the house it occupies.

On an interpersonal level, this means that when we encounter someone, the transformations that make up the natal adult and child characteristics of that person reside in certain houses in our natal chart. This is how we will experience their transformations. Briefly stated, we see their qualities through our filters.

Depending on our own personal

balance and sensitivity, we may be able to distinguish what is truly them and what is just our perceptual framework. However, it is not uncommon for us to blur the two. In Nine Star Ki terms, this means mistaking the transformation qualities of the other person for the house qualities and the interactions between the transformation and the houses that we experience. An example will quickly clarify this concept and how it impacts on our perceptions and relationships.

Let us look at a three-tree/space year.

In a three-tree/space year, one-water sits in the House of Three-Tree. A three-tree person encountering a one-water person generally finds them supportive, as water is the mother of tree/space. However, the internal perception of the three-tree

person will go further than that. For the three-tree, the one-water person sits in the tree house of ideas, inspiration and new energy. Thus the three-tree person may find that they are nourished with these qualities by the one-water person.

This is fine in itself. It gets distorted, however, when the three-tree person expects the one-water person to interact and respond in accordance with the energetics of the House of Three. The three-tree may not see the cautiousness and reflection that has gone into the ideas the

*Figure 25. Universal Chart for a three-tree/space year*

243

one-water presents to them. Thus they may overlook the one-water's reserved nature and expect bouncing enthusiasm. With such a distortion communications with the one-water may become stifling. Inner perception here is not congruent with outer reality.

We can all fall prey to such a way of viewing others. The issue here is not that it is wrong. Rather we must learn to distinguish between what the basic energetic patterns of the other person are and what their energetics become when viewed from our particular frame of reference. It is a useful self-reflective process to observe how our own energetics change on a month-by-month basis, depending on what houses our own natal numbers reside in. As we come to be more sensitive to this within ourselves, it becomes easier to see others more clearly. If nothing else, it relaxes our tendency towards fixation.

## INTERACTING

If we relate to our world only on the basis of our inner perceptions, in other words our filters, we are in for a rude awakening. In some ways the inner perceptions view is useful in so far as it shows us how we take in our world. In extending back out into the world by communicating, a change of focus is needed.

It seems quite evident these days that communications between individuals, couples, groups and nations are rife with problems. These problems may simply stem from the fact that we are responding to the world only from the standpoint of our perceptions of our needs and assuming that everything and everyone else operates in the same way.

Being who we are, our relationship to the world is based on our own natal year numbers being in the centre of the Magic Square. This being the case, it is almost as if all inner perceptions are cancelled. As everyone in a relationship is speaking from their centre (with their natal year number at the centre), it is almost as if no one is in the centre. Relating creates balance. We have to get out of our heads and relate to what is in front of us. If we don't, misunderstanding is inevitable.

On a practical level, what this means is that the standard Five Transformation chart is the best way to identify what the actual elemental energetics are in a relationship. The Magic Square and its houses can thus be simplified as in Figure 26.

Once set in this standard configuration, one can plot the natal month and year numbers of each individual within a particular interaction with the given transformations. From this, the responses and reactions that occur in the course of the relationship can be examined based on transformation energetics. Of course there are the house influences and monthly and yearly variations to be taken into account. However, the configuration of energetics as presented on the basic Five Transformation chart will be the underlying core dynamic in the relationship.

## TAKING A COUPLE AS AN EXAMPLE

What we shall now do is look at a relationship. The steps suggested in the example will be the ones you can take to look at any relationship.

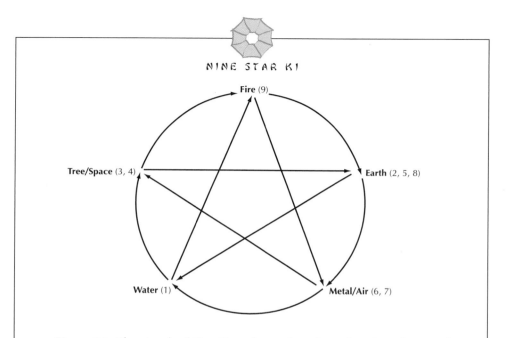

*Figure 26. The standard Five Transformation chart showing elemental energetics in a relationship*

John was born on 18 March 1947 and his wife, Jennifer, was born on 6 August 1953. They come to a Nine Star Ki counsellor wanting to gain more insight into their relationship.

To do this, the following method is recommended.

*First, study the information pertaining to your own natal year adult and natal month child numbers.* Note the adult potentials and the potential and stress patterns of the natal month number. Read the material about transformation combinations and gender energetics.

In John's case, 18 March 1947 makes him a 8*m*(l*m*) seven*f*. He should see that he is a deep thinker, strong in masculine character, and not very expressive emotionally. He likes to take his time deliberating over matters and is a hard worker. He may be too serious and may often find himself taking things too literally. As earth (eight) is his adult and controls water (one) as his child, John is rather self-controlled and self-critical, he does not take criticism from others well. His more fluid child side is suppressed in many areas and thus will exhibit one-water stress-related problems. He may at times seem withdrawn and depressed. Initial signs of stress may be the result of trying to please people or having fears which he tries to mask so as not to upset those around him. Although a generally caring man, his masculine/masculine, hence same/same gender energetics can sometimes make him naïve, or oblivious to the needs of women. He may even idealize the women in his life, not recognizing how this can set them and him up for disappointment or failure.

In Jennifer's case, 6 August 1953 makes her a 2*f* (6*m*) nine*f*. Briefly, Jennifer has both primal mother (two-earth) and primal father (six-metal) characteristics. A generally caring individual, Jennifer may find that she is other people's confidant, and involved excessively in their lives. Her two-earth nature makes her very

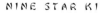

sympathetic. Yet because earth is the mother of metal (and her six), Jennifer may find that she leaps from concern to judgements and actions in other people's lives before the time is appropriate. She may even be rather argumentative in such circumstances, pushing her point a bit too far. However, as people see her as a responsible person, they may allow her to take over, abdicating their own responsibility. Thus, Jennifer may tend to burn herself out.

Stress for her may manifest as anxiety which then precipitates rigid stubbornness or a sense of hysteria that is somewhat ill-focused. There are many 'shoulds' in her life. Her female/male or same/opposite gender energetics generally allow her to feel at ease in herself and she can relate well to either sex. This ease, together with her socializing ways may make others see her as flirtatious, perhaps superficial. As a result she may find that partners are jealous and covetous.

*Second, after this brief character evaluation, plot the natal year and month numbers of the other person in the relationship on your chart, that is, with your natal year in the House of Five.* Simply put, with your natal year number in the centre, you are looking at the houses in which the other person's number resides. This will give you your inner perception or experience of the other person on transformation and house level.

Let's look at John's chart in Figure 27 to see where Jennifer fits in.

Jennifer's two-earth adult sits in John's House of Eight, while her six-metal child sits in the House of Three. This means that John sees Jennifer in

| 7 | 3 | 5 |
| 6 | 8 | 1 |
| 2 | 4 | 9 |

*Figure 27. John's chart*

details and perhaps when he is bogged down, to pull him up. Being emotionally unexpressive, John may find it difficult to understand when Jennifer is emotional. Also, Jennifer's six-metal sits in John's House of Three. As tree controls earth, John may experience Jennifer as coming up with lots of ideas, but those ideas, although pragmatic and seemingly logical, may challenge or threaten him and his plans.

Now let's look at Jennifer's chart in figure 28 to see where John fits in.

her adult nature as someone with whom he probably sees eye to eye. Because the two-earth, which is softer in its quality, occupies the House of Eight, John may overlook Jennifer's softer nature. He may expect her to be stoical and hard-working, someone who drives herself as hard as she can. He may also look to Jennifer as someone to sort out

John's eight-earth adult sits in Jennifer's House of Two while his one-water child sits in the House of Four. Here we have a situation where John and Jennifer's internal percep-tions almost match, thus possibly creating many expectations and assumptions. John's eight-earth in the

| 1 | 6 | 8 |
|---|---|---|
| 9 | 2 | 4 |
| 5 | 7 | 3 |

*Figure 28. Jennifer's chart*

House of Two leads Jennifer to feel that both she and John see the world in the same way. However, Jennifer, being more expressive, may be confused by John's lack of expression and the way he gets caught up in situations and considers things that Jennifer sees as trifling. She may ask, 'Why he is taking things so seriously?'

Jennifer finds John very caring, but may expect him to be more malleable and expressive than he is capable of being. At the same time, John's one-water is in her House of Four. Thus John may come up with ideas for Jennifer that are both well thought out and meaningful, but at the same time, challenge Jennifer's two-earth nature and irritate her need for control and for feeling responsible (six-metal aspect). She may nevertheless look to John for creativity and inspiration, and view his lack of expressiveness as a way of concealing things from her. She may even think that he is basically angry with her or that when he doesn't say what is on his mind, it is an act of hostility.

*Third, use the standard Five Transformation chart to plot both numbers. Use lower case letters to*

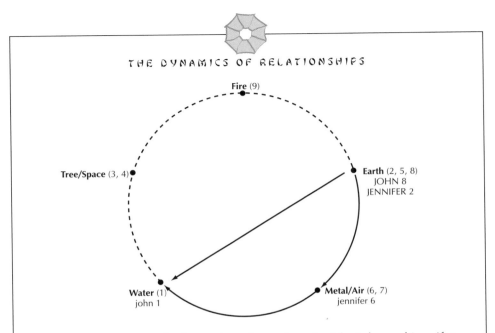

Figure 29. The standard Five Transformation chart for John and Jennifer

indicate the child transformation and capitals to indicate the adult transformation. Place the number beside the name in each case. Such a chart will give you the actual basic energetics occurring during interaction.

Based on such a map one can make the following observations of John and Jennifer's interactions.

Both John and Jennifer have their adult numbers in the earth transformation, indicating that they see eye to eye in many ways and that the yin (two) of Jennifer and yang (eight) of John create enough of a difference in expression to make their relationship dynamic. (If both were eight or two, although there would be much in common, there might also be a sense of stagnation in the relationship, as if nothing is moving forward. *This can be true of any relationship where the numbers of the respective partners are the same.*) Both John and Jennifer like to get on and do things.

In general, Jennifer feels more supported by John than vice versa. Here John's eight-earth adult is the mother element to Jennifer's six-metal child. Jennifer's two-earth is also the mother to her six-metal child. The result may be that as Jennifer has a natural tendency to slip into her six-metal child anyway, such a pattern is reinforced by John as

well. Thus within the relationship, Jennifer may act more out of her child than her adult transformation. Six being the primal father number, she may find herself taking on too many responsibilities, being somewhat confrontational or argumentative, and being more concerned about the relationship than John appears to be. As this six-metal is reinforced by both John's 8 and Jennifer's 2, the dominance of six-metal in the relationship may encourage more one-water responses from John. Thus while eights are generally reserved in their communication, John may be even more cautious and uncommunicative as Jennifer's six-metal dominates interactions. John may even appear enigmatic as he feels less inclined to communicate directly what is on his mind. This may further upset Jennifer as she expects things to be on the surface and 'up front'.

Another dominant scenario in their interactions is that John is rather self-critical and controls his own behaviour (adult eight-earth controlling child one-water), so John may also feel Jennifer is being rather critical of him as her two-earth also controls one-water. Thus there are times when John almost feels emotionally set up by Jennifer; the mother–son relationship of John and Jennifer's numbers precipitates their child patterns, yet when activated into his one-water child response patterns, Jennifer's adult two-earth response can add insult to injury as John is already trying to get a grip on himself emotionally.

John's own self-doubt will be compounded by Jennifer's smothering and controlling tendencies. Whereas she may wish to act to clear the air, to a large extent John just wants to be left alone to think about things in his own time. Because Jennifer's numbers are supportive of each other and because she trusts that John does care for her and is supportive of her, his lack of response at times may be seen as stubbornness or an unwillingness to share. In fact even in the best of circumstances it takes John some time to get to the point. It's not that he doesn't feel things; indeed, he feels very deeply. If Jennifer can be patient, she will find that what John conveys to her has depth and can bring new levels of meaning to their relationship. From Jennifer, John can learn that letting people know what is going on strengthens relationships. His tendency to isolation and silence can only weaken a relationship over time.

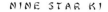

## WHAT IS THE VALUE OF SUCH INFORMATION?

As I have often said in this volume, no situation is unworkable. However, we get it into our minds that when communication is awkward or situations run counter to expectations there must be something wrong and something, therefore, must be fixed. A couple like John and Jennifer may find themselves in counselling trying to change something which is nothing more than a basic transformation dynamic expressing itself in social and psychological arenas.

If the significance of these dynamics is realized, the more supportive aspects of their relations could be emphasized and a more humorous and spacious approach could be adopted when they see some of the more conflicting patterns emerging in stressful situations. Obviously this can be more difficult than we would like, simply because most of us take our lives rather seriously and have particular definitions of who we are and what our relationships should be like. However, if we can begin by taking into account basic energetics and the patterns they create we may be able to come up with creative ways to bridge the gap between reality and our desires. If our desires are devoid of any basic reality, then we shall always pursue a self-identity and lasting meaningful relationships in vain.

As we accept reality, life becomes less and less of a problem. Drama gives way to relative *dharma* or truth.

## APPLICATION IN WORK AND BUSINESS

In the realm of personal relationships

and family matters, the usefulness of Nine Star Ki can be seen in the example of John and Jennifer. But how might it apply in other relationships, such as in the workplace? For it is a fact of most adults' experience that most of their waking hours are spent at work.

In 1985 and 1986, a good friend, Rex Lassalle, and I were doing some work and training with a Kentucky-based accounting firm. One of the sidelines of this firm was a computerized personality testing and evaluation service for employers looking for employees who would fit into their corporate settings. Over the years, technology in this field has become so precise in determining psychological and social make-up and character that not only are more firms relying on such testing but there have been fewer lawsuits by state and federal boards investigating discrimination when such tests are used compared to personal interviews by company personnel departments. It seems that such testing is more objective and accurate in creating the right employer-employee task mix.

Although effective, many of those tests are quite time-consuming to administer and costly to evaluate. The firm in this situation was using two separate systems. Mr Lassalle and I offered the use of Nine Star Ki at no cost, to see if the ki could pick up the same information just by having access to the prospective employees' birth-dates.

While we were not surprised at the results, the head of the firm was. The ki *can* be used to look at the numerous variables that employers want to know about; personalities, authority issues and likely responses, skills and general responses under stress. Looking at the profiles and descriptions found in this volume, such information is evident. Beyond this, however, the ki can also be used to determine how such an individual will interact with fellow workers.

The model presented for evaluating the relationship of our example couple is applicable here. The ki can be used to look at a new employee coming into an already existing system. This can be good news for personnel departments as it can not only be an effective evaluation tool, but also an exceedingly cost-effective one. But apart from new employees, all personnel departments are called upon to deal with morale and task issues of employee/staff teams. Creating a Nine Star Ki map of all employees or working units is useful in that it can

not only highlight all the individual strengths, weaknesses and potentials within a group, but also be used to determine routes of support, pockets of potential conflict, as well as the overall strengths, weaknesses and balance of an entire group at once. I have devised a systematic evaluation process that is useful for any group being studied.

This evaluation is broken down into four distinct phases in order to make data more coherent and usable for supervisors or team evaluators. Phase One involves questions a supervisor or evaluator should try to answer regarding individual team members. Phase Two is a chart where the adult and child natal numbers of each team member are plotted out under each of the nine numbers and their associated management or emphasized interaction skill. This chart will give supervisors or evaluators a visual picture of where the strengths, weaknesses and gaps in team functioning exist. At the bottom of the chart are management strategies that should be adopted to support, enhance or control various tendencies or individuals. Phase Three is an actual Five Transformation map with all the individuals plotted on it in their adult and child aspects. A narrative of group dynamics follows where each of the individuals in relation to others is highlighted. Phase Four is general comments and recommendations.

## CARDIOVASCULAR LAB EVALUATED

The following example is a Nine-Star Ki evaluation of a cardiovascular lab of a large hospital system. The names used in the example are fictitious, but the birth-dates are actual ones. The people in this situation are not prospective but actual employees who have been working under the same supervisor for some time. The purpose of the evaluation here is thus to look at the individuals within and the operation of the entire team.

Please be aware that while the phases as they are presented and the language used in the discussion that follows regarding the cardiovascular lab will refer to 'supervisor' and 'employees', the participants can be members of a family, a counsellor looking at the dynamics of a therapy group, or any other group situation one may want to look at from a Nine Star Ki perspective. The usefulness of giving the specific details of this group evaluation is that they demonstrate Nine Star Ki's potential in identifying, clarifying and sorting out processes in group settings.

## Phase One

In Phase One of an evaluation, a supervisor or evaluator needs to ask the following four questions regarding members of the staff team:

1. What are the employee's adult and child numbers and what are the characteristics found within these numbers that best correspond to the employee's job description? Attention should be paid to the occupations as listed in the number profiles as well as the general and business relationship narratives.

2. Of the management skills as listed in the profiles and the relationship styles as described in the narrative of both adult and child numbers, which are most in keeping with the employee's job description, particularly in the area of interactions expected with other employees?

3. From which number (child or adult) do you see the employee operating generally?

4. What situations do you know of that bring out the employee's adult traits? What situations bring out the employee's child traits?

As we have already done basic character evaluations in our description of John and Jennifer (see above), no descriptions of the various employees is given here. You are advised when using the system suggested to follow the questions in Phase One to get the information you need to proceed to the other three phases.

## Phase Two

In the mid-eighties, Warren Bellows and Nancy Post of the Merriam Hill Centre in Cambridge, Massachusetts developed an organization theory where types of managing and work skills were classified as yin or yang aspects of one of the Five Transformations. Using this as a base, it has not been difficult to ascribe numbers to each of the skills classified. The Phase Two chart (Figure 30), especially the left-hand portion of it, is based on the Bellows-Post model. The right-hand portion of the chart deals with action strategies. As one will usually want the adult natal year strength to be dominant, *supportive* strategies are suggested to activate those strengths. Where child natal month responses are evident and a supervisor or evaluator considers that it is a transition situation, *enhancing* strategies are recommended. *Controlling* strategies are recommended when an employee seems to be caught in habitual child responses, thus in their most stressful mode. All strategies are based on the mother–son transformation relationships and the ko (control) cycle.

As regards the strategies on the right of the chart, the purpose is not to manipulate people so much as to find a way that will actually help them to bring out their potential. As this is an energetic innovation, the suggestion here is to try the strategies to see how

*Figure 30. (overleaf) Group Energetic Evaluation chart for the Cardiovascular lab*

| NUMBER | MANAGING SKILLS | PEOPLE INVOLVED |
|--------|-----------------|-----------------|
| ① | **YIN – Allocator:**<br>containing, storing, delineating<br>boundaries, managing resources<br><br>**YANG – Motivator:**<br>generating, energizing, providing<br>direction, reflection | DAVE<br>TANYA<br>jim |
| ② | **Supporter**<br>sustaining, supporting, retaining<br>assimilating, anchoring, centring | |
| ③ | **Planner**<br>mapping, visioning, defining borders,<br>strategizing, adapting, organizing | JOHN<br>DOROTHY<br>dorothy<br>JANE<br>MIKE<br>mike<br>dave |

## STRATEGY

| NO. 1<br>**Support for adult activation** | NO. 2<br>**Enhance to move person out of child activation** | NO. 3<br>**Control inappropriate child action** |
|---|---|---|
| **Metal/Air Action:**<br>provide historical data, provide summations, get No. 1 to consider the broader social implications, provide space for reflection and response, fatherly support | Strategy No. 1 followed by<br>**Tree/Space Action:**<br>be enthusiastic, show them what potential there is, let them know where things need to go, ask for their energy and gleanings from their reflections | **Earth Action:**<br>ground them, listen to them. Get details from them regarding vague fears. Acknowledge but challenge hesitancy |
| **Fire Action:**<br>be direct, be convincing, promote excitement, be joyful, overcome anxieties, demonstrate appreciation, find out what else they need, sell them the idea | Strategy No. 1 followed by<br>**Metal/Air Action:**<br>monitor quality, make them accountable, ask for progress reports, accept what's offered, show social/historical importance of work done | **Tree/Space Action:**<br>clarify person's situation, initiate conflict if necessary, restructure person's situation, define limits, prioritize |
| **Water Action:**<br>communicate general trends of situation, delineate boundaries for person, energize them to move in given direction, be a well spring, gentle action with reserve | Strategy No. 1 followed by<br>**Fire Action:**<br>show them what is possible, weave them into a greater plan or network of people, be enthusiastic, clarify their ideas | **Metal/Air Action:**<br>make person accountable, spell it out, establish order in their activity, list consequences, refer to team commitment, social order, morality, avoid direct confrontation |

| NUMBER | MANAGING SKILLS | PEOPLE INVOLVED |
|---|---|---|
| 4 | **Decision-Maker**<br>clarifying, individuating, scheduling,<br>initiating conflict, structuring | DENISE |
| 5 | **Consolidator**<br>catalysing, leading, sorting, critiquing,<br>also traits for 2 and 8 | john |
| 6 | **Inspirer**<br>equilibrating, resonating, receiving,<br>balancing, establishing order | denise<br>tanya |

| | STRATEGY | |
|---|---|---|
| **NO. 1**<br>**Support for adult activation** | **NO. 2**<br>**Enhance to move person out of child activation** | **NO. 3**<br>**Control inappropriate child action** |
| Same as 3 tree/space but appeal to their sense and maturity to see things clearly. Support in prioritizing | Same as Strategy No. 1 for 3 tree/space but make sure encouragement allows them to stick to one direction and within time limits set | Same as 3 tree/space in Strategy No. 3, but over-ride their muddledness. Overcome confusion by refining, giving a clear evaluation of the situation, bringing balance to their perspective |
| **Fire Action:**<br>same as for 2 earth but here over-ride indecisiveness, appeal to intellect, stimulate catalysing nature, define role, create trust, be supportive | Same as Strategy No. 1 in 2 earth followed by<br>**Metal/Air Action:**<br>critically weigh up options, help person adjust to change, establish order, encourage person to produce results, balance action | As Strategy No. 3 for 2 earth, getting person to commit themselves, over-ride sentimentality, encourage indepence, provide time limits, give commands, help person to vision |
| **Earth Action:**<br>nurture, provide adequate details, be an anchor, listen | Strategy No. 1 followed by<br>**Water Action:**<br>reflect back, be receptive, manage resources, overcome rigidity by proving larger perspective | **Fire Action:**<br>spell it out, challenge dualistic (blank/white) thinking, overcome arrogance, clear air before grudges are set |

| NUMBER | MANAGING SKILLS | PEOPLE INVOLVED |
|--------|-----------------|-----------------|
| ⑦ | **Evaluator:**<br>accounting, refining, eliminating,<br>evolving, managing change,<br>quality control | |
| ⑧ | **Producer**<br>nuturing, transporting, supporting,<br>producing, attention to details,<br>integrating | jane |
| ⑨ | **YIN**<br>**Sorter:** selling, problem solving,<br>discriminating transforming and **networker**–<br>team builder, socializing, atmosphere builder<br><br>**YANG**<br>**Coordinator:** coordinating, defining roles,<br>directing, cooperation-building; and<br>**Communicator:** appreciating, creating<br>trust, expressing protecting | JIM |

| STRATEGY | | |
|---|---|---|
| **NO. 1**<br>**Support for adult activation** | **NO. 2**<br>**Enhance to move person out of child activation** | **NO. 3**<br>**Control inappropriate child action** |
| Same as Strategy No. 1 for 6 metal, but more anchoring and centring, offer positive criticism, help to sustain momentum | Strategy No. 1 followed by<br>**Water Action:**<br>as with 6 metal but here be more conservative, provide more direction, facilitate more truthful responses | **Fire Action:**<br>don't buy smooth talk, challenge sense of entitlement, overcome any melancholy, keep person task-focused, appeal to social values and importance of the team |
| Same as Strategy No. 1 for 2 and 5 earth, but help person to relax more, provide enthusiasm, lightness and clarity, help with discrimination and priority | Strategy No. 1 followed by<br>**Metal/Air Action:**<br>help to eliminate excess, refine, help person to focus beyond task, engage in play | **Tree/Space Action:**<br>snap person out of wallowing or hopelessness, encourage independent thinking, provide vision, even reframe structure, provide time frames |
| **Tree/Space Action:**<br>provide ideas, give vision, enthusiasm and excitement, stimulate, map the territory to be explored, provide supportive muscle, create context | Strategy No. 1 followed by<br>**Earth Action:**<br>get it all focused, encourage to act, spell out the end product, encourage diligence, provide realistic outlook and expectations, help person to match talk and actions | **Water Action:**<br>listen, provide reflection, express caution, demand focus and direction, challenge flamboyance, facilitate direct communication, point out possible undertones |

well they work rather than viewing and applying them in some dogmatic fashion. For one thing, people relate to their adult and child natal energetics according to circumstances, conditioning, etc. My experience is that once a person discovers what their actual energetic potentials are, a greater fluidity of expression emerges.

For Phase Two, all the birth-dates of the employees are needed. The birth-dates and Nine Star Ki birth-date configurations of the employees

of our example are presented here:

Using the chart, the strengths and weaknesses of each individual in the lab can be noted. The adult natal year number is written in capitals and the child natal month number is written in lower case letters. It should be borne in mind that adult traits are those from which the individual's greatest sense of strength and self-expression will emerge. The child traits are also skills and potentials, but they are subject to more past condi-

| | | |
|---|---|---|
| Jane: | 11 August 1961 | 3*m*(8*m*)one*m* |
| Jim: | 5 July 1964 | 9*f*(1*m*)six*m* |
| Mike: | 13 January 1962 | 3*m*(3*m*)five*m*/*f* |
| Dorothy: | 11 April 1934 | 3*m*(3*m*)five*m*/*f* |
| Dave: | 22 July 1963 | 1*m*(3*m*)seven*f* |
| John: | 27 November 1961 | 3*m*(5*m*/*f*)seven |
| Tanya: | 10 January 1955 | 1*m*(6*m*)one*m* |
| Denise: | 20 April 1951 | 4*f*(6*m*)seven*f* |

tioning, as well as being a potential source for stress. Where the adult and child numbers are the same, as in our example with Mike and Dorothy, their individual tasks are to overcome their past conditioning in order to turn what is a potential source of stress into a strength.

As can be observed in the chart of lab employees, there is a dominance of planners (threes), both in adult and child expression. This group has a lot of ideas about almost every phase of the lab's activities. Endless possibilities may be discussed as to what could be done, with no particular goal in mind. Conversations may be loud, gestures bold, with an air of excitement, but this may have little to do with what is actually attained in the process. In terms of stress, irritation and frustration may be quite marked. Impatience and anger may

dominate transactions with authority. As three-tree is the most independent of the numbers, this could easily be a case of 'too many chiefs, not enough Indians'.

The only other concentration in the chart is in the one-water area. Here there are two 'adults', Dave and Tanya, and one 'child', Jim. This is a group which is capable of seeing how things have gone, getting a sense of what is needed to change direction and providing encouragement and direction for all the planners in the group to investigate. As regards the group dynamic, although we shall go into this more in Phase Three, it is useful for this group to have a concentration in this area as it provides some sense of support for all the threes, as well as the supervisor.

If we look at the decision-making,

interestingly enough, we find that the one who needs to focus the group, clarify and structure what actually goes on, turns out to be the supervisor, Denise. When it comes to getting things done, however, the group is lacking. Nine-fire people can catalyze things and bring them into some form, but it is in the areas of earth (two, five and eight) and metal/air (six and seven), that the consolidation, maturation and end products emerge. In the earth position, we have John and Jane who can get on in this area, but because it is their child natal month expression, it is a strain (not to mention the fact that their tree/space adult natal numbers have a controlling, hence limiting, effect on their earth expression). John and Jane may, in fact, find that much of their time and effort goes into worry and caretaking for the emotional needs of the group rather than the actual completion of tasks.

Tanya can put the final touches on things, balance efforts and be somewhat supportive to the supervisor, Denise. However, neither Tanya nor Denise comes out of a position of strength (that is, adult expression) in this situation. Tanya and Denise may find that much of their effort goes into trying to establish order, finding themselves on the defensive and putting an inordinate amount of time into dealing with the three-tree/space energy that dominates the group. Denise may find that she views situations in black and white terms, always being pushed to state the bottom line. And there is no one in the seven-metal/air position to act as an evaluator as the process of the group unfolds.

## Phase Three

There are two ways to look at and evaluate data in Phase Three. First of all what is needed is a Five Transformation chart upon which each individual's natal adult and child numbers can be plotted. In dealing with a group, each individual's interactions with other members can be plotted on a one-to-one basis, as in our couple's example of John and Jennifer. This is certainly useful in assisting individuals in their interactions with the others in the group. However, a Five Transformation chart, where all individuals are plotted at once, best serves an evaluator or supervisor in looking at overall group dynamics. Although we shall look at the Five Transformation map more closely, the one-to-one model is still useful to

have in so far as individuals do run into problems with each other that are more specific than could be explained by a group gestalt. (The one-to-one model would be used by taking one individual, let us say Jane, and making maps and couple-type narratives of her in relation to Jim, Mike, Dorothy, etc.)

Figure 31 shows a Five Transformation chart for the cardiovascular lab.

The basic theme of the lab staff is excitement and ideas. There is an endless stream of new ideas that people generate in this group – and a lot of talk about those ideas. The air is therefore usually charged. If it is charged in a negative way, rather than there being ideas and excitement, there can be agitation, anger and a chaotic feeling about daily operations.

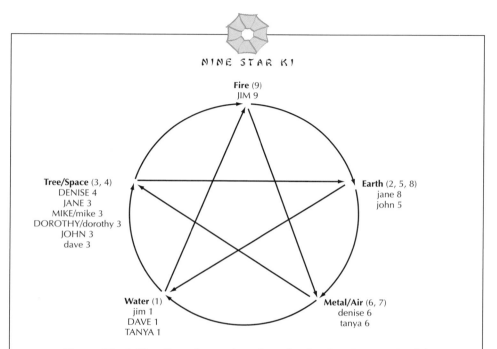

NINE STAR KI

**Fire** (9)
JIM 9

**Tree/Space** (3, 4)
DENISE 4
JANE 3
MIKE/mike 3
DOROTHY/dorothy 3
JOHN 3
dave 3

**Earth** (2, 5, 8)
jane 8
john 5

**Water** (1)
jim 1
DAVE 1
TANYA 1

**Metal/Air** (6, 7)
denise 6
tanya 6

*Figure 31. A Five Transformation chart for the Cardiovascular lab*

When expressing their adult natal characteristics more, this group holds together. This does not mean that there are no problems, but they are more internal and personal than rela-tional. Social interaction runs smoothly as water (Dave, Tanya and Jim) supports tree/space (Denise, Jane, Mike, Dorothy, John and Dave), which in turn supports fire

(Jim). While this dominance of water, tree/space and fire creates a supportive network, it does not lead to a coordinated or consistent effort in the accomplishment of tasks. As three-trees are usually animatedly busy, there can be an appearance of accomplishment, while the effort is disproportionate to the actual results.

Internal and personal areas of tension arise where child natal numbers are activated or are in control positions relative to adult natal numbers. This is also true where child and adult numbers are the same.

Jane and John may be the task completers for the group, but this role is a strain on them in that it is a manifestation of their child natal energetics. They also put a lot of pressure on themselves as their adult natal tree/space aspect controls their child natal earth aspect. Dorothy and Mike, whose House of Five position gives them an earth quality, may also expend a lot of energy in task completion, but not without a lot of internal pressures as well.

These four are the workhorses of the group, but generally they do not feel good about it, either consciously or unconsciously. Their internal pressures and stress may be projected outwards in which case they can feel judged or watched over by the other three- and four-tree/space members of the group. This may create a feeling of resentment or a type of co-dependency where because the other three-tree/-space numbers either identify with or go through the same internal dynamics, they can all unite in complaining about how stressful the situation is, how hard the work is and how insensitive the supervisor (Denise) is. It may be difficult for them to see that they are themselves the authors of their clash with authority, that they naturally have this struggle because of their tree/space and earth configurations. Moreover, it is a fact that unless they can run their own show, three-tree space individuals will inevitably run into difficulties with anyone or anything that inhibits their autonomy or independence.

Their situation is not helped by the fact that three-tree/space and four-tree/space people do not see eye to eye and there is some tension in their interaction. Here, the supervisor, Denise, tries to clarify and put order into what Jane, John, Dorothy and Mike generate. She may at times see what it is that they are trying to accomplish, but not why it has to be done the way it is being done. Denise likes to do one thing at a time and the timing of what is done is important for her. Likewise, her job makes time management a signpost to demonstrate effective cost and task supervision. To her, the way three-tree/space people operate seems time-consuming if not random – even chaotic.

Because her communication with three-tree/space people goes awry at times, she may easily slip into her six-metal/air child patterns. Her four-tree/space skills of initiating conflict may thus snap into open confrontation, where she makes black-and-white declarations of how she wants to run things. Sensing her weakness in such an approach as, again, this is not a dominant (i.e. adult natal) strength for her, her employees may not take her seriously and may just brush her off. Because her suggestions in this situation arise out of her stress and are usually mundane or consolidating, the three-trees will usually find them at best uninteresting and at worst an insult to their sense of brilliance and spaciousness.

What can temper and bring balance in this particular arena of conflict is Denise's relationship with Dave and Jim. Generally, Jim feels supportive both of the three-tree/-space team members and of four-tree/-space Denise. Jim finds Denise supportive, especially as he can be a catalyzing force for the tree/space ideas generated and can keep operations moving forward. As regards the three-tree group, Jim may find that in times of crisis, he becomes their spokesman to Denise. As Jim feels supported by both the group and Denise, he may find himself in a quandary and not know where to stand. If Denise's six-metal child is activated in an attempt to control three-tree energy, Jim may become confrontational. His adult nine-fire energy may keep Denise's six-metal at bay, in which case she may become empowered to use more adult metal strategies. It all depends on how safe Jim feels in his relationship with Denise. There is a tendency, however, for Jim to retreat into his one-water position of cautiousness and reserve. Denise's six-metal behaviour may even activate Jim's one-water child tendencies.

As regards Dave, Denise's six-metal behaviour in times of stress may activate Dave's one-water adult. As water supports tree/space and Dave's child is a three-tree/space, he can identify with the group tensions, but can act as a support for both the group and Denise by reflecting back to them what he sees and possibly acting as a bridge between the group and Denise. This, of course, depends on how much Dave identifies with his adult or child characteristics. If he is living out of his child (three-tree/space) expression, which is his tendency as his one-water adult precipitates a three-tree/space expression, he may just identify with the three-tree/space crowd, in which case, because his three-tree/space is his child expression, he may be the most vocal in dissent.

Another area of energetic interaction revolves around Dave, Tanya and Jim. As I have said, Jim has a tendency to become less expressive in the group as his one-water child cautiousness can undermine his nine-fire adult potentials. This tendency is reinforced by both Dave and Tanya. Jim may feel that Dave has some influence on him, but there is a controlling aspect to this. At the same time, Dave's three-tree/space child traits may lead him to look to Jim as a source of inspiration, especially to help him with his frustration at times. The resulting dynamic may make Jim feel that Dave idealizes or has great expectations of him.

Tanya likewise reinforces Jim's water tendencies, but equally feels under pressure from Jim as her six-metal child is controlled by Jim's nine-fire adult. As Tanya identifies with and can feel under pressure from Jim, his actions from his nine-fire adult potential, may lead her to doubt herself. This may lead her to put more pressure on him, in which case their relationship may be an insidious triangle of energetics that leaves both feeling stultified.

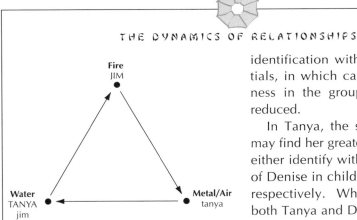

identification with his child potentials, in which case Jim's effectiveness in the group will be greatly
reduced.

In Tanya, the supervisor Denise
may find her greatest ally. Tanya can
either identify with or be supportive
of Denise in child and adult aspects
respectively. When under stress,
both Tanya and Denise have similar
responses and thus may reinforce
each other in their child natal expression. However, Tanya can slip out of
this pattern more easily, coming into
her one-water adult aspect. As water
is the mother of tree/space, Tanya's
adult expression, her ability to
reflect, respond with consideration
and communicate well with all
tree/space individuals, may provide
Denise with the kind of clarity and
support she needs to come back into
her adult four-tree/space expression.

*Figure 32. A Five Transformation
chart for Tanya and Jim*

This particular triangle has the
potential for being the most volatile
in the group process. However, this
all depends on how much Jim acts
out of his nine-fire adult potential. If
he experiences his water transformation as more dominant, then Tanya's
six-metal child and one-water adult
are nurturing and reinforcing an

A final comment needs to be made regarding the tree/space energetics within this group. The natural air of excitement and ideas holds a lot of positive possibilities for the group. However, since three people have their child aspects in this position (Mike, Dorothy and Dave), there is a strong likelihood that the group will lapse into frustration and dissent. This will, in turn, undermine group spontaneity, sabotage Jane and John's efforts, starve Jane of support and put Denise on the defensive, where she issues ultimatums that only Tanya is willing to accept.

## Phase Four

The strategies within Phase Four can vary according to the group being addressed and the circumstances in which it operates. Recommendations can be of a relational nature, such as how to address specific personal dynamics or general group interaction patterns, or circumstantial, in which case suggestions made may include activities and environmental changes.

In the case of the cardiovascular lab, without making staff changes it is imperative that supervisory efforts be made to tap into the creative energy of three-tree/space that dominates the group. It is with this foremost in mind that the following recommendations are made.

1. Dave and Tanya should be encouraged to share their perspective on the overall running and atmosphere of the lab. Their reflections and comments could be used as a basis for inspiring Jim, Mike, Dorothy, John and Denise. Communications

between these one-water adults and the three- and four-tree/space group may need to be encouraged, especially as it is in the nature of one-water people to be cautious in what they present to others and how they do it. Once Dave and Tanya have presented to the others, feedback from Jane, Mike, Dorothy and John should be encouraged to ensure that what Dave and Tanya have shared is clearly understood.

2. Give the three-tree/space adults a diversity of tasks. Use them for brainstorming new ways of operating. Get them to learn all the different jobs in the lab so that they can not only fill in for one another, but possibly even change positions at will from time to time.

3. Encourage Jim to overcome his

caution and 'run with the ball'; to catalyze whatever it is that Jane, Mike, Dorothy and John come up with. Ideas from Mike, Dorothy and Dave may at times be impulsive, because of their attempts to overcome self-doubt (especially Mike and Dorothy), but Jim should hear them out. His comments and actions on their suggestions may improve their overall response in the group.

4. In times of stress, Mike, Dorothy and Dave may be the focal group for frustration and anger within the lab. To balance this tendency, meetings should be arranged where the adult three-tree/space qualities of Jane and John are utilized, together with the structuring and conflict management skills of Denise. Tanya can provide support for a more mature approach

from Dave and support others in allowing the adult, rather than the child, quality of the three-tree/space transformation to emerge. She can also be a helpful ally for Denise.

5. Given the fact that no one in the lab is in an adult earth or metal/air position energetically to complete tasks, Jim should be encouraged to provide moral support to John, Jane and Tanya in their efforts. What may thwart this is that Jane can lapse into hopelessness and John into indecisiveness and worry given their three-tree/space controlling adult energetics. However, because they also naturally empower Jim, they may be able to over-ride their personal tendencies as they interact with him. Jim's relationship to Tanya may not directly support task completion. However, it may help her to overcome her tendency to take on too much responsibility and any sense of guilt in her functioning in the lab.

6. This staff team has a lot of physical energy. People should be encouraged to take exercise at lunch time, or at least once a day. Organize group walks or even stress management sessions where stretching, breathing and relaxation exercises are taught. Rechannelling such physical energy will improve morale and relations. Even the encouragement of a good hug between workers during the day may go a long way in breaking up any tension. (This is based on the fact that the primary ways in which three-tree/space people feel nurtured is through touch and contact.)

7. With a dominance of three-

tree/space energy in the group, lighting, colour and a sense of spaciousness in the working environment are important. Lighting should be as natural as possible; replace fluorescent bulbs with full-spectrum and incandescent ones. There should be green and blue colours throughout the physical space – plants would be a good idea. Water and tree/space people are sensitive to electromagnetic influences. Computer display terminals should have protective screening and be turned off when not in use. The use of asynchronous natural sound and music can also help to mellow the naturally intense atmosphere that such a group generates.

8. A suggestion box and other means of facilitating the expression of the constant flood of ideas coming from the team is essential. Innovation need not imply revolution. However, if one does not acknowledge their innovative ways, there will be revolutions.

9. When interviewing for new staff in the future, look for more earth and metal/air adults. Being service-oriented, they will enhance the success and bring balance to the lab and staff.

## ONE STEP FURTHER: BIRTH CHARTS FOR ORGANIZATIONS, GROUPS AND EVENTS

As I said in the Introduction, all things must go through a process of conception, gestation, maturation and manifestation. This applies to both the animal and the vegetable kingdoms.

In the realm of human beings, it also applies to our endeavours. For example, two people meet, they like each other, they court and they get married – the marriage being a manifest statement of their love for each other. The same applies to a business or organization. A person or a group gets an idea, they work out the details, and, at some point, that idea becomes an entity – a product or enterprise of some sort.

In the Orient, the time at which one establishes an enterprise or embarks upon a venture is not left to chance. Astrologers are consulted for auspicious dates and times. Geomancers are consulted regarding the appropriate place, construction, etc. Recently, while living in Kentucky, I observed how a major Japanese motor car company which was trying to establish a plant in that state, used numerology and astrology to come up with the right place and the right offer at the right time. One can also ponder the actions of Ronald Reagan, who seemed to get apparently unpopular ideas approved, and to act in ways that probably would have caused more of a stir had he not chosen the right timing. People scorned the Reagans' use of astrology. Considering their success and popularity, however, it may behove others to look more closely at this approach and consider whether it is not more than mere superstition. In early 1991, the United States decided to go to war with Iraq. The deadline for the initiation of military action was set for 15 January of that year. Was it just coincidence that this day also corresponded to a new moon and a solar eclipse, and was a day that was very significant in Tibetan astrology?

Trying to arrange events in accordance with Nine Star Ki merely requires knowing how to calculate the numbers for given dates and what energetics you want to have present when the event occurs. The more you study the profiles, narratives and various aspects of the number combinations, the more you will have a clearer sense of what the dynamics will be at the time of the venture.

Besides this predictive quality, when analyzing the dynamics of an event, group or enterprise that already exists, you can treat the origination date, be it an event, the date of incorporation of a company, or the signing of a contract, as the birthdate and calculate the dynamics present at the time just as you would do for an individual.

## What is the value of such calculations for groups or businesses?

Just as individuals go through peak times, challenging times and low times, the same is true for any venture. In a business, you can see when operations have gone smoothly; when they have not; whether there are noticeable cycles in financial growth, times of expansion and times of recession or slow down; and whether there are times when personnel work better together than others.

Treating the origination date of a group or business as a birth-date, you can also look at the dynamics of the enterprise as an entity in relation to the people working for it. Given the dynamics of an enterprise, how have individuals within that enterprise functioned? Are they well placed? How can you create a more cohesive support system for your enterprise?

The implications of using Nine Star Ki in such a manner are far-reaching. Not only can a business or organization be steered in accordance with the energetics of the time, but changes needed within (such as staff appointments, re-configurations, hirings or redundancies) can be tailored to give the optimal internal dynamics for the desired external results, whether they be increased production, profit or anything else.

## SOME GENERAL REMARKS

After making such detailed observations of individual and group behaviours and listing specific recommendations as found in Phase Four, the steering of a group in such a way may often seem awkward or contrived. In order to manifest our adult natal potentials, there has to be a sense of personal empowerment, a certain level of basic confidence and trust in who we are. When this is not present, it is an indication that our child natal potentials persist and may even dominate our lives on various levels. To create an atmosphere in a group process where the adult natal potentials are expressed more than the child potentials and the resultant personal stress patterns is a challenge, but it is necessary for healthy personal and interpersonal growth and interaction. Thus it is a goal worth pursuing.

One of the first issues that needs to be addressed in working towards this goal is to confront the denial that the group is operating out of the child natal patterns. In fact, denial promotes elevated stress and disease – more so even than the child natal energetics themselves. Confrontation of this denial can take the form of any number of strategies, the intention of which is to make it less and less of a viable option in our behaviour and ways of thinking. Once the breakthrough is achieved and we get in touch with and can accept the way that we are living our lives, the space created in our expression gives room for the adult natal characteristics to emerge.

My personal observation in seeing this happen is that individuals in a group are hesitant at first, begin gradually to see and experience the truth of Nine Star Ki, and then express in a more whole-hearted way traits and ways of being that feel new, yet natural at the same time. It is almost as if a large burden had been lifted from their shoulders. Then people learn to assert themselves naturally, no longer apologizing for who they are.

Not apologizing for who they are does not mean that they become pig-headed or obnoxious in their interactions. In fact, I have observed that as people accept themselves more, they relax, become less defensive and have more compassion and time for those around them. So much of the pain in relating is our own self-uncertainty and projected neuroses. As these become less solid, the barriers between individuals become less and less significant. Openness, humour and inquisitiveness emerge as natural ways of interacting.

This does not mean that the adult natal way of being doesn't possess challenges. It is just that being personally empowered, being in and

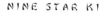

relating to the world we live in is less of an effort. There may still be exertion. There remains the fact that the combinations of some transformation energetics are smoother than others, both within our own being and when relating to others. But whereas effort implies history and working against or in spite of something – usually limitations we impose on ourselves or think others are imposing on us (more often than not, a projection) – exertion in its purest sense is dynamic, present-moment, intentional movement. The past is no longer something that we have to work our way out of. Rather it becomes a foundation upon which new and creative directions in our lives can be built.

# A Final Word

Our migration through the years and all their transformations gave us the opportunity to experience and appreciate life in all its possible elemental permutations. We are given a chance to become whole, mature individuals just by remaining open to what life offers us. The gift of relating to others is that this whole process is speeded up. Each individual that walks into our lives provides us with an on-the-spot opportunity to expand and share in a dance, a weaving and blending of natal energetics and potentials that can enrich our lives, if we only remain open and allow ourselves to view the world in wholeness, rather than in separation.

Opening our hearts and minds, the fiction of separation dissolves of its own accord. In the end, the way we relate to ourselves is the way we relate to our world and to others. If we do not see ourselves as separate from the world or other people, then we are not. If that is so, then every moment and every interaction becomes a spontaneous expression of life, of transformational forces in a beautiful, harmonious dance. As we embrace others in this spirit, we embrace the world and ourselves.

Towards that end, may this book be of benefit.

# Anecdote
## A Personal Account
### by Marcia Sutton, PhD

'How was your dream trip to Europe, Marcia?' I was asked many times when I returned from two months of field research in Italy, France and the British Isles in the summer of 1990. My friends expected a positive answer, rave reviews. After all, how could it be a hardship to visit Europe's ancient sacred places to gather data for a forthcoming book.

But it *was* hard, up to a point.

Before leaving home, I had received a Nine Star Ki astrology reading from my friend Bob Sachs. The reading showed an amazing pattern when it was overlaid on my European itinerary. Without exception, every time I planned to turn north, east, south or west, I would be facing a difficult or troublesome aspect. I would not be in danger, but wonderful experiences (the norm of my life) wouldn't be plentiful either. Never mind. I had planned this trip for a year and I would proceed, even though the preparations had become tedious rather than fun. It *had* to be the right time to go, because I could, I wanted to, I would do it.

It was uncanny how the timing and directions of my itinerary pointed me at the most taxing aspects of myself every time. Bob said I would be facing my adult self. I could meet the challenges as a wanting, needing child and feel affronted, or I could meet them as a capable, mature person and grow with each opportunity.

Before leaving home, as I absorbed this astrological reading, of course I assumed that I would take the mature path. Once I was on the road, however, I did not always feel I had the strength to be so objective.

So what happened? I was to leave on Monday, after turning in grades the previous Friday for the courses I taught at the university. That week, my eighty-year-old father was suddenly hospitalized and needed a pacemaker. Was this a sign that I should stay in the States? I flew to Pennsylvania to be with him and then went on to London. But in London, there was no hotel reservation for me because the travel agent had not confirmed it in writing. That hotel was full but they found me a room nearby. On a hunch I phoned ahead to Paris to my next hotel: no reservation because of no written confirmation, but they would make room for me for a night or two. Fine.

A world-famous museum in London that I had waited a decade to see was disappointing; the exhibits I was most interested in were not on display. The old church of the Knights Templar was closed. But many things went right. The weather was decent. The Underground was an efficient transport system. Two

'walking tours' of old London revealed fascinating, mysterious parts of the city. Next stop, Paris.

The same pattern occurred. Fortunate events (such as getting the last ticket to a flamenco dance appearance) were balanced by unfortunate events (such as the most important window in Chartres Cathedral having been removed for cleaning, my hotel being torn apart for remodelling and the parrots in the breakfast room gone, being shoved out of line by German tourists).

By this time I realized that my biggest mistake was to think I could wrench myself away from my network of loving family and friends without emotional loss. I had never been so lonely! I had never needed comfort and support so badly. I had expected to meet lots of 'interesting people' but everyone seemed to be connected already except me. Every single person I had planned to see, whether friend or professional contact, couldn't make it: sick/phone disconnected/out of town – the reasons varied but the result was the same. When I found out that the Dalai Lama would be in northern Italy the same week that I was there, I tried every way to rearrange my schedule so I could see him. But there were no hotel rooms, or when he would be close enough for me to travel by train or bus for a day trip, he was not having any public audiences that day.

I was catching on to the meaning of the astrological reading. A series of small challenges was coming at me like tennis balls: here, hit this one. Here, field that one. The trip continued like that for weeks.

My husband joined me for a tour of France. We were disappointed at the Disney-World atmosphere pervading the more famous sacred sites we visited. This wouldn't do at all for the book I had in mind.

This buffeting of good and ill fortune went on until I re-routed myself. Instead of going to Spain as planned, my husband and I reversed direction and went to England. From that moment on, our fortunes improved. We spent time at powerful sacred sites, so remote and uncommercialized that one had to hunt diligently in the fog to locate them. We had a seaside picnic on a cliff at Land's End, stayed in a big Victorian room, drove down country lanes so narrow that the mirrors on both sides of the car were brushed by the growing crops. We were touched by the beauty and the mystery of the sites we were privileged to visit and the people who were making similar pilgrimages.

So when my friends back home asked how my trip had been, I answered, 'Difficult, memorable, challenging, well worth it. I learned as much about myself as I did about the sacred places of Europe.'

# Appendices

# 1 ASPECTS OF THE FIVE TRANSFORMATIONS

| Element | Tree/Space | Fire | Earth | Metal/Air | Water |
|---|---|---|---|---|---|
| **Season** | Spring | Early Summer | Late Summer Solstices & Equinoxes | Autumn | Winter |
| **Colour** | Green | Red | Yellow | White | Black |
| **Direction** | East | South | Centre | West | North |
| **Associated Nine Star Ki Numbers** | 3,4 | 9 | 2,5,8 | 6,7 | 1 |
| **Associated Yin organs** | Gall Bladder | Small Intestine, Triple Warmer | Stomach | Large Intestine | Bladder |
| **Associated Yang organs** | Liver | Heart, Heart Governor | Spleen/Pancreas | Lungs | Kidneys |
| **Time of day activated** | Gall Bladder (11pm–1am) Liver (1–3am) | Small Intestine (1–3pm) Triple Warmer (9–11pm) Heart (11am–1pm) Heart Governor (7–9pm) | Stomach (7–9am) Spleen/Pancreas (9–11pm) | Lower Intestine (5–7am) Lungs (3–5am) | Bladder (3–5pm) Kidneys (5–7pm) |
|  |  |  |  |  |  |

NINE STAR KI

| Element | Tree/Space | Fire | Earth | Metal/Air | Water |
|---|---|---|---|---|---|
| **Associated body formation** | Connective Tissue, Muscles | Blood Vessels | Flesh | Skin, Body Hair | Bones, Head Hair |
| **Associated sense organ** | Eye (Sight) | Tongue (Speech) | Mouth (Taste) | Nose (Smell) | Ears (Hearing) |
| **Associated secretion** | Tears | Sweat | Saliva | Mucus | Urine |
| **Taste** | Sour | Bitter | Sweet | Pungent | Salty |
| **Emotion (& extremes)** | Irritability (Anger) | Joy (Hysteria) | Empathy (Obsessiveness) | Reflection (Sentimentality) | Caution (Fear) |
| **Voice expression** | Shout | Laugh | Sing | Weep | Groan |
| **Faculty** | Spiritual | Inspirational | Intellectual | Vital | Will |
| **Illness first detected in** | Throat & Neck | Chest & Ribs | Spine | Shoulders & Back | Loins & Thighs |
| **Time of acute problems** | Spring | Early Summer | Any Time | Autumn | Winter |
| **Time of chronic problems** | Autumn | Winter | Any Time | Spring | Summer |
| **Celestial influence** | Jupiter | Mars | Earth | Venus | Mercury |

*Figure 33. Aspects of the Five Transformations*

# 2 THEORY SUPPORTING NINE STAR KI

## HEAVEN, EARTH AND MAN: THE PRINCIPLE OF MACROCOSM AND MICROCOSM

One of the basic principles implicit in Oriental thought is that we are a microcosm of a greater macrocosm: that we are integrally connected with the world that we perceive, that our outer world is a reflection of our inner world, and vice versa. The separation between the two is illusory. Distinctions between the seeming two are merely linguistically useful and mundanely convenient. If taken too literally or seriously the resulting dualism leads to all sorts of confusion, misunderstandings and a host of personal and planetary problems.

Ultimately it is being ignorant of our inter-connectedness with our world that is the source of all our human mischief.

History tells of the many men and women throughout time and around the world who from a yearning for truth devised systems to explore both our inner and outer reality. Amongst those searchers were the philosophers and sages of the East who came to see that the laws that governed the energetic properties in nature applied not only to plants and animals, but to all life, including humans. For example, the I Ching arose out of an intuitive understanding of the relationship between what the literature describes as heaven, earth and man. Yearly and seasonal cycles, human psychology and physiology, social and political law and reform and the art of geomancy – *Feng shui,* to name a few aspects of life, all arise from a common knowledge base. Thus in describing politics it is not unusual to find metaphors from nature or human physiology. And it is not unusual for corollaries to be drawn from one aspect of nature to another. That different aspects of reality share similar properties, energetics and ways of functioning is one way the sages were able to prove the macro-cosmic/microcosmic premiss.

## THE ENERGETICS OF NATURE, ACUPUNCTURE THEORY, AND THE FIVE TRANSFORMATIONS

One of the most profound of ancient sciences was the understanding of energetics and principles of change as found in the acupuncture system. This system was not only for understanding human functioning, ailments and cures, but it also had a cosmic vision.

Masters of this system observed that there is a central magnetically charged core to the human form: an electromagnetic field running from the crown of the head to a point just behind the scrotum in a man or back of the vagina in a woman. There is a positive and a negative pole to this core. Around this core are two central electrical lines (or meridians – the acupuncture term) constantly circulating the energy from this charged central core. Off these two primary meridians arise the twelve other major meridians that are either more positively or more negatively charged. These twelve form the electromagnetic basis for the growth, sustenance and demise of all major body organs, systems and their related functions. These meridians are not a random phenomenon, but a power grid which runs throughout the body, on the body's surface and out to a distance of one hand span from the body surface. There are circuit breakers – areas of low electrical impulse – along all of these meridians. These are the acupuncture points.

The central core of the body runs at about a 23° tilt from the polar end at our heads to the polar end between our legs. Interestingly enough, this is the same tilt as the Earth has on its axis as it moves through space. We also know that there are electromagnetic lines which weave around the Earth's North and South Poles. The Van Allen belts are akin to the body's

aura. Ley lines – known to earth mystics, geomancers, and diviners – are like the Earth's acupuncture meridians with sacred or power spots like the body's acupuncture points. (It is even interesting to see how over such points, civilizations have erected pyramids, obelisks and various monolithic structures as if they were giant acupuncture needles pulling in cosmic energies in the same way that needles applied to the body's acupuncture points are used to stabilize the electromagnetic force in a meridian by changing or draining it.)

As the human electromagnetic patterns are similar to planetary electromagnetic patterns, it stands to reason that if planetary electromagnetic patterns are altered, a similar shift would be observed on the microcosmic (human) level. And

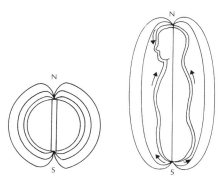

Figure 34. The electromagnetic fields
of earth and man

The electromagnetic forces in nature and in the human form undergo five seemingly distinct but interdependent transformation phases. These are the gestation, maturation, consolidation, completion and resting phases. The Chinese acupuncture theory gives these transformations more elemental names: wood or space, fire, earth, metal or air, and water respectively. All life forms, be they plant or animal (including human), go through and are embodiments of all these elemental transformations. And while a plant or animal may be more obviously going through one particular transformation phase, all the other phases are present on a more subtle level. From the most observable expressions of living organisms right down to the cellular level, these transformations are going on continuously.

although Chinese and other Oriental sages were not familiar with the language of modern physics, their keen sense of observation led them to detect subtle changes in the electromagnetic forces around them; changes that have a cyclical nature, affecting plants, animals, human characteristics, consciousness and interaction, and the world in general.

At the same time, while all these transformations can be observed in all things, each has its own seat – a place or system in which the particular way in which a transformative phase expresses itself is more dominant. Thus, in the case of humans there are organs, systems and ways of being in the world that are – in the language of acupuncture – more wood/space-like, fire-like, earth-like, etc. (When we speak of organs, systems and ways of being, we include levels of consciousness, as Oriental thought does not draw a distinction between physiological and psychological, or body and mind, manifestations and functions. All physiological and psychological phenomena, including body gestures, speech and inflections, thought dominance – to name but a few – are linked and interdependent in a way that is observable and classifiable in accordance with the Chinese Law of Five Transformations.)

Oriental sages observed that although these Five Transformations are taking place continuously, there are variations in the dominance of one transformation over the others according to time: the time of day and the months and seasons as well as the years. Each hour of the day is dominated by either wood/space, fire, earth, metal/air or water transformative-type energy. Spring is associated with wood or space; early and mid-summer with fire; solstices, equinoxes and late summer with earth; autumn with metal or air; and winter with water.

To live in accordance with the cycles of the days, the months and the seasons helps to create balance and health on a day-to-day basis.

However, sages could also see that the larger cycles, and more particularly a cycle of nine years, has a more profound and lasting influence on our condition and basic psychophysical constitution.

## WHY NINE STAR AND WHAT IS KI?

Although our planet's polar axis is tilted at 23° with the star Polaris in Ursa Minor above its northern pole, this is not a constant. Modern astronomers know that approximately every 26,000 years the Earth 'flops' to a position where the star Vega in the constellation Lyra becomes the pole star. This shift is fairly dramatic. However, there is a less dramatic wobbling that our planet makes on its axis, a wobbling that invariably alters the north-south polarity.

Sages of the past were able to observe nine distinguishable electromagnetic phases in this wobbling. Astrology and astronomy were both sciences in those days, so it was determined that as there are nine stars in the northern sky closely centred around the northern end of the Earth's polar axis – Polaris, Vega and the seven stars that make up Ursa Major (the Big Bear) – they are responsible for the slight electromagnetic shift that occurs. Thus, as Nine Star Ki theory has it, each star is integrally a part of and responsible for each of the distinguishable electromagnetic phases.

When our planet is under the influence of one of the particular electromagnetic phases, one of the transformation phases or transformations mentioned earlier becomes accentuated. Thus there are fire years, earth years, water years, and so on with all elemental or transformation phases represented within a nine-year cycle. The cycle begins with a fire year, followed by an earth year, followed by two metal/air years, followed by an earth year, then two wood/space years, another earth year, and finally a water year which leads us back into another fire year to begin a new cycle. As particular transformations are accentuated from year to year, so it is also that each of the transformation's more positive and negative charges is accentuated. This leads us into a brief discussion of yin, yang and ki.

'Ki' must first be mentioned. This is the Japanese term for *chi* in Chinese, and *prana* in Sanskrit. Roughly translated into English it is 'life force'. It is a force that pervades all of life. It is associated with con-sciousness and the will. Its source is the subject of philosophical and theological speculation. It is the mastery of 'ki' which is at the central core of martial arts. The various yogic systems of Buddhism, Hinduism, Taoism and other traditions utilize the awareness of this subtle force and our ability to work with it in order to achieve the end states or realization as perceived by such systems.

On a fairly crude level, the presence of ki is detected by the presence of an electromagnetic force, which again is detected on subtle or crude levels: the aura, the psychic channels and vortices (chakras) of the body, the acupuncture meridian system, the autonomic system and finally the central nervous system. Such electromagnetic force is only noticeable when there is a slightly more positive or negative charge present. And for movement and life to be present, there must be a continuous fluctuation in the dominance of positive and negative charges. The acupuncture system goes on to point out that with a more positive charge, life forms or functions seem to go into a relatively more contractive state as opposed to a more expanded, relaxed state when the negative charge is dominant. Using the macrobiotic theories of George Ohsawa we classify the positive/contractive state as being yang and the negative/expansive state as being yin. This differs from classical Chinese acupuncture theory, which would reverse the terminology. This does not alter the functional or usable aspects of this theory, so the macrobiotic interpretation is what I have used in this volume.

## YIN AND YANG

Nothing is solely yin. Nothing is solely yang. The flow of ki means that the apparent opposite is present when there is a positive or a negative electromagnetic dominance.

In Figure 35, we are looking at a static representation of yin and yang force. If we were to look at each one of the transformation phases, we would see a dominance of either the lighter area (yang) or the darker area (yin). Even then, such a representa-

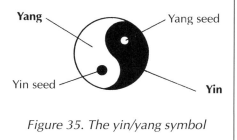

*Figure 35. The yin/yang symbol*

tion would need a third dimension to demonstrate the subtlety of this system.

To summarize briefly, life force or ki pervades all life and is detected or experienced in a relatively more yin or yang state. The fluctuation between yin and yang is continuous, with certain states of balance represented as one of the Five Transformations. As our planet wobbles through space, the ki flow of our world is altered. Thus different transformation phases with a relatively more yin or yang expression of the ki flow become accentuated.

Being interested in systems and ways of codifying data within systems, sages who worked with the Five Transformations and the laws of yin and yang began at some point in time – perhaps in accordance with the history presented – to ascribe numerical values to each of the trans-

formations. Numerical values and the construction of lined trigrams and hexagrams representing numerical value – hence transformations – is the basis of the I Ching, probably the most complete presentation of Chinese thought and source from which a *fully* systematized Nine-House or Nine Star Ki astrological system emerged. Thus, when looking at a Nine Star Ki astrological chart, rather than seeing elements or signs as in other astrological systems, one sees a system of numbers that have been systematically calculated for a given individual.

Figure 36 shows all nine years of a cycle with transformation phase, yin/yang dominance, numerical value and trigram structure.

The Nine Star Ki system most widely used has the numbers and their respective transformation

| Transformation Phase (Element) | Yin/Yang | Number | Trigram | |
|---|---|---|---|---|
| Fire | Yin | 9 | ☲ | (Li) |
| Earth | Yang | 8 | ☶ | (Ken) |
| Air/Metal | Yin | 7 | ☱ | (Tui) |
| Air/Metal | Yang | 6 | ☰ | (Ch'ien) |
| Earth | Yin/Yang | 5 | ⭘ | |
| Tree/Space | Yin | 4 | ☴ | (Sun) |
| Tree/Space | Yang | 3 | ☳ | (Chen) |
| Earth | Yin | 2 | ☷ | (Kun) |
| Water | Yang | 1 | ☵ | (Kan) |

*Figure 36. The relationship between year number and transformation phase*

phases descending in order through time, nine to one. Nine (fire) is considered the most yin or expanded number with each successive number being more contracted, even though the numbers become more intense as they approach 'one', each number reveals a more yielding or open (yin), or active and insular (yang) side to its nature. Figure 37 is a graph of the cycle of nine years based on the contracting movement with yin and yang variations.

Excluding the peculiarities of each of the transformation phases for a moment, the general trend of intensification of the years over a nine-year cycle can be observed. For example

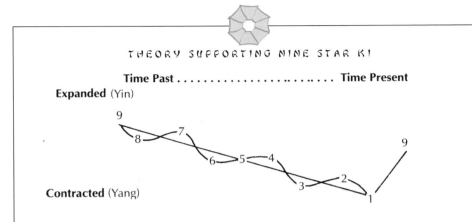

**Time Past . . . . . . . . . . . . . . . . . . . . .. . . . Time Present**

**Expanded** (Yin)

**Contracted** (Yang)

*Figure 37. Nine years along a time continuum*

there are years when we feel that events and our lives are moving rather slowly, other years when they move more quickly. It could be argued that this is a subjective experience, that it just has to do with our personal experience. However, there is another level of subjectivity: our basic human experience which transcends our individual subjective peculiarities. It is this level of subjectivity that we are addressing.

On a more observable level, sages noted that certain vegetation and animal life was more dominant or active, relatively speaking, in a particular year. They would see how in one year apples or carrots might be more prolific while in other years they would do poorly while squashes and melons did well. This was observed to have more to do with yearly cycles than with the results of human effort.

As with the plant or animal kingdoms – and here more specifically human beings – it was noted that certain physiological and psychological characteristics are dominant in given years with changes of the months and years producing people of different qualities. For example, people born in certain years seem to be more physically agile than those born in other years. Some years, it was noted, produced people who are more philosophical; other years, natural born leaders. And in the lifespan of any person, just like a carrot, there are easy months and years and difficult months and years, determined by the interaction of original birth characteristics with changes in transformation dominance in the cycle of months and years.

This is difficult for modern individualistic humans to accept only because of a basic lack of understanding of the world, an attachment to preconceived ideas and a determination to hold on to what seems familiar and deny anything or anyone that indicates the contrary. The resulting insensitivity to the inter-connectedness we have with the world around us puts us under the influence of arrogance – the function of our ignorance, attachment and aggression – where any serendipitous event or connections we feel towards others are regarded as the products of our individual efforts.

## THE SPECIAL QUALITY OF NINE STAR KI AS AN ASTROLOGICAL SYSTEM

It is interesting to note that just as there are twelve houses or zodiac signs in conventional astrology, there are twelve major acupuncture meridians that run along the human body. Being electromagnetic in nature, as we saw earlier, the stars and planets within the conventional zodiacal system have their influence, and that influence can be far-reaching.

At the same time, acupuncture theory postulates that the general constitutional strengths of the twelve

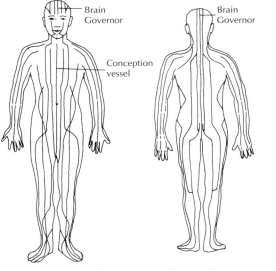

*Figure 38. The two central meridians*

meridians of the body are determined by the yin/yang balance and ki flow of two other – and more central – meridians: the brain governor and the conception vessel. These two meridians run vertically along the central vertical plane of the body, the central core of which is the north/south polar axis of the body.

Conventional astrology has always demonstrated the interconnection between mind, body and spirit, pointing out how certain signs impact on certain organs, systems of the body or states of mind. This is true for Nine Star Ki as well. However, whereas one may find that one shares similar experiences and life situations with those of a similar astrological sign, the traits that one shares with others whose Nine Star Ki numbers are the same seem to run much deeper. The issue is no longer what one experiences, but how one experiences in the first place. 'What' implies product; 'how' implies process.

By analogy, whereas conventional astrology can present you a tapestry of your life, the images and quality of which you can learn to accept and move along with based on what is presented, Nine Star Ki is like looking directly at the quality of the threads within the images. If one knows the colours, textures and qualities of the threads, one has greater latitude in tightening or loosening the weave, even changing the image in so far as conditions allow. What both I and Nine Star Ki expert Rex Lassalle have observed is that sidereal-based astrologies, such as the Indian Vedic system, come closest in being able to identify as central to a person's being, the core traits that are readily identified by the Nine Star Ki.

Like other astrological systems that speak of the migration of houses and coming under the dominance of various planets in various increments of time, this is also true of Nine Star Ki. What the ki takes into consideration is that given one's particular transformation phase dominances and the specific time frame with its dominant characteristics, obvious and fairly predictable ways of feeling and experiencing the world will occur, based on how various transformations interact as postulated in acupuncture theory. This adds texture to our basic ways of being and will be the backdrop upon which the events of our lives will be laid out. In *An Anthology of I Ching*, Sherrill and Chu summarize this point most appropriately and provide an excellent overview of the value and purpose of Nine Star Ki:

*In Nine House astrology a man or woman is not simply born in a particular 'house', but during his or her lifetime migrates through the yearly, monthly, daily and hourly sequences many times. The belief behind this is that man can and should become as perfectly balanced as possible through facing and overcoming all the varied experience presented to him as a result of the influences of the various 'houses'. People follow different patterns because of the influences permanently imprinted upon them at their particular times of birth. The rules that carry them through these cycles remain constant, and it depends upon their state of wisdom as to how well they apply them. The different situations different people face are determined by their state of evolution at the time they re-enter this world. The strength and intensity of troubles or good fortune depend on the strength and (cosmic) maturity of the individual. These considerations lend Nine House astrology a philosophical aspect as well.[7]*

# 3 THE TWENTY-FOUR SEASONS

With this twenty-four season concept, the year is divided into thirteen months with shorter time increments around the winter solstice. Rather than starting the monthly calendar close to the start of the Chinese New Year, it begins right after the winter solstice. Thus the ascribing of natal month numbers at that time of year differs from Figure 5 on page 27. You are advised to see whether the chart in Figure 5 or the following chart based on one shown in Sherrill and Chu: *An Anthology of I Ching,* is more appropriate for you.

NINE STAR KI

**In the year**

| Approximate dates | 1, 4, 7 | 2, 5, 8 | 3, 6, 9 | 24 Seasons | |
|---|---|---|---|---|---|
| 22 Dec–5 Jan | 1 | 4 | 7 | (1) winter solstice | |
| 6 Jan–3 Feb | 9 | 3 | 6 | (2) little cold | (3) severe cold |
| 4 Feb–5 Mar | 8 | 2 | 5 | (4) spring begins | (5) rain water |
| 6 Mar–4 Apr | 7 | 1 | 4 | (6) excited insects | (7) vernal equinox |
| 5 Apr–5 May | 6 | 9 | 3 | (8) clear and bright | (9) grain rains |
| 6 May–5 Jun | 5 | 8 | 2 | (10) summer begins | (11) grain fills |
| 6 Jun–7 Jul | 4 | 7 | 1 | (12) grain in ears | (13) summer solstice |
| 8 Jul–7 Aug | 3 | 6 | 9 | (14) slight heat | (15) great heat |
| 8 Aug–7 Sep | 2 | 5 | 8 | (16) autumn begins | (17) limit of heat |
| 8 Sep–8 Oct | 1 | 4 | 7 | (18) white dew | (19) autumnal equinox |
| 9 Oct–7 Nov | 9 | 3 | 6 | (20) cold dew | (21) hoar frost descends |
| 8 Nov–7 Dec | 8 | 2 | 5 | (22) winter begins | (23) little snow |
| 8 Dec–21 Dec | 7 | 1 | 4 | (24) heavy snow | |

*Figure 39. Descending natal month numbers according to the twenty-four season concept*

# 4 DESCENDING AND ASCENDING NUMBERS THROUGH TIME: A CONSIDERATION FOR BOTH SEXES

Although the descending order of numbers from nine to one through the years is used for both men and women in the Japanese system, this is not so in the Chinese system. The direction of numbers from nine to one is considered to be an overall contracting (yang) direction, even though there are both expanding (yin) and contracting (yang) variations in the numbers movement. The Chinese considered this yang direction to be more masculine and hence ascribed it to men (as yang is associated with masculine/male energy). For them, therefore, there also had to be a more yin or expanding cycle within the years – and numbers – over time that would be best suited to feminine energy. Thus the numbers for women are considered to go in the opposite direction, that is one to nine through the years, with the number three being the only year common to men and women. This also means that in any given year there is, in this Chinese system, a different transformation phase that is dominant for men and women.

It has been my experience and the experience of Nine Star Ki specialist Rex Lassalle that the Japanese system of descending numbers through the years works best for both men and women as regards personal characteristics and stress patterns on both physiological and psychological levels. However, this may only be because of what appears to be the dominance of and emphasis on the masculine persona in this time period. This being the case, it may even be that women, on physiological and psychological levels, are sacrificing something innately feminine in their being, and are identifying – either consciously or unconsciously – with this persona. Thus they could manifest the same patterns or tendencies as their male counterparts of any particular year.

Taking this hypothesis out of a gender context, Nine Star Ki master Michio Kushi contends that the reason why the descending (yang) order works best for both men and women in this time is that the yang order represents a more materialistic way of being and that the world culture at present is currently more caught up in such a way of thinking and being. The yin or ascending progression represents a more spiritual direction.[8]

In my consultations with many clients and from the discussions I have had with noted Italian astrologer Annamaria Poclen, the significance of the ascending order appears to be emerging. And it seems to be significant for men as well as women. This is in keeping with both contemporary Western and Vedic astrology which both indicate the beginnings of a shift, occurring now, out of the depths of materialism towards a more spiritual orientation. Of course, we would all like to believe that this 'New Age' is the dominant paradigm at this point in time. But, if we look around, it is self-evident that we still have a long way to go.

In any event, as women self-actualize, they may notice that more and more of the traits connected to the numbers associated with the ascending order surface in their lives. For women, this change is very empowering, as is indicated by, for example, the re-emergence of the goddess archetype in Western culture. It is clear that this is a time when, increasingly, the roles of women extend beyond conventional sexual stereotypes, affecting the nature of business, families and virtually every social institution. And for men, we see the emergence of a recognition of the female aspect of being, but the issue is more murky. I would argue that for many of them the emerging need to attend to their feminine side can initiate doubts about their core sexuality, thereby leading to what I and Annamaria Poclen witness as being faux-homo-sexuality – in which some men believe they are gay primarily because they are confronted by feelings and impressions that appear to fly in the face of the dominant, but fading, male paradigm of the times.

Therefore, although – as each individual makes their towards self-actualization in this current world situation – the descending order is of utmost importance and needs to be addressed as a priority, the ascending order should be studied for more in-depth Nine Star Ki evaluations and, at least, recognized as an emerging force in the process of a person becoming whole.

Although the descending (yang) natal number progression is easy to calculate mathematically with the given formula, this is not so for the yin pattern. To make calculations easier and avoid confusion for everyone, a chart for a significant part of this era and the future using the yin or ascending natal number progressions for both years and months is presented here (Figures 40, 41 and 42).

| Year | Number | Year | Number | Year | Number | Year | Number |
|------|--------|------|--------|------|--------|------|--------|
| 1896 | 1 | 1925 | 3 | 1954 | 5 | 1983 | 7 |
| 1897 | 2 | 1926 | 4 | 1955 | 6 | 1984 | 8 |
| 1898 | 3 | 1927 | 5 | 1956 | 7 | 1985 | 9 |
| 1899 | 4 | 1928 | 6 | 1957 | 8 | 1986 | 1 |
| 1900 | 5 | 1929 | 7 | 1958 | 9 | 1987 | 2 |
| 1901 | 6 | 1930 | 8 | 1959 | 1 | 1988 | 3 |
| 1902 | 7 | 1931 | 9 | 1960 | 2 | 1989 | 4 |
| 1903 | 8 | 1932 | 1 | 1961 | 3 | 1990 | 5 |
| 1904 | 9 | 1933 | 2 | 1962 | 4 | 1991 | 6 |
| 1905 | 1 | 1934 | 3 | 1963 | 5 | 1992 | 7 |
| 1906 | 2 | 1935 | 4 | 1964 | 6 | 1993 | 8 |
| 1907 | 3 | 1936 | 5 | 1965 | 7 | 1994 | 9 |
| 1908 | 4 | 1937 | 6 | 1966 | 8 | 1995 | 1 |
| 1909 | 5 | 1938 | 7 | 1967 | 9 | 1996 | 2 |
| 1910 | 6 | 1939 | 8 | 1968 | 1 | 1997 | 3 |
| 1911 | 7 | 1940 | 9 | 1969 | 2 | 1998 | 4 |
| 1912 | 8 | 1941 | 1 | 1970 | 3 | 1999 | 5 |
| 1913 | 9 | 1942 | 2 | 1971 | 4 | 2000 | 6 |
| 1914 | 1 | 1943 | 3 | 1972 | 5 | 2001 | 7 |
| 1915 | 2 | 1944 | 4 | 1973 | 6 | 2002 | 8 |
| 1916 | 3 | 1945 | 5 | 1974 | 7 | 2003 | 9 |
| 1917 | 4 | 1946 | 6 | 1975 | 8 | 2004 | 1 |
| 1918 | 5 | 1947 | 7 | 1976 | 9 | 2005 | 2 |
| 1919 | 6 | 1948 | 8 | 1977 | 1 | 2006 | 3 |
| 1920 | 7 | 1949 | 9 | 1978 | 2 | 2007 | 4 |
| 1921 | 8 | 1950 | 1 | 1979 | 3 | 2008 | 5 |
| 1922 | 9 | 1951 | 2 | 1980 | 4 | 2009 | 6 |
| 1923 | 1 | 1952 | 3 | 1981 | 5 | 2010 | 7 |
| 1924 | 2 | 1953 | 4 | 1982 | 6 | 2011 | 8 |

*Figure 40. Years and the yin, or ascending, year numbers*

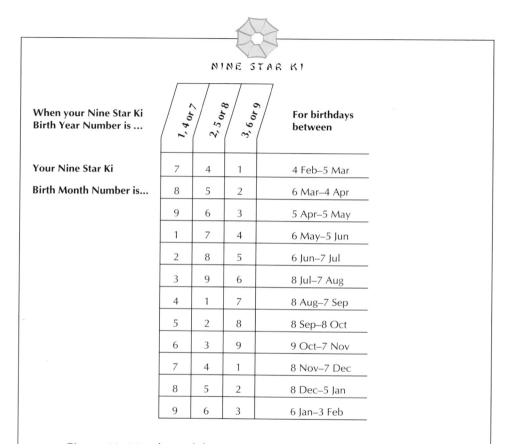

NINE STAR KI

| When your Nine Star Ki Birth Year Number is ... | 1, 4 or 7 | 2, 5 or 8 | 3, 6 or 9 | For birthdays between |
|---|---|---|---|---|
| Your Nine Star Ki Birth Month Number is... | 7 | 4 | 1 | 4 Feb–5 Mar |
| | 8 | 5 | 2 | 6 Mar–4 Apr |
| | 9 | 6 | 3 | 5 Apr–5 May |
| | 1 | 7 | 4 | 6 May–5 Jun |
| | 2 | 8 | 5 | 6 Jun–7 Jul |
| | 3 | 9 | 6 | 8 Jul–7 Aug |
| | 4 | 1 | 7 | 8 Aug–7 Sep |
| | 5 | 2 | 8 | 8 Sep–8 Oct |
| | 6 | 3 | 9 | 9 Oct–7 Nov |
| | 7 | 4 | 1 | 8 Nov–7 Dec |
| | 8 | 5 | 2 | 8 Dec–5 Jan |
| | 9 | 6 | 3 | 6 Jan–3 Feb |

*Figure 41. Months and the yin, or ascending, natal month numbers*

**In the year**

| Approximate dates | 1, 4, 7 | 2, 5, 8 | 3, 6, 9 | 24 Seasons | |
|---|---|---|---|---|---|
| 22 Dec–5 Jan | 5 | 2 | 8 | (1) winter solstice | |
| 6 Jan–5 Feb | 6 | 3 | 9 | (2) little cold | (3) severe cold |
| 4 Feb–5 Mar | 7 | 4 | 1 | (4) spring begins | (5) rain water |
| 6 Mar–4 Apr | 8 | 5 | 2 | (6) excited insects | (7) vernal equinox |
| 5 Apr–5 May | 9 | 6 | 3 | (8) clear and bright | (9) grain rains |
| 6 May–5 Jun | 1 | 7 | 4 | (10) summer begins | (11) grain fills |
| 6 Jun–7 Jul | 2 | 8 | 5 | (12) grain in ears | (13) summer solstice |
| 8 Jul–7 Aug | 3 | 9 | 6 | (14) slight heat | (15) great heat |
| 5 Aug–7 Sep | 4 | 1 | 7 | (16) autumn begins | (17) limit of heat |
| 8 Sep–8 Oct | 5 | 2 | 8 | (18) white dew | (19) autumnal equinox |
| 9 Oct–7 Nov | 6 | 3 | 9 | (20) cold dew | (21) hoar frost descends |
| 8 Nov–7 Dec | 7 | 4 | 1 | (22) winter begins | (23) little snow |
| 8 Dec–21 Dec | 8 | 5 | 2 | (24) heavy snow | |

*Figure 42. Ascending natal month numbers according to the twenty-four season concept*

# 5  GROUP ENERGETIC EVALUATION CHART

| NUMBER | MANAGING SKILLS | PEOPLE INVOLVED |
|--------|-----------------|-----------------|
| (1) | **YIN – Allocator:**<br>containing, storing, delineating<br>boundaries, managing resources<br><br>**YANG – Motivator:**<br>generating, energizing, providing<br>direction, reflection | |
| (2) | **Supporter**<br>sustaining, supporting, retaining<br>assimilating, anchoring, centring | |
| (3) | **Planner**<br>mapping, visioning, defining borders,<br>strategizing, adapting, organizing | |

| STRATEGY | | |
|---|---|---|
| **NO. 1**<br>**Support for adult activation** | **NO. 2**<br>**Enhance to move person out of child activation** | **NO. 3**<br>**Control inappropriate child action** |
| **Metal/Air Action:**<br>provide historical data, provide summations, get No. 1 to consider the broader social implications, provide space for reflection and response, fatherly support | Strategy No. 1 followed by<br>**Tree/Space Action:**<br>be enthusiastic, show them what potential there is, let them know where things need to go, ask for their energy and gleanings from their reflections | **Earth Action:**<br>ground them, listen to them. Get details from them regarding vague fears. Acknowledge but challenge hesitancy |
| **Fire Action:**<br>be direct, be convincing, promote excitement, be joyful, overcome anxieties, demonstrate appreciation, find out what else they need, sell them the idea | Strategy No. 1 followed by<br>**Metal/Air Action:**<br>monitor quality, make them accountable, ask for progress reports, accept what's offered, show social/historical importance of work done | **Tree/Space Action:**<br>clarify person's situation, initiate conflict if necessary, restructure person's situation, define limits, prioritize |
| **Water Action:**<br>communicate general trends of situation, delineate boundaries for person, energize them to move in given direction, be a well spring, gentle action with reserve | Strategy No. 1 followed by<br>**Fire Action:**<br>show them what is possible, weave them into a greater plan or network of people, be enthusiastic, clarify their ideas | **Metal/Air Action:**<br>make person accountable, spell it out, establish order in their activity, list consequences, refer to team commitment, social order, morality, avoid direct confrontation |

| NUMBER | MANAGING SKILLS | PEOPLE INVOLVED |
|--------|-----------------|-----------------|
| ④ | **Decision-Maker**<br>clarifying, individuating, scheduling,<br>initiating conflict, structuring | |
| ⑤ | **Consolidator**<br>catalyzing, leading, sorting, critiquing,<br>also traits for 2 and 8 | |
| ⑥ | **Inspirer**<br>equilibrating, resonating, receiving,<br>balancing, establishing order | |

| | STRATEGY | |
|---|---|---|
| **NO. 1**<br>**Support for adult activation** | **NO. 2**<br>**Enhance to move person out of child activation** | **NO. 3**<br>**Control inappropriate child action** |
| Same as 3 tree/space but appeal to their sense and maturity to see things clearly. Support in prioritizing | Same as Strategy No. 1 for 3 tree/space but make sure encouragement allows them to stick to one direction and within time limits set | Same as 3 tree/space in Strategy No. 3, but over-ride their muddledness. Overcome confusion by refining, giving a clear evaluation of the situation, bringing balance to their perspective |
| **Fire Action:**<br>same as for 2 earth but here over-ride indecisiveness, appeal to intellect, stimulate catalyzing nature, define role, create trust, be supportive | Same as Strategy No. 1 in 2 earth followed by<br>**Metal/Air Action:**<br>critically weigh up options, help person adjust to change, establish order, encourage person to produce results, balance action | As Strategy No. 3 for 2 earth, getting person to commit themselves, over-ride sentimentality, encourage indepence, provide time limits, give commands, help person to vision |
| **Earth Action:**<br>nurture, provide adequate details, be an anchor, listen | Strategy No. 1 followed by<br>**Water Action:**<br>reflect back, be receptive, manage resources, overcome rigidity by providing larger perspective | **Fire Action:**<br>spell it out, challenge dualistic (black/white) thinking, overcome arrogance, clear air before grudges are set |

| NUMBER | MANAGING SKILLS | PEOPLE INVOLVED |
|--------|-----------------|-----------------|
| ⑦ | **Evaluator:**<br>accounting, refining, eliminating,<br>evolving, managing change,<br>quality control | |
| ⑧ | **Producer**<br>nuturing, transporting, supporting,<br>producing, attention to details,<br>integrating | |
| ⑨ | **YIN**<br>**Sorter:** selling, problem solving,<br>discriminating, transforming and<br>**Networker**: team builder, socializing,<br>atmosphere builder<br><br>**YANG**<br>**Coordinator:** coordinating, defining roles,<br>directing, cooperation-building; and<br>**Communicator:** appreciating, creating<br>trust, expressing protecting | |

| NO. 1<br>**Support for adult activation** | NO. 2<br>**Enhance to move person out of child activation** | NO. 3<br>**Control inappropriate child action** |
|---|---|---|
| Same as Strategy No. 1 for 6 metal, but more anchoring and centring, offer positive criticism, help to sustain momentum | Strategy No. 1 followed by<br>**Water Action:**<br>as with 6 metal but here be more conservative, provide more direction, facilitate more truthful responses | **Fire Action:**<br>don't buy smooth talk, challenge sense of entitlement, overcome any melancholy, keep person task-focused, appeal to social values and importance of the team |
| Same as Strategy No. 1 for 2 and 5 earth, but help person to relax more, provide enthusiasm, lightness and clarity, help with discrimination and priority | Strategy No. 1 followed by<br>**Metal/Air Action:**<br>help to eliminate excess, refine, help person to focus beyond task, engage in play | **Tree/Space Action:**<br>snap person out of wallowing or hopelessness, encourage independent thinking, provide vision, even reframe strucure, provide time frames |
| **Tree/Space Action:**<br>provide ideas, give vision, enthusiasm and excitement, stimulate, map the territory to be explored, provide supportive muscle, create context | Strategy No. 1 followed by<br>**Earth Action:**<br>get it all focused, encourage to act, spell out the end product, encourage diligence, provide realistic outlook and expectations, help person to match talk and actions | **Water Action:**<br>listen, provide reflection, express caution, demand focus and direction, challenge flamboyance, facilitate direct communication, point out possible undertones |

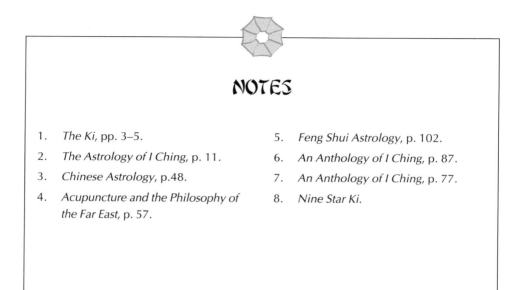

# NOTES

1. *The Ki*, pp. 3–5.

2. *The Astrology of I Ching*, p. 11.

3. *Chinese Astrology*, p.48.

4. *Acupuncture and the Philosophy of the Far East*, p. 57.

5. *Feng Shui Astrology*, p. 102.

6. *An Anthology of I Ching*, p. 87.

7. *An Anthology of I Ching*, p. 77.

8. *Nine Star Ki*.

# FURTHER READING

Gagne, Stephen and Mann, John. *The Nine Ki Handbook*, Spiral-bound Books, Rochester, 1984.

Hersey, Paul and Blanchard, Kenneth. *Management of Organizational Behavior*, Prentice Hall, Englewood Cliffs, NJ, 1982.

Kushi, Michio and Esko, Edward. *Nine Star Ki*, One Peaceful World Press, Becket, Massachusetts, 1991.

Lassalle, Rex. *Grasshopping through Time ... Using Ancient Wisdom*, Rex Lassalle, London, 1998.

Lin, Jami. *Feng Shui Today: Earth Design; the Added Dimension*, Earth Design Inc, Miami Shores, Florida, 1995.

Muramoto, Naboru. *Healing Ourselves*, London, Michael Dempsey, 1975.

Ohsawa, George. *Acupuncture and the Philosophy of the Far East*, Tao Publications, Boston, Massachusetts, 1973.

Sandifer, Jon. *Feng Shui Astrology: Using 9 Star Ki to Achieve Harmony and Happiness in Your Life*, Piatkus, London, 1997.

Sherrill, W. A. and Chu, W. K. *An Anthology of I Ching,* Routledge & Kegan Paul, London, 1985.

Sherrill, W. A. and Chu, W. K. *The Astrology of I Ching*, Samuel Weiser, York Beach, Maine, 1980.

Spear, William. *Feng Shui Made Easy*, HarperCollins, San Francisco, 1995.

Taguchi, Sinda. *Bai Hwa Zhong-guo Qi Xue Ming Li Ru Men*, Tokyo edition: B. Sunday, Publishing, 1984.

Tara, William. *Macrobiotics and Human Behavior*, Japan Publishing, Tokyo, New York, 1985.

Tulku, Tarthang. *Knowledge of Freedom*, Dharma Publishing, Berkeley, 1984.

Walters, Derek. *Chinese Astrology*, Aquarian Press, Wellingborough, Northants, 1987.

Wilheim, Richard and Baynes, Cary, F., editors. *The I Ching*, Routledge & Kegan Paul, London, 1975.

Yamamoto, Shizuko. *Barefoot Shiatsu,* Japan Publishing Inc., Tokyo.

Yoshikawa, Takashi. *The Ki,* St. Martin's Press, New York, 1986.

# GLOSSARY

*Adult Number or adult natal year numbers*: The number associated with the transformation dominant in the year that a person was born. It represents a person's self-actualizing potential.

*Child Number or child natal month numbers*: The number associated with the transformation dominant in the month that a person was born. Stress is more often than not associated with this number. It represents conditioning that a person experiences in their struggle to self-actualize or become more independent.

*Feng Shui*: A Chinese term literally translated as 'wind and water'. The geomantic tradition of Feng Shui explains the optimum arrangement of space in and out of doors. The same as *Vastu Shastra* (India) and *Sa Che* (Tibet).

*I Ching*: An ancient Chinese divination system. Symbols of the I Ching are hexagrams derived from the trigram line markings that appeared on a tortoise in ancient times. To work the I Ching, a person asks a question and then performs certain ritual procedures in order to arrive at a hexagram which answers the question in the most auspicious way.

*Ki*: A Japanese term for life force; the same as *chi* (Chinese), *lung* (Tibetan) and *prana* (Sanskrit).

*Ko Cycle*: One of the Laws of Five Transformations, having to do with the way certain transformations control others when there are major disturbances in the life process. It is also called the cycle of death because as all things die, the order in which the organs or systems associated with certain transformations break down is in this particular order. Because it also reflects the dynamic tension between paired transformations that are, in fact, the humours of Ayurvedic medicine, I prefer to call this the cycle of dynamic transformation.

*Lamaistic*: 'Lama' means meditation master in Tibetan. In this context the term refers to an association with Tibetan Buddhist tradition in a monastic setting.

*Law of Five Transformations*: Guidelines discovered in ancient times which identify the factors and energetics that arise from the birth-to-death cycle of all phenomena.

*Magic Square*: Also referred to as Universal Chart. Originally found on Fu Hsi's tortoise and thus considered a sign from divine forces. It represents the qualities, order, and movement of all phenomena here on earth as expressed in the Law of Five Transformations. Each of nine blocks in the magic square is a 'house' which bears certain qualities. This square is the cornerstone of Nine Star Ki astrology as it is used in China, Tibet and Japan.

*Mother–Son*: One of the Laws of Five Transformations where there is an intimate and direct relationship between two transformations. This relationship can be supportive, excessive, non-nurturing or depleting in nature.

*Transformation*: An aggregate of specific characteristics that is inclusive, but falls within a continuum. Originally, the translation of the Chinese for this term was 'element' as there is a kind of building-block quality. However, the term did not convey the dynamic quality of the aggregates, hence modern theorists have chosen 'transformation' as the term most suitable.

*Trigram*: A shorthand way of conveying certain qualities in nature, somewhat like calligraphy. Originally the line markings that are the trigrams were said to have appeared on a tortoise in antiquity.

*Universal Charts*: *see* Magic Square

*Yang*: A force in nature which exhibits contraction as a primary characteristic. Often associated with masculine energy.

*Yin*: A force in nature which exhibits expansiveness as a primary characteristic. Often associated with feminine energy.

# USEFUL ADDRESSES

To receive Nine Star consultations or to study more about Nine Star Ki, contact:

Robert Sachs
Diamond Way Ayurveda
PO Box 13753
San Luis Obispo
CA 93406
Toll Free (USA) 877 964 1395 or
800 484 6283, ext. 7816
Email:
diamond.way.ayurveda@thegrid,net
Or write c/o Element Books Ltd

Rex Lassalle
*In Europe:*
PO Box 12174
London N19 4LR
England

*In USA:*
2232 S. Nellis Blvd, Suite 140
Las Vegas
NV 89104
USA
Email: grasshopping@compuserve.com

## USEFUL ADDRESSES

Jon Sandifer
PO Box 69
Teddington
Middlesex TW11 9SH
England
Tel/Fax: 0181 977 8988
Email: 106140.2645@compuserve.com


For courses on Oriental philosophy,
Macrobiotics, or Nine Star Ki contact:

Kushi Institute International
PO Box 7
Becket
MA 01223
USA
Tel. 413 623 5741 (Toll Free, USA)
800 975 8744
Email: kushi@macrobiotics.org

For Nine Star Ki daily calendars
for the year, contact:

J. Koji Higa
9 Ki Resources
PO Box 638
Great Barrington
MA 01230
USA
Tel: 413 528 3260
Email: nineki@juno.com

# INDEX